Missionaries of the Light

Chico Xavier

Missionaries of the Light

Dictated by the Spirit
André Luiz

Translated by Darrel W. Kimble and Ily Reis

FEB

Second Edition – 9/2020

Original title in Portuguese:
MISSIONÁRIOS DA LUZ
(Brazil, 1945)

ISBN 978-65-5570-140-1

Published by
BRAZILIAN SPIRITIST FEDERATION
Av. L2 Norte – Q. 603 – Conjunto F (SGAN)
70830-106 – Brasília (DF) – Brazil
www.febeditora.com.br
editorial@febnet.org.br
+55 61 2101 6198

INTERNATIONAL DATA FOR CATALOGING IN PUBLICATION

L953n Luiz, Andre (Spirit)

Missionaries of the light / dictated by the spirit André Luiz ; [received by] Francisco Cândido Xavier ; [translated by Darrel W. Kimble and Ily Reis]. – 2st edition – Brasília, DF (Brazil) : FEB, 2020.

348 p.; 21 cm

Original title: Missionários da luz

ISBN 978-65-5570-140-1

1. Spiritism. 2. Psychographic works. I. Xavier, Francisco Cândido, 1910-2002. II. Brazilian Spiritist Federation. III. Title. IV. Series.

CDD 133.93
CDU 133. 7
CDE 00.06.02

Table of Contents

On Facing The New Era

As long as a story speaks about the intervention of fairies when referring to tutelary genii, hidden palaces and the wonders of an unknown forest, children are all ears, showing happiness and interest on their enrapt faces. However, when the storyteller changes his or her approach in order to focus on instructive realities, the infantile mind retracts, upset and bored... It does not understand the promise of the future life, with its work and responsibilities.

Hearts that are still tender love dreams and expect easily-won heroism; they prefer making the least effort possible and they do not immediately understand the divine labor involved in ongoing perfection; hence, they withdraw, amazed and surprised, from any real teaching. Nevertheless, life is waiting for them with its unchangeable laws, and it gradually reveals the truth to them, without spectacular noises, but with the serenity of a mother.

The pages by Andre Luiz remind us of that image.

As long as wise and benevolent spirits bring a vision of heaven, thereby broadening the arena of human hope, our incarnate brothers and sisters ecstatically and joyously listen to us. It is the sublime consolation, the comfort for which they have longed. Souls gather to receive messages from heaven. On the other hand, if messengers from the higher realms reveal certain angles of the spirit life, speaking to them about work, personal effort, personal responsibility, constructive struggle, necessary study and self-improvement, they cannot hide their displeasure.

Contrary to what they believed at first, they do not see a heaven of ease or a region of privilege, nor do they witness miraculous events or see restful beatitude. Instead of paradise surrounding them, they feel they are in the vicinity of an industrious workshop, where workers do not evolve by means of the privilege of protectionism, but rather at the cost of their own effort; thus, victory or defeat comes from their own conscience. They perceive the imperishable law, which, without making erroneous decisions, has control over lives in the name of the Eternal One. They understand that the seashores of divine beauty and the enchanted palaces of peace await the spirit on other vibrational continents of the universe, but they also realize that it is their responsibility to sweat and struggle, to be industrious and to improve themselves in order to reach them by swimming across the great sea of experience.

Most become frightened and try to retreat. They expect a heaven of ease after the death of the body, one that may be had by means of mere doctrinal affirmations. No one, however, will gainsay the divine law; truth will always be victorious and the life eternal will continue to teach, slowly, with maternal patience.

Christian Spiritism today has a great and sublime task in the world.

It is not enough simply to define its venerable characteristics as the Consoler of Humankind; it is also necessary to reveal its facet as a liberating movement aimed at consciences and hearts.

Physical death is not the end. It is merely the next chapter in the book of evolution and improvement. At its arrival, no one should expect final and definitive solutions, for we know that one hundred years of activity in the world represent but a relatively small fraction of time for any type of spiritual growth in the life eternal.

An infinite field of service awaits the dedication of workers of truth and the good. Massive problems challenge the brave spirits incarnated at this time with the glorious mission of preparing the new era and contributing to the restoration of living faith and the widening of human understanding. It is crucial to come to the aid of religion, entombed in the theological archives of churches of stone, and to support science, which has become a satanic genius of destruction.

Victorious spirituality is traveling the world, regenerating its moral sources and awakening individuals to a realistic picture of their acquisitions. There are new warnings calling to disbelieving men and women of the 20th century, pointing out broader horizons to them and showing them that the spirit lives above the civilizations that war transforms or consumes in its millenary dragon-like voracity.

On facing this new era, and considering the great endeavor of renewal, the cooperation of all faithful servants of truth and the good is requested so that, more than anything else, they may live the new faith, each and everyone improving and uplifting themselves on the way to a better world so that the teachings of Christ may prevail over the mere words of fine-sounding ideologies.

In the execution of this lofty task, incarnates and discarnates of goodwill are coming together, building the bridge of light over which humankind will cross the abyss of ignorance and death.

It is for this reason, dear reader, that Andre Luiz once again comes to you to tell you something about the divine service of the "Missionaries of the Light" and to explain that humans are eternal spirits, temporarily inhabiting the living temple of terrestrial flesh; that the perispirit is not a body of nebulous mist, but rather a living structure to which physical cells are molded; that in all places the soul receives according to its personal creations; that the ties of love and hatred follow us into every arena of life; that other activities besides the common struggle of everyday life are carried out by the incarnated consciousness; that reincarnation is guided by sublime spiritual powers; and that beyond the grave, the soul continues to struggle and learn, to perfect itself and to serve the Lord's designs, continuing to grow toward the immortal glory to which the Father has destined us.

If in reading this book you become frightened, if the statements of the Messenger seem revolutionary to you, turn to prayer and thank the Lord for the learning experience, asking him to clarify and enlighten you so that illusion does not keep you trapped in its web. Remember that the revelation of truth is progressive, and as you appeal for divine help for your soul, pay heed to the sacred duties that the earth has arranged for you each day. Be aware that the death of the body will not lead you to stagnation, but to new arenas of improvement and labor, of renewal and blessed struggle, where you will live much more, and more intensely.

EMMANUEL
Pedro Leopoldo (MG)[1], May 13, 1945.

[1] Pedro Leopoldo is a Brazilian city located in the state of Minas Gerais, the birthplace of the medium Francisco Candido Xavier. – Tr.

1
The Psychographer[2]

Once the conversation regarding the problems of interaction with the inhabitants of the physical realm was over, Instructor Alexandre, who performs important functions on our spirit plane, said to me kindly:

"I can understand your wish. If you would like, you may come with me to our center when the opportunity arises."

"Yes," I replied, delighted, "the subject of mediumship is a fascinating one."

Alexandre smiled benevolently and agreed:

"That is certainly the case for those who examine its moral influence."

Later, the evening for my visit was set and I awaited the practical instruction with undisguised interest.

---

[2] A medium who writes messages dictated by spirits. (See Allan Kardec, *The Medium's Book* (International Spiritist Council) – Tr.

When the time came, I used Alexandre's prestigious influence to enter the large old hall where he carries out his leadership duties.

Of the dozens of chairs set out in rows, only eighteen were taken by incarnate individuals. The rest were occupied by the mass of spirits invisible to the ordinary eyes of the physical realm.

It was a large gathering of suffering souls – a large and needy audience.

I noticed that luminous filaments divided the assistants from the spirit world into different groups, each displaying its own characteristics. Guards were posted around the access areas, and because of the noise of voices on the outside, I realized that here too the entry of discarnates was subject to strict control. The needy spirits who were let inside remained silent and circumspect.

I entered carefully, without attracting the attention of the audience, who was listening excitedly to the caring and edifying words of the center's hardworking instructor.

A large number of spirit coworkers were attentively keeping watch, and as the devoted mentor spoke from his heart, the eighteen incarnates kept their thought strictly focused on high and pure purposes. It was lovely to feel their individual vibrations. Each one emitted luminous rays that differed greatly from each other in intensity and color. These rays came together at approximately sixty centimeters[3] from the individuals' physical bodies and established a current of power quite different from the energies of our realm. This current was not limited to the circle in which it moved; at certain points it would pour out vital elements like a miraculous spring with its source in the human hearts and minds that were meeting there. The incarnates'

[3] About twenty-four inches. – Tr.

energies mingled with the robust fluids coming from the large number of workers from our plane. These fluids formed a precious dispensary of benefits for the unfortunate spirits who were still strongly attached to physiological sensations.

Such mental energies are not illusory, though they might seem to be so from an earthly point of view that is less enlightened regarding the infinite reserves of potential that lie beyond denser matter.

After the consoling discourse had ended, I was pondering these new additions to my learning experience, when my friend asked me to attend a mediumistic session.

Because he was interested in taking full advantage of the time available, he kept his greetings short.

"We don't have a minute to waste," he said.

And pointing to a small group of six spirits nearby, he explained:

"Our authorized friends are waiting."

"For a communication?" I asked.

The instructor nodded and added:

"However, not all will achieve their aim at the same time. Some will have to wait for weeks, months, years..."

"I didn't imagine that the task would be so hard," I added, surprised.

"You'll see," said Alexandre kindly.

And nodding toward a young man who was deep in concentration and surrounded by assistants from our plane, he explained attentively:

"There are six spirits who could potentially give a communication, but presently only one medium at this meeting is in a condition to be of use. So, we are forced to consider the fact that the group of terrestrial learners and workers will only be able to receive messages related to the overall interests of the group. There is no possibility for any work beyond the ordinary.

"I thought a medium was above all simply a machine," I stated.

"A machine can wear out," Alexandre remarked, "and we are looking at machinery that is extremely delicate."

Noticing my look of surprise, he continued:

"First of all, we must realize that, when it comes to mediumistic work, moral factors prevail. In order to be faithful to a higher mandate, the medium needs to be clear and serene, like the crystalline mirror of a lake's surface. Otherwise, the waves of disquietude would upset the projection of our spiritual energies upon earthly materiality, in the same way that turbulent waters cannot reflect the sublime images of the sky and surrounding nature."

Pointing to the medium, the instructor continued in a firm voice:

"This brother is not simply an instrument. He is a spirit who must be as free as we are, and in order to be useful for the desired communication, he must deny himself with selflessness and humility, the first factors required to gain access to interaction with the higher realms. He must remain silent so that others may speak; to give of himself so that others may receive. In short, he must serve as a bridge where diverging interests meet. Without this conscious understanding of the spirit of service, he would be of no use for spiritually constructive purposes. Of course, he is responsible for maintaining inner resources such as tolerance, humility, a fraternal disposition, patience and Christian love; however, we too must do our part so as to maintain his outer support, because if our friend here doesn't have any nourishment or relative peace, or if he lacks help in acquiring the simplest things, we cannot ask for his self-sacrificing cooperation. Our responsibilities, therefore, are linked to the smallest details of the task at hand."

As I pondered the idea that a medium should happily wait for divine compensation, Alexandre replied:

"Nevertheless, my dear friend, we must remember that we are still dealing with work that is not yet complete. The matter of payment will come later."

At this point in the conversation, he invited me to approach the "mediumistic instrument"[4], and putting his right hand on the medium's forehead he said:

"Observe. This man is an ordinary psychographer. Before beginning the task he is undertaking at this moment, our assistants prepared his faculties so that his physical health would not be harmed. The transmission of the message will not entail merely 'using his hand'. There are intricate and complex processes involved."

Because of my profound scientific curiosity, the instructor offered me the magnetic assistance of his energetic personality and I was able to observe a large laboratory of vibrant energies in the medium's body. My power of visual perception now exceeded that of X-rays – it had much broader characteristics. The young man's glands had become luminous centers resembling perfect electrical workshops. I focused on his brain in particular. The medullar conductors formed a long wick, sustaining the mental light that resembled the generous flame of a candle of immense proportions. The metabolic centers filled me with surprise. The brain showed flashes of light in intricate designs. The cerebral lobes reminded me of dynamic currents. The cortical cells and the fine tendrils of the nerve fibers were very delicate conducting elements of concealed and imponderable energies. Within this array enveloped in an indefinable mental light, the pineal gland emitted intense, bluish rays.

---

[4] The Spirits frequently refer to a medium as a "mediumistic instrument." – Tr.

"Done with your observation?" asked the instructor, interrupting my astonishment. "Transmitting messages from one realm to the other in the work of human spiritual edification," he continued, "demands effort, goodwill, cooperation and a consistent purpose. Of course, the medium's training and willing cooperation facilitate the work; at any rate, however, serving as a medium is not automatic ... It requires a lot of understanding, opportunity and awareness."

I was impressed.

"Do you think a medium can improvise the receptive state?" he asked. "Not in the least. A medium's spiritual preparation must be never-ending. Any incident can upset the medium's sensitive apparatus like a strike from a rock interrupting the work of a receiving valve. Furthermore, our magnetic cooperation is fundamental for the execution of the task. Examine the matter carefully. We are now observing the peculiarities of the perispiritual body. You can see that every glandular center is an electrical power source. In any type of mediumistic practice, the pineal gland plays the most important role. By means of its well-balanced energies, the human mind intensifies the power of the sending and receiving of rays peculiar to our realm. It is in the pineal gland that human beings' new sense lies; however, in most people the divine potential still sleeps in an embryonic state."

In fact, I realized that the medium's pineal gland was emitting an increasingly intense luminosity.

Shifting his attention from the brain to the corporeal apparatus in general, the instructor continued:

"The process of receiving the message is not at all simple, and incarnate workers are unaware of its intrinsic mechanism, just as children who are provided for in their home environment are unaware of the cost of living and the sacrifices made by their parents. Long before the meeting that is now taking place, this spiritual servant was already the object of our special attention so that coarse thoughts would not weigh on his inner realm. He was prepared appropriately for the task, and the moment he sat down here, he began to be assisted by several workers from our plane. Before anything else, his nerve cells received a new magnetic coefficient so that there would be no harmful losses from the tigroid fundus (Nissl's bodies) needed for the mental processes. The sympathetic nervous system – in particular the autonomous area of the heart – received energy support and the central nervous system was appropriately assisted so that the health of our well-intentioned worker would not be compromised. Under our influence, the vagus was fortified against any shock from the viscera. The suprarenal glands received additional energies in order to accelerate the production of adrenaline, which is needed to help with the eventual loss of neural reserves."

At that moment, I noticed that the medium seemed almost discarnate. His dense, corporeal expressions seemed to have disappeared, so intense was the light that surrounded him originating from his perispiritual centers.

After a long pause, Alexandre continued:

"From our perspective, he is not a calcium framework covered in carbohydrates and proteins, but instead, he represents the more significant expression of the immortal being, the child of the Eternal God. According to this new way of looking at his anatomy, observe the glory of each miniscule unit of the body. Each cell is an electric motor that needs fuel to work, live and serve."

Unconcerned with my astonishment, the instructor changed his attitude and stated:

"Let's put our observations on hold for now; we need to take action."

He waved to one of the six communicants, who happily came over to us.

"Calixto," Alexandre said seriously, "there are six friends available for the communication, but the possibilities are not great. You will be the only one to write. Take your position. Remember your mission of consolation and avoid anything of a personal tone. The opportunity at hand is very limited and we need to bear in mind the overall interest."

After quickly acknowledging us, Calixto stood beside the medium, who received him with obvious signs of joy. Calixto embraced him with his left arm, and raising his hand to the young man's brain, he touched his memory center with the tips of his fingers, as if collecting materials from the medium's memories. Little by little, I could see that the communicator's mental light started to mingle with the medium's radiations. His motor area took on a different color and luminosity. Alexandre drew closer to the pair and placed his right hand on the medium's frontal lobe as if controlling the inhibiting fibers and trying to avoid any interference with the mediumistic apparatus as much as possible.

Calixto expressed great joy on his face, like a happy servant who rejoices in the blessings of service. Showing signs of profound gratitude to the Lord, he started to write, assuming control of his companion's arm and beginning the task with these beautiful words:

"May the peace of Jesus be with you!"

2
The Pineal Gland

While Calixto was communicating using the medium's body as an instrument, I employed the magnetic energies furnished to me by Alexandre and concentrated all my attention on the medium. The more I observed the brain's details, the more I marveled at the increasing light the pineal gland was emitting. The tiny gland had become a radiating nucleus and its rays formed a lotus flower of sublime petals around it.

I carefully examined the other incarnates. This gland displayed some degree of luminosity in all of them, but in none did it shine as it did in the acting medium.

A gentle light descended from the higher realms onto the nucleus, which looked like a resplendent flower, and I realized that very delicate vibrations were in play, imperceptible to me.

I had studied the pineal gland's function during my modest work as a doctor on the earth, where, according to classic authors, its function was restricted to sexual control during infancy. It was nothing more than a controller of the instincts until the wheels of sexual experience could glide with regularity down the pathways of human life. Afterward, it decreased in strength, abated, and almost disappeared so that the genital glands could succeed it in taking over this field of energy.

My current observations, however, were now clashing with the definitions of the official circles.

Since for someone who is ignorant the best recourse is to wait for someone who is more knowledgeable, I waited for Alexandre to enlighten me after the meeting was over.

After a few minutes, the kind mentor approached.

He did not wait for me to explain myself.

"I understand your perplexity," he said. "At one point I experienced it too. The pineal gland has now become a revelation to you."

"It sure has," I added.

"It isn't a dead organ as previously supposed," he continued. "It's the gland of mental life. During puberty it awakens the creative forces in the human organism, and thereafter it continues to function as the most advanced laboratory of a human being's psychic elements. Regular neurologists don't understand it very well. Some day, psychiatrists will grasp its secrets. Conventional psychologists overlook it. Freud failed to interpret it correctly when he exaggerated the influence of 'libido' in the study of human congenital dysfunction. During the period of childhood development – the readjustment phase for this important center of the preexistent perispiritual body – the pineal gland seems to restrain the manifestations of sex; however, these observations need to be rectified.

"At the age of fourteen, approximately, the pineal gland goes from a stationary state regarding its essential attributes and begins to function again in the reincarnate person. What once represented control now becomes a creative source and an escape valve. The pineal gland readjusts itself to the body's organic order and reopens its wonderful world of sensations and impressions in the realm of the emotions. The individual yields to the recapitulation of his or her sexuality and examines the inventory of passions experienced in the past, which reappear under strong impulses."

I was profoundly surprised.

After a pause in his exposition, Alexandre continued:

"As an organ of the ethereal body's highest expression, it presides over the neural phenomena of the emotions. In a certain way, it unravels the divine links of nature that connect the existences in the series of struggles for the perfecting of the soul, and it allows for a glimpse of the greatness of the creative faculties with which humans are endowed."

"Amazing!" I exclaimed. "And the genital glands? Where do they stand?"

The instructor smiled and explained:

"They are too mechanical to store the subtle and almost imponderable generative principles. They are entirely controlled by the magnetic potency of which the pineal gland is the main source. The genital glands secrete the sex hormones, but the pineal gland – if I may put it this way – secretes the 'psychic hormones' or 'power units', which act positively on the generative energies. The chromosomes in the seminal sac cannot escape the pineal gland's absolute and determining influence."

Alexandre made a significant gesture and considered:

"However, we are not examining problems of embryology. Let's stick to the initial subject and analyze the pineal gland as the gland of a person's spiritual life."

In my astonishment I kept strict silence, eager for new explanations.

"By secreting subtle psychic energies," he continued, "the pineal gland maintains control over the entire endocrine system.

Connected to the mind through electromagnetic principles in the vital field – which ordinary science has not yet been able to identify – it commands subconscious powers under the direct determination of the will. The neural webs form its 'telegraph wires' for giving immediate orders to all cellular areas, and under its direction psychic energies are supplied to all the autonomous storage areas of the organs. As one of the most important creative sources, its attributes are extensive and fundamental. In its capacity as controller of the world of the emotions, its position in sexual experiences is basic and absolute. In general terms, all of us, either now or in the past, have corrupted this sacred focal point of creative energies, transforming it into a lax magnet amidst the base sensations of our animal nature. How many lifetimes have we wasted by channeling our spiritual potential toward the lowest denominators of materialistic pleasure? Unfortunately, divorced from the law of usage, we embrace emotional dissipation, and that is the reason, my dear friend, for our multi-millenary corruption of the generative energies, and why we have become burdened with moral commitments toward all those whom we have hurt with our insanity and thoughtlessness. The regrettable contempt for this sacred potential causes the heartrending phenomena of physiological heredity, which should invariably constitute a cache of blessed and pure acquisitions. From any evolutionary point of view, the perversion of our conscious mental plane causes the perversion of our unconscious psychism, which is in charge of carrying out our innermost desires and orders in the realm of automatic actions. An unbalanced will deregulates the focus of our creative potential. From there arises the need of moral rules for those who are truly interested in the eternal acquisitions of the spirit. Self-sacrifice, selflessness, sexual continence and emotional discipline are not mere precepts of a religious nature. They are measures with a scientific content for the effective enrichment of our personalities. We will never escape the law, whose articles and paragraphs from the Supreme Legislator encompass the universe. Nobody will ever fool nature. Unbalanced vital centers will force the soul to remain in states of imbalance. At the time of physical death it does no good to rely on conventional gestures and words if the individual has not considered his or her own purification. The justice that governs eternal life has never bent. It is true that the profound sentiments of the final moment of the incarnate spirit play a major part in the process of regeneration beyond the grave, but they do not represent the needed accomplishment."

The instructor spoke in a sublime tone – so it seemed to me. For the first time I was hearing commentaries about conscience, virtue and sanctification based on strictly logical and scientific concepts in the field of reason.

My thoughts on the matter were obviously becoming clearer. To receive a body granted by reincarnation is not like being given a boat for a new adventure and being left to chance; instead, it means being given a definite responsibility in the work of learning, elevation or reparation in our evolutionary or redeeming efforts.

"Now do you understand that the functions of the pineal gland lie in the mental growth of human beings and in the enrichment of the values of the soul?" the instructor asked.

"Yes..." I answered, strongly impressed.

"By secreting 'energy units'," he continued, "it can be compared to a powerful mill that needs to be used and controlled in the work of enlightening, refining and benefiting our personality; it is not to be lessened by an excessive expenditure of psychic supply on base emotions. To wallow in the mud of the lower sensations like hogs is to keep it in the toxic currents of the excesses of the animal nature, and through the excessive waste of subtle energies, it will prove very difficult for humankind to raise itself from its terrible immersion in darkness – an immersion that is prolonged beyond physical death. In light of this, it is imperative to pay close attention that our supply of energies is employed in every honest endeavor aimed at developing the higher faculties. Materialists of pure reason, masters of vast intellectual heritages, have long perceived such realities, and with the purpose of preserving youth, beauty and eugenics, they have fostered the practice of all kinds sports. As a means of combating the potential dangers of the excessive accumulation of neural energies – as the electrical secretions of the pineal gland are called – they have advised the youths of all countries to practice rowing, ball games, jumping, pole vaulting, and running. In this way, the legitimate and normal organic qualities would be preserved for the functions of heredity. This measure, although satisfactory in part, is nevertheless incomplete and defective. Undoubtedly, work-outs and controlled exercise are valuable health factors; honest sports competition is an invaluable foundation for socialization; it can, however, be restricted solely to providing benefits for the bones, and sometimes it can degenerate into the motive behind less-worthy passions. On earth there are still very few of those who recognize the need to conserve psychic energies for the enrichment of the eternal spirit. Humans have forgotten that Jesus taught virtue as the sport of the soul, and they do not always remember that, regarding the problem of inner improvement, it is not the shadow of the substance that must be corrected, but rather the substance itself."

I listened to his lesson with emotion and great wonder.

"Do you now understand how important self-denial is? Can you perceive the greatness of the law of spiritual growth by sacrifice? Bleeding stimulates the production of life-sustaining cells in the bone marrow; pruning brings beauty, newness and fruitfulness to trees. The person who truly practices the good lives amid the constructive and sanctifying vibrations of gratitude, happiness and joy. This is not simply a theory of hope. It is a scientific principle, and without its application in day-to-day living, the soul cannot free itself, because it has become decentralized by corruption in the lowest realms of nature."

Alexandre noticed that his lesson was taking too long, so he concluded:

"So, according to what we have stated, the function of the pineal gland in mental life is very important."

"Yes," I offered, "I can now understand its substantial influence on sex, and I can also understand humankind's long and heartbreaking sexual tragedy. I can clearly perceive the reason for the dramas that are taking place one after the other without interruption, the afflictions that seem to be never-ending, the anxieties that lead to crime, the entanglement of suffering involving homes and hearts."

"And because human beings are always willing to corrupt the sacred centers of their personality," Alexandre concluded solemnly, "they are always ready to contract new debts, but they are rarely determined to rectify or pay them off."

"I understand, I understand."

Harboring a number of questions, I started to ask:

"Wouldn't it be more reasonable..."

The instructor interrupted me and clarified:

"I already know what you want to ask."

And smiling:

"You would like to ask if it wouldn't be better to cease all sexual experiences, and to bury the possibility of physical rebirth. Such a question, however, is unfounded. Nobody must act against the law. The respectable use of life's treasures, ennobling union and dignified togetherness comprise the program of spiritual growth. Hence, it is crucial to distinguish between harmony and imbalance, thereby avoiding remaining at a standstill in a deadly abyss."

With these words, Alexandre became silent, like a wise mentor who gives his disciple the time needed to digest the lesson.

3
Mediumistic Development

My normal duties did not allow for long or frequent trips with Alexandre; however, I took advantage of all my time off.

There was always something to learn, and I found great pleasure in following this active missionary of mediumistic communication activities.

"Tonight," said my devoted friend, "you will observe a few demonstrations of mediumistic development."

I awaited the learning experience with great interest.

At the appointed time, I went to the group meeting.

Even before our incarnate fellow spirits entered, much activity was already taking place in the realm of the spirit world. There was a considerable number of workers, and much work of a spiritual nature.

I was admiring the characteristics of magnetic assistance given to suffering spirits, when Alexandre pointed out:

"For the time being, our efforts are more fruitful in the circle of unfortunate discarnates. The beneficent activities of this center are focused mainly on them, because incarnates, even those who already show an interest in Spiritist practice, are very rarely committed to taking real advantage of the true worth of our cooperation."

And after a long pause, he continued:

"The transition between dense animality and higher spirituality is very slow and difficult. And in that sense, among humans there is always an ocean of words and only a few drops of action."

At that moment, the first of our friends from the physical realm entered the room.

"We shall see..." a man with a large moustache was saying. "Today, we shall see if we have any luck."

"I haven't been coming to the sessions regularly," a young man remarked, "because I'm very discouraged ... how long have I been holding the pencil in my hand to no avail?"

"That's a pity!" another man answered. "Difficulties are discouraging, in fact."

"It seems to me that we are not deserving of anything in the area of encouragement on the part of our invisible benefactors!" added an elderly woman. "How many months have I been trying in vain to develop mediumship? At certain times, I feel intense spiritual vibrations near me; but I can't get beyond the initial manifestations."

The talk continued, interesting and colorful.

After a few minutes, with the presence of a few other small groups of experimenters who had eagerly arrived, the development session began.

The director offered a touching prayer, and all those present followed along in thought.

Eighteen people were sitting in a state of expectancy.

"Some," Alexandre explained, "are hoping for psychography; others are attempting incorporation[5]. Unfortunately, almost all

[5] Mediumistic incorporation or Psychophony: Communication by spirits through the voice of a speaking medium (*The Medium's Book*, op. cit.). – Tr.

of them confuse psychic powers with physiological functions. They believe in the absolute mechanism of the endeavor and expect eventual and problematic progress, but they forget that all edification of the soul requires discipline, education, effort and perseverance. Constructive mediumship is the tongue of fire of the Holy Spirit, a divine light for which it is necessary to maintain the wick of Christian love, the oil of pure goodwill. Without the necessary preparation, the journey of those who try to rush their entrance into the invisible kingdom almost always winds up being a trip to the realms of darkness. They experience strong sensations and run up against heartbreaking perplexity. They make surprising discoveries and end up in endless anxiety and uncertainty. Nobody can betray the law with impunity, and in order to grow spiritually, no soul can dispense with its own efforts at inner improvement."

Addressing those around him in particular, the instructor recommended:

"Let us observe."

He stood beside a young man in an expectant posture, pencil at the ready, immersed in deep silence.

Alexandre offered me his vigorous magnetic assistance and I looked at the young man closely. His glandular centers were emitting pale radiations. His pineal gland, in particular, resembled a tiny seed that glowed somewhat.

"Observe the genital system," the instructor advised gravely.

I was astonished. The generative glands were emitting a very weak luminosity that seemed to be compressed by swarms of black corpuscles that displayed a surprising mobility. They originated under the urinary bladder and they vibrated all along the spermatic cord, forming compact groups in the seminal vesicles, in the prostate and in the mucus masses of the urethra; they invaded the seminal canals and fought with the sexual cells, destroying them. The most vigorous of these microscopic beasts were located in the epididymis, where they were greedily absorbing the delicate embryos of organic life. I was shocked. What was the meaning of this mob of little dark organisms? They seemed magnetized to one another on the same destructive wavelength. Could these be little-known expressions of syphilis?

Although I had silently asked myself this question, Alexandre explained to me:

"No, Andre. What we are looking at is not Schaudinn's Spirochaeta pallida or any other new form that is capable of material analysis by human bacteriologists. They are psychic bacilli of sexual torment, produced by the feverish hunger for pleasures of the lowest kinds. The world's medical dictionary knows nothing about them, and in the absence of a definition that is suitable to your knowledge, let's simply call them 'larvae'. They have been cultivated by this fellow worker, not only because of his incontinence in the domain of the emotions per se through various sexual experiences, but also through his contact with coarse spirits who are in tune with his predilections, entities that frequently visit him in the manner of imperceptible vampires. The poor young man cannot yet understand that the physical body is only a vague shadow of the perispiritual body. He has not grasped the fact that prudence in sexual matters is the balance of life, and when he receives our warnings regarding temperance, he believes he is listening to old lessons of a dogmatic character that belong exclusively to the arena of religious faith. Under the pretext of accepting the empire of pure reason within the realm of logic, he believes that sex has nothing to do with spirituality, as if spirituality were not existence per se. He forgets that all is spirit, divine manifestation and eternal energy. Our friend's mistake is the same as that of all religious persons who think that the soul is completely separate from the physical body, when, in fact, all psycho-physical manifestations originate from the spirit's influence."

New worlds of thoughts were dawning on me. I was beginning to discern definitions that were more forthright about what had been terrible unknowns for me in the area of general pathogenesis. I had not yet recovered from my indescribable surprise, when the instructor called my attention to an older gentleman who was attempting psychography.

"Observe this friend," he said knowingly. "Do you smell something familiar?"

Around that pale face an unpleasant atmosphere was indeed noticeable. His body seemed like a barrel of whimsical configuration, from whose inside certain light vapors escaped continuously. One could see his difficulty in maintaining his train of thought with relative serenity. I had no doubts. He surely must be using alcohol on a regular basis.

I took advantage of the circumstance to observe his organic particularities.

The gastrointestinal system seemed to be drenched in liquor, because this substance invaded all the corners of the stomach. Beginning by making its presence felt in the walls of the esophagus, it manifested its influence all the way down to the fecal bolus. The size of his liver surprised me. Minuscule, horrifying figures posted themselves voraciously along the hepatic portal vein, desperately fighting with the newer blood elements. The whole structure of the organ had been altered and it was terribly engorged. The modified cylindrical lobules harbored sick and weakened cells. The spleen displayed strange anomalies.

"Alcohol," Alexandre explained in a serious tone of voice, "is slowly destroying him. You are examining the lesser abnormalities. This fellow has strayed completely from his centers of vital balance. The whole endocrine system has been affected by the toxin's action. In vain the bone marrow works to improve his circulation. In vain the genital centers make efforts to bring order to their specific functions, because excessive alcohol causes depressing modifications in the chromatin itself. The kidneys are also working in vain, trying to excrete the corrosive elements, because the pernicious actions of the substance in question destroys a large number of nephrons every day. The corrupted pancreas cannot tend precisely to its function of breaking down food. Destructive larvae are killing the hepatic cells. Profound alterations are modifying the dispositions of the vegetative nervous system, and were it not for the sweat glands, the continuation of his physical life would perhaps become impossible."

Alexandre indicated the diseased points and explained the matter with such great wisdom and simplicity that I could not hide the astonishment that had come over me.

Next, the instructor placed me beside a nice elderly lady. After carefully examining her he added:

"Observe this sister. She is a candidate for the development of incorporation."

A very weak light emanated from her mental organization, and right away I noticed her obesity. Her stomach was terribly stretched and the intestines seemed to have undergone strange modifications. Her greatly enlarged liver displayed indefinable agitation. We also could see large anomalies from the duodenum to the sigmoid colon. It seemed that I was looking not at the work of a normal digestive system, but rather at a large distillery full of meat pastes and fatty broths, smelling of a strong vinegar condiment. In a large part of the food-overloaded abdominal area, there were many familiar parasites, but besides these, other corpuscles similar to voracious slugs formed large colonies from the muscles and fibers of the stomach up to the ileocecal valve. These parasites were attacking the nutritional juices with frightening destructive potency.

Noting my amazement, the instructor helped me out:

"This poor friend has given in to excessive eating. All her glands and neural centers are working to meet the demands of the digestive system. Uncaring about herself, she has fallen into gross gluttony and has become a prisoner of entities of a low condition."

And because I remained silent, unable to say anything in light of such new teachings, Alexandre considered:

"According to what you have seen, you can judge the extent to which education is needed in the physical realm. The incarnate mind has embellished itself with intellectual accomplishments and has created the cult of pure reason, but it has forgotten that human reasoning needs divine light. Ordinary human beings notice very little and feel even less. Due to the emergence of new knowledge, and in light of Spiritualism's regenerating wave – which is reaching the more educated nations of the earth, distressed for so long by collective suffering – we need to put forth our best capabilities of cooperation in order for our fellow men and women to value their blessed opportunities of service and redemption."

I realized that Alexandre was referring obliquely to the great Spiritist movement, because we were present at the activities of a doctrinal center. I was not mistaken, because the kind mentor continued gravely:

"Christian Spiritism is the revival of the Gospel of Our Lord Jesus Christ, and mediumship is one of its living fundamentals. However, mediumship is not limited to so-called 'mediums'. All individuals possess it because it entails spiritual perception, something which should be encouraged within us. Nevertheless, it is not enough just to perceive it. It is essential to sanctify this faculty, making it an active ministry of the good. The majority of candidates for this type of development, however, are not willing to undergo the preliminary work of cleansing the receptive vessel. They relentlessly separate matter and spirit into opposing camps, whereas we, the students of truth, have not yet been able to strictly define the boundaries between one and the other. We are certain that the entire universal organization is based on pure vibrations. Of course, dear friend," and he smiled, "we don't want to make the world a graveyard of sadness and desolation. To take part in the sanctifying mission of sex in its respectable sense, to have an ordinary aperitif, or to enjoy a good meal does not in any way indicate a spiritual deviance; however, excesses represent a lamentable waste of energies, which retains the soul in the lower realms. Therefore, for those who have incarcerated themselves in the prisons of darkness, it is not easy to develop advanced perceptions. We cannot consider constructive mediumship apart from constructive balance in the sublime science of healthy living for those who want to practice it."

"Oh!" I exclaimed. "So why not tell our brothers and sisters here about all this? Why not give them a stern warning?"

Alexandre smiled kindly and emphasized:

"No, Andre. Let's be patient. We are in the work of evolution and training. Our friends are neither intentionally rebellious nor evil. They are spiritually misguided and ill. They cannot change themselves overnight, so it is our duty to help them on the educational path."

The instructor stopped, smiled, and added:

"It is true that they dream of building marvelous castles without foundations, of making great outer discoveries without studying themselves. However, they will slowly come to understand that higher mediumship or edifying perception do not constitute mechanical activities of the personality, but rather conquests of the spirit, and for this achievement one cannot dispense with the painful beginnings and the necessary work, in addition to systematic and persevering self-education. However, except for their childlike illusions, they are good companions in the struggle. We affectionately care for them not only because they are our younger brothers and sisters but also because they deserve credit for the frequent cooperation they offer us, many times unconsciously. The tender green shoots of today will be the robust trees of tomorrow. The primitive tribes of yesterday comprise humankind today. For this reason, all our meetings are beneficial; and while their steps might be hesitant along the way, we will do everything to defend them against the dangerous mesh of vampirism.

4
Vampirism

According to what I deduced from the incarnate friends' conversation, the mediumistic development session had accomplished very little. However, this was not the case on our plane, where all the faces displayed great satisfaction, starting with Alexandre, who was jubilant.

The work had taken more than two hours, and although I had not said a word as I pondered the evening's lesson detail by detail, I did observe the intense effort made by workers from our realm. Large numbers of them had not only helped our earthbound fellow spirits, but had also assisted long lines of suffering spirits on our plane.

Alexandre, our devoted instructor, had acted in a thousand different ways. And touching on the issue that had impressed me the most during my observations of those worthy services, he approached and pointed out happily:

"Thank the Lord, we had a very fruitful night. We accomplished a lot of work against vampirism."

Oh! So vampirism was the subject with which I was concerned. I had seen the strangest bacilli of a psychic nature, which were completely unknown to the most advanced microbiology. They were neither spherical in form like the coccaceae nor rod-shaped like many types of bacteria; however, they did form dense and dreadful colonies. I had observed their attack on the vital elements of the physical body as they acted with great destructive power on the more delicate cells.

What was the meaning of that new world? What agents were they, characterized by an indefinable and pernicious power? Were all humans subject to their influence?

I could not hold back. I openly exposed my doubts and fears to my guide.

Alexandre smiled and considered:

"Very good! Very good! You came to observe the workings of mediumship and you are trying to fit it in to your role as a physician. That's natural. If you had specialized in another profession, you would have identified other aspects of the matter in question."

And encouraging me fraternally, he added:

"You are showing that you are well-prepared for the spiritual medicine that awaits your study."

After a long pause, he continued:

"Blood-sucking bats aside, a vampire, as understood by humans, refers to the ghosts of the dead that leave their crypt in the middle of the night to feed on the blood of the living. I don't know who the author of such a definition was, but deep down it is not wrong. All we need to remember is that for us a vampire is any idle entity that unduly uses others' potential; and, as for vampires who visit humans, it is necessary to realize that they carry out their sinister purposes any time they can find shelter in the envelope of human flesh."

Alexandre stopped briefly, letting me grasp the fact that he had just expounded the preliminary to more-serious explanations, and then he continued:

"You are aware of the fact that in the realm of earthly diseases each microbe species has its preferred environment. The pneumococcus normally lodges in the lungs; Eberth's bacillus is found in the intestines, where it produces typhoid fever; the Klebs-Loeffer bacillus settles in the mucous membranes, where it causes diphtheria. When the body offers special conditions, Hansen or Koch bacilli proliferate. But do you think that such microscopic formations are restricted only to transitory flesh? Don't you know that the macrocosm is full of surprises in varied forms? In the infinitesimal field, the findings follow the same surprising order. Andre, my friend, psychic illnesses are much more deplorable. The pathogenesis of the soul manifests in many different heartrending ways: anger, intemperance, sexual dissipation and varying degrees of degradations produce inferior creations that deeply affect one's inner life. A sick body almost always indicates a diseased mind. As understood in the realm of earthly thinking, the physiological organization goes no further than the vessel of clay within the pre-existent mold of the spiritual body. When this mold is affected in its structure by the blows of inferior vibrations, the vessel immediately reflects it."

I understood where my instructor wanted to go with this. However, his thoughts on these new microbial views were raising certain questions. What about the problem of their initial formation? Could psychic disease be fitted into the same symptomatic framework that I had known until now regarding organic illnesses in general? Might diseases of the soul be contagious? And would it be possible for this to occur in the sphere where the pathological phenomena of the flesh should no longer exist?

Virchow[6] stated that the human body "is a cellular country, where each cell is a citizen, and that disease is a conflict among these citizens, caused by the invasion of outside elements." In fact, from the cradle onward, human beings must fight against many types of climatic afflictions, between poisons and bacteria of various origins. How could I explain the new picture that now confronted my scant knowledge?

I could not restrain my curiosity. Resorting to Alexandre's admirable experience, I asked:

"Listen, my friend. How do the morbid processes of psychic origin occur? Doesn't illness result from the attack of outside forces? How can we explain this in our realm? Is it the corruption of the spiritual personality that produces the vampiristic creations, or do these creations dominate the soul, imposing certain illnesses on it? In the latter hypothesis, may we consider the possibility of contagion?"

My guide listened carefully and explained:

"First comes the sowing; then the harvest. Upon finding the appropriate soil, the seeds of both wheat and torpedo grass will produce in their own way and at the same rate. In this reply from nature to the farmer's efforts, we simply see an expression of the law. You are observing the area of larvae with justifiable wonder. Have no doubt. In diseases of the soul, just as in illnesses of the physical body, environment precedes outbreak. Actions produce effects, sentiments generate creations, and thoughts give rise to forms and consequences in infinitely different ways. And because each spirit represents a universe in and of itself, each one of us is responsible for the energies that we emit to circulate in the currents of life. Anger, despair, hatred and vices offer an open field to dangerous psychic germs in the realm of the soul. And

[6] Rudolf Virchow, 1821–1902, German pathologist (*Random House, Webster's College Dictionary*, 1991). – Tr.

just as happens with the diseases of the body, contagion here is a consummate fact once carelessness or the need to struggle establishes the appropriate environment amongst spirits of the same level. Of course, in the realm of denser matter this law functions violently, whereas amongst us it develops with natural alterations. Besides, it could be no other way; you are aware of the fact that many people tend to throw themselves into the abyss. Each individual corruption of the personality produces the dark forms that result from it, and these forms – just like weeds that spread through the soil due to the laxity of the person responsible – extend to nearby areas where the spirit of vigilance and defense does not prevail."

Demonstrating extreme caution in the examination of the facts, and warning me against any unworthy judgment in the evaluation of the Divine Work, he added:

"I know that your perplexity is enormous; however, you mustn't forget our condition as former backsliders in the abuse of the law. From the first day that reason took hold in the human mind, the idea of God has created religious principles that suggest rules for good living. However, as intellectual knowledge has become more refined, it seems that humans have less respect for the sacred gifts. With few exceptions, parents are the first corrupted sentinels, acting to their children's detriment. Usually, by age twenty and due to the inertia of the home's 'sentries', a woman has become a doll and a man a mannequin of sickly futilities: both are much more interested in the precision of their tailors than in being enlightened by their teachers. And upon reaching the time of marriage, they are often excessively ignorant or extremely degraded. We must further realize that, over the course of our earthly experiences, in the majority of cases we ourselves have been the champions of hardening and perversity against our own vital forces. Amid abuses of sex and food from our earliest years, we do nothing more than develop our inferior tendencies, crystallizing malignant habits. So is it any wonder that we have so many diseases of the body and so much psychic degenerateness? The Higher Realms never deny resources to the needy of all types, and, using every circumstance, they help brothers and sisters in humanity to restore their patrimony, either by working with nature or by inspiring the discovery of new medical or restorative sources. In our turn, as we rid ourselves of the denser fluids through physical death and to the extent that we evolve in understanding and competence, we become people's direct helpers. Despite this fact, however, the tangle of ignorance is still very thick. And vampirism is still very significant, because if the Father is supremely merciful, he is also infinitely just. No one will thwart his designs, and the death of the body almost always surprises the soul in a dreadful parasitic condition. Therefore, promiscuity is widespread among incarnates who are indifferent to divine law, and among discarnates who have been unresponsive to it. Completely unprepared and having lived much more from animalized sensations than from pure sentiments and thoughts, human creatures beyond the grave in very many cases continue to be magnetized to the home environments that used to nurture their emotions. Deplorable ignorance holds their minds, which are filled with particularities and imprisoned in earthly magnetism, deceiving themselves and fortifying their old delusions. The larvae that you observed are the habitual fare for the unfortunate individuals who have fallen into this type of parasitic condition."

"My God!" I exclaimed, greatly surprised.

Alexandre added:

"Such larvae possess a powerful animal magnetism."

Noticing perhaps that many distressing questions were clashing within my mind, my instructor considered:

"Of course, the microbial fauna in question cannot 'be served on plates'; instead, it is enough for the discarnate spirit to cling to its incarnate fellow spirits like a harmful weed clinging to the branch of a tree and sucking out its vital substance."

I could not hide my astonishment.

"Why so surprised?" asked my attentive guide. "What about us when we were in the physical realm? Weren't our tables maintained at the cost of the viscera of cattle and birds? Under the pretext of looking for sources of protein, we killed countless chickens and sheep, pigs and goats. We extracted their muscle tissues and chewed on their bones. Not content with killing the poor beings that were asking us for support on their path of growth and learning so that they could better tend to the Father's work, we increased the skill of our millenary exploitation and inflicted on many of them certain conditions so that they could most effectively serve our palate. The common pig was placed by us on a fattening diet, and the poor animal, often at the cost of waste, had to create reserves of fat for our use until it became completely prostrate under the weight of sickening and abundant lard. We placed geese on a fattening regimen for their livers to hypertrophy so that we could obtain pâtés for famous delicacies, unconcerned about the wrongs we were committing, supposedly on behalf of enriching culinary qualities. We felt no sorrow at seeing the touching picture of cows going to the slaughterhouse so that our pans could be filled with a good aroma. With scientific responsibility, we raised our need for a variety of proteins and fats, but we forgot that our minds, so productive in the discovery of convenience and comfort, might have the resources to find new elements and means of enhancing the supply of proteins in the organism without resorting to the industries of death. We overlooked the fact that increasing dairy products to enrich our diet would comprise an uplifting task, because a time will come for earthly humankind in which the stable, like the home, will also be sacred."

"But my friend," I stated, "the idea that many people on earth live at the mercy of invisible vampires is obviously disagreeable and disturbing. What about protection from the higher planes? And the assistance of angelic spirits and the loving defense of our superiors?"

"Andre, my dear fellow," said Alexandre kindly, "we need to affirm the truth, even if it goes against us. In all areas of creation, God our Father put high and low order beings to work on evolving by means of cooperation and love, management and obedience. Would we dare state, for instance, that we have been good to the beings beneath us? Haven't we devastated their lives, personifying diabolical entities on their paths? Of course we do not wish to create a principle of false protection for irrational individuals, compelled as they are – as are we – to cooperate to the best of their abilities and energies for the growth and harmony of life, nor do we wish to suggest the dangerous conservation of elements known to be harmful. However, we need to clarify the fact that, in the chapter of indifference concerning the fate of animals, in which we take part in the area of human activities, none of us, in good conscience, would be able to cast the first stone. The lower and needy creatures of the planet do not regard us as their generous and intelligent superiors, but rather as cruel persecutors. They trust the raging storm that disturbs the forces of nature, but they desperately flee at the approach of humans of any condition – except for domesticated animals, which, trusting our words and attitudes, yield to the cleaver at the slaughterhouse, almost always with tears of affliction, incapable of discerning with their embryonic reasoning where our wickedness begins and where our understanding ends. If we neither protect nor educate those whom the Father has entrusted to us as fragile seeds of reasoning in the heavy vessels of instinct; if we broadly abuse their inability to defend and preserve themselves, how can we demand help from our benevolent and wise superiors, whose simplest instructions are difficult to bear due to our deplorable condition as breakers of the law of mutual assistance? In your role as a physician, you cannot ignore the fact that if an embryologist were to look at the human fetus in its first days and away from its natural setting, he or she would not be able to say with any certainty whether he or she was looking at the beginnings of a man or a horse. A coroner finds it difficult to tell if a bloodstain found at a crime scene is that of a human, a dog or a monkey. Animals too have their endocrine system, their reserves of hormones, their own particular processes of reproduction in each species, and for that reason they have been precious and faithful helpers of science in the discovery of the most effective work of curing human diseases, actively taking part in the defense of civilization. Meanwhile..."

My instructor interrupted himself, and considering the seriousness of the subject, I asked emotionally:

"How can we solve such heartbreaking problems?"

"They are our problems," my kind friend clarified serenely. "It is not our place to condemn anybody. As we abandon the stages of our primitivism, we must awaken our consciousness to collective responsibility. The mission of superiors is to help and educate inferiors. And our abuses of nature have been crystallized in all countries for many centuries. We cannot renew the economic systems of nations overnight, nor can we suddenly replace the deep-rooted and corrupting habits of improper nourishment; these too reflect our multi-millenary errors. But in our status as children indebted to God and nature, we must continue the work of education, awakening our more experienced and enlightened incarnate fellow spirits to the new era in which humans will cultivate the soil of the earth out of love, and animals will be used in a spirit of respect, education and understanding."

After a short pause, my instructor remarked:

"Such a realization is of the utmost importance in human life, because without love for those beneath us, we cannot expect the watch-care of those above; without respect for others, we cannot hope for respect from others. If we have been insatiable vampires of the fragile creatures that surround us in earthly form, abusing our reasoning power in light of the weakness of their intelligence, it is not surprising that most humans, due to the animal nature that holds them in its grip, fall into situations of illness due to the vampirism of spirits who are attuned to them in the invisible realm."

Alexandre's explanations were ministered without presumption or criticism, yet they pierced me deeply. Something new awakened within my being. It was the spirit of veneration for all things, the effective recognition of the Paternal Power of the Lord of the Universe.

My kind guide interrupted my inner wonder of adoration for the Father, pointing out:

"As you can see, authentic mediumistic development is a problem of candidates' spiritual ascension to sublime perceptions. Nevertheless, Andre, it doesn't matter that our friends, anxious for psychic growth, have come here without due preparation. Although they are beginners in the subject, they have profited a lot because they have been helped against poisonous and destructive vampirism. You were surprised by the larvae that were sapping their spiritual energies; now you will see the exploiting spirits that have remained outside the room, awaiting their return."

"Outside?" I asked, alarmed.

"Yes," replied Alexandre. "If our brothers and sisters were to succeed in using the desirable blows of discipline on themselves, they would gain a lot of strength against the influence of the unfortunate spirits who follow them; regrettably, however, rare are those who are able to maintain the necessary willpower when it comes to the living application of the light they have received. After our magnetic circle, set up during the course of each meeting, is broken, most attendees forget the blessings they have received and they return to the same deplorable state they were in hours before, subjugated by obstinate and cruel vampires."

"Oh! What a lesson!" I exclaimed.

Noticing that our incarnate friends were about to leave, the instructor invited me:

"Come with me onto the street and see for yourself."

5
Exerting an Influence

I was now able to notice the difference in the environment.

For us, discarnate spirits, the atmosphere inside had been impregnated with soothing, regenerative elements; but outside the air was heavy. I had become hypersensitive to the coarse emanations of the street. The electric lights were like little globes emitting a very weak light, isolated by heavy darkness.

Breathing in the new currents of air, I noticed the indefinable difference. The oxygen seemed to be tinged with an unpleasant magnetism.

Once again, I understood the sublimity of prayer and the work of higher spirituality within people's inner selves.

Prayer, uplifting meditation and edifying thought transform the atmosphere, purifying it.

Instructor Alexandre interrupted my inner considerations:

"The change is obviously inexpressible. Between the harmonious vibrations of the scenario inside the center – illuminated by prayer – and the public street – full of inferior emanations – there are striking differences. Lofty thought sanctifies the atmosphere around it and possesses electrical properties that common folk can't even begin to imagine. The street, on the other hand, is an ancient repository of antagonistic vibrations in the midst of dark psychic materials and dangerous bacteria of various sources, because the majority of passers-by continuously put into circulation not only immense colonies of various microbes but also wrong thoughts of all types."

While I was pondering this lesson, I noticed that several groups of unfortunate and restless spirits were standing around nearby. One could hear the most interesting and colorful conversations; they were, however, nonsensical and improper at best.

Alexandre pointed out a small group of apparently highly imbalanced discarnates:

"That group of friends makes up the almost permanent cohort of our incarnate fellow spirits now returning to their homes."

"Really?" I asked without meaning to.

"Yes," added my teacher attentively. "Such unfortunate spirits are not allowed to enter the premises during specialized sessions such as the one tonight; they are allowed to come to meetings aimed at general assistance. This evening, however, we needed to assist other friends in order to attenuate the damaging consequences of the vampirism victimizing them."

I was impressed by the excellence of his explanation. Everything involving such work obeyed a pre-established order; everything was calculated, programmed and foreseen.

"Now," a good-humored Alexandre continued, "notice our earthly coworkers as they leave. Observe the way in which they instinctively return to the arms of the ignorant spirits who are exploiting them."

I watched carefully. They were all intent on leaving the room peacefully.

At the door next to us, they all began saying their goodbyes:

"Thank the Lord!" exclaimed a woman of refined manners. "We said our prayers in peace with great results."

"How much better I feel!" one of the more elderly friends said. "The session brought me relief. My soul was burdened with worries, but now I feel comforted and happy. I believe that the prayers removed the heavy clouds from my heart. By listening to them and taking part in the attempts at mediumistic development aimed at helping our neighbor, we have received a lot of assistance! Ah! How generous Jesus is."

A distinguished looking gentleman remarked:

"Spiritism is our comfort. In light of such truth, our commitments are very extensive. It is not without reason that the Lord has placed in our hands the sublime torch of faith. Suffering people weep all around us and the ignorant stray onto the broad pathway of evil. The tools for our work come to us from heaven. We must work hard to render ourselves faithful coworkers of the New Revelation!"

"Precisely!" agreed someone in the group, moved by his exhortation. "We have great duties to fulfill; we cannot waste any time. The comforting doctrine of the Spirits[7] is our treasure of light and consolation. Oh, my friends, how much work we have to do! Jesus calls us to serve; it is essential that we respond."

As I recognized the characteristics of gratitude and praise in the conversation, I expressed my sincere admiration and praised the faithfulness of the center's coworkers. They showed themselves to be fervent in their faith, trusting in the future and

[7] A reference to the high order spirits involved in formulating the Spiritist Doctrine codified by Allan Kardec. – Tr.

interested in extending the divine benefits on behalf of the pain and needs of others.

Noticing my laudatory thoughts, Alexandre smiled and remarked:

"Don't be too impressed. The problem is not one of enthusiasm but of persistent effort. We cannot rush results that will take time. Few friends can maintain uniformity of emotion and idealism in their spiritual growth. I have been actively participating in this group with few interruptions for almost nine years, and every month I see a parade of new promises and vows of service. However, at the first collision with the real needs of the endeavor, only a small number actually remain faithful to their consciences. During times of calm, great praise; during times of difficulty, desertions camouflaged under the pretext of not being understood by others. I must say that, in the majority of cases, our brothers and sisters are helpful and charitable toward their neighbors regarding material needs, but they almost always continue to be less kind to themselves because they forget to apply the evangelical light to their practical lives. They promise too much with words, whereas they work very little in the area of the sentiments. With exceptions, they get upset at the first contact with a harder struggle after having reaffirmed the soundest of intentions of renewal, and usually, when they return to their place of prayer each week, they are in the same condition, requesting comfort and outside assistance. It is difficult for them to fulfill the promise they made to themselves to cooperate with Christ, the fundamental basis of true enlightenment."

As Alexandre became silent, I carefully observed the bystanders. The incarnates were all still radiating the joy and peace reaped from the short time spent with their invisible benefactors. Remarkable rays of spirituality were emanating from everyone's forehead.

With an indicating gesture, my instructor explained:

"They are still under the radiations of the shower of light they received through their submission to spiritual work coupled with prayer. If they were able to maintain this mental state by putting into practice the rules for perfection that they learn, comment on and teach, it would be easy for them to reach the higher levels of life; however, Andre, just like we ourselves used to be, they too are inexperienced and fragile. Each of the unworthy habits acquired by the soul during the incessant course of centuries works as a living entity in the world of our sentiments, driving us toward disturbed regions and offering elements that connect us to the unhappy spirits dwelling at a lower level. Examine our incarnate friends very carefully."

I observed them with interest. They were politely exchanging their final greetings of the night, displaying luminous joy.

"Let's accompany the group that is most strongly affected by sexual disturbances," exclaimed my teacher, offering me a valuable experience.

A young man, accompanied by an elderly lady and a young woman – whom I soon perceived to be his mother and sister – was on his way home.

We followed them closely.

A few yards beyond the place where our companions-in-struggle had held the meeting, the overall atmosphere of the street was becoming even heavier.

Three spirits of a gloomy appearance, completely blind to our presence due to the low vibratory level of their perceptions, approached the trio.

One of the spirits leaned on the elderly lady and instantaneously I noticed that her forehead became opaque, strangely dark. Her facial expression changed. Her radiant joy disappeared and gave way to the signs of deep worry. She had become completely transfigured.

"Oh, my children!" exclaimed the mother, who seemed to be patient and kind. "Why are we so different during our spiritual work? After we leave our joint prayer service, I wish I could retain the same level of good cheer and inner peace. But that's not the case. Once I rejoin the path of practical struggle, I feel that the essence of the evangelical readings remains within me, but in a vague sort of way, without the clarity of the initial moments. I make a sincere effort to continue in the same state of spirit, but I lack something that I cannot define exactly."

At that moment, the two other spirits, who had been keeping their distance, casually took the young man's arms, and I witnessed the same phenomenon. His mental clarity became foggy and two wrinkles of concern and despondency marked his face, which lost its aura of luminous and confident happiness. He answered in a slow and sad voice:

"That's true, Mother. Our imperfections are enormous. Believe me; my situation is even worse. You feel anxious, downhearted and sad ... That is very little for someone like me, who feels himself a victim of evil thoughts. I got married less than eight months ago, and notwithstanding my wife's devotion, my heart is at times full of inappropriate temptations. I ask myself why I have these strange ideas, and quite frankly, I have no answer. The invincible attraction to spiteful environments confuses my spirit, which I feel is inclined to goodness and proper behavior."

"Who knows, dear brother? You might be under the influence of less enlightened spirits," the polite young woman considered.

"Yes," sighed the young man. "That's why I've been attempting to develop my mediumship – to locate the cause of this situation."

At that moment, my guide whispered kindly:

"Let's help this friend out by talking to him."

He put his right hand on the young woman's forehead, keeping it under a vigorous magnetic influx while transmitting benevolent thoughts to her. I noticed that when it touched the young woman's curly hair, his protective hand let off luminous sparks, which only I could perceive. The young woman seemed to become more poised and dignified in her almost childlike expression. She answered firmly:

"In this case, I would say that the development of mediumship should be the last resort, because before we can face our enemies, the offspring of ignorance, we must arm our hearts with the light of love and wisdom. If you were to discover invisible persecutors around your activities, how could you offer them any Christian benefit without the necessary spiritual preparation? An intelligent educational reaction against evil is always our duty, but before considering psychic development – which might perhaps be premature – we must try to uplift our ideas and sentiments. We cannot count on good mediumship without the consolidation of our good intentions, and in order to be useful in the realms of the spirit, we first need to learn to live spiritually, albeit still in the flesh."

Although this reply was surprisingly valuable to me, it did not generate much interest in the other two, who had become almost neutralized by the action of their vampires.

Mother and son showed they were deeply annoyed by the remarks they had just heard. The girl's words, full of true light, were unsettling.

"Dear child, you are not yet old enough to offer an opinion on the matter," exclaimed her elderly mother, aggravated.

And like a good cultivator of old sufferings, she remarked:

"When you have traveled the paths that my feet have trod; when hopeless disillusionment comes your way, then you will see how hard it is to keep peace and light in your heart!"

"And if one day you experience the struggles that I have known," the sad young man added, "you will see that I have my reasons for complaining against my fate and that I have no other recourse but to remain in the circle of indecision that afflicts me. I do what I can to free myself from dark ideas and I continually struggle against unexpected temptations; nonetheless, I feel far-removed from the spiritual freedom I need. It's not that I'm unwilling, but..."

Alexandre removed his hand from the young woman's forehead, and told me in reply to my bewilderment:

"The spirit attached to our sister used to be her husband, a man who did not develop his spiritual potential and who lived in tremendous selfishness at home. The two unhappy spirits clinging so hard to the young man are two ignorant and disturbed companions whom he acquired in contact with prostitution."

In light of my astonishment, the instructor continued:

"The ex-husband did not see his marriage as anything more than the union of bodies to fulfill the carnal tendencies of human life; and because he spent his time of earthly learning without any ennobling ideals and was interested only in enjoying every gratification of the senses, he does not feel strong enough to leave his domestic circle, where his companion, only now, after his discarnation, has begun to concern herself with issues relating to spiritual life. As for the young man, in moving from one thoughtless act to the next, he created strong ties to spirits still bogged down in the swamp of sensations in the area of prostitution; the two, more persistent ones now clinging to him are almost wholly attuned to his personal magnetic field. The poor fellow did not realize the perils he was facing and became an unwitting prisoner of invisible companions who are as weak and addicted as he is."

"But isn't there any way to free them?" I asked, moved.

The guide smiled paternally and considered:

"Who should break their shackles, except themselves? They never lacked the outside help of our continuous friendship; however, they themselves nourish each other in the realm of subtle sensations, something impossible to compute for those who cannot probe their inner mechanism. Of course, they are now seeking the elements for their liberation. They draw near to the source of elevated enlightenment; they feel tired of the situation and they do, in fact, have the desire for a new life; but this wish comes from the lips instead of the heart, and it constitutes a very vague, almost non-existent longing. If they were actually to cultivate a positive resolution, they would transform their personal energies, rendering them the determining factors in the area of regenerative action. However, they expect unacceptable miracles and deny their own energies, the only levers available for accomplishing their desire."

"But couldn't we make these unconscionable vampires leave?" I asked.

"The parties in interest would simply make them return," explained Alexandre, smiling. "The attempt you are suggesting has already been made with the purpose of benefiting them indirectly, but our sister declared that she missed her husband too much, and our male friend stated that he felt less of a man on the inside, mistaking humility for cowardice and taking detachment from the lower impulses as a doom to boredom. Their emission of mental complaints got to the point that their inner thoughts became veritable evocations, and due to the strong magnetism of an incessantly fed desire, their unfortunate companions joined up with them once more."

"Are they magnetized to each other like that wherever they go?" I asked.

"Almost always. They mutually fulfill each other in their continuous exchange of emotions and innermost feelings."

Concerned about doing something good, I offered:

"Couldn't we guide these spirits to acquire the strength they need? Wouldn't it be right to instruct them, urging them on to spiritual balance and self-respect?"

"That recourse," said Alexandre serenely, "has not been ignored. Such measures are being carried out with determination using the appropriate method; however, since this is a case in which these incarnates have become powerful magnets of attraction, it requires time and fraternal forbearance. A large number of workers on our plane are dedicated to the task, and we are waiting for the sowing of teachings to bear fruit. In any case, you can rest assured that every type of assistance has been given to our friends here. If all of them have not yet advanced in the land of higher spirituality, it is because of the weakness and ignorance to which they have willingly enslaved themselves. They are reaping what they sowed."

We again focused our attention on the conversation at hand:

"I'm doing all I can," the young man repeated, discouraged, "but I just can't seem to find inner peace."

"Me either," remarked the forlorn mother. "I only feel some improvement at our group prayers. Afterward, the worst emotions assault my spirit. I live without peace, without support. Oh, my children! It's so cruel to have to roll around like this in the world like a castaway without direction!"

"I know what you mean, Mother," replied the son, as if pleased to be feeding the noxious thoughts filling his mind. "I know what you mean, because temptation has turned my life into a jungle of heavy darkness. I don't know what else to do to resist these disturbing thoughts. Woe to us if Spiritism had not come into our lives as a sacred source of sublime consolation!"

Alexandre once again put his right hand on the young woman's forehead, and she translated his thoughts in a respectful and affectionate tone:

"I agree that Spiritism is our fount of consolation, but I cannot forget that the Doctrine is a blessed preparatory school. If we remain attached to our demands for comfort, we might end up forgetting that we must work. I believe that the teachers of spiritual truth wish above all for our inner reform so that we may partake of the higher life, but if we look only for consolation, without building up our strength, we will be nothing but spiritual children. If we seek the company of benevolent guides with only the intention of enjoying personal advantages, where will we acquire enlightenment? Aren't we here on the earth to learn? Upon being reborn, did we receive our body simply to sit around? We cannot believe that our friends from the higher spheres are here to deprive us of our ability to walk on our own two feet. Of course, our benefactors from the Beyond do not want us to be the needy of God's house forever, but to be fellow spirits in the glorious work of the good, and to be as generous, strong, wise and happy as they themselves already are."

And wanting to demonstrate the daughterly affection that vibrated in her soul, she changed her tone of voice:

"Mother, you know how much I love you, but something deep inside my conscience won't allow me to comment on our needs in any other way than this, by adjusting myself to the higher teachings that the Doctrine has been engraved on our hearts. I cannot comprehend Christianity without our practicing Christ's example fully."

Alexandre halted the magnetic operation, and because I found myself perplexed by the ease with which the young woman had received his thoughts after I had observed the complexity involving psychography, I voiced the questions that had assailed my mind.

Without hesitation, Alexandre explained:

"Andre, you have been witnessing the simple activity of mental transmission, and you cannot forget that the exchange of thought is a free movement in the world. Discarnates and incarnates in all areas of earthly activity live within the widest exchange of ideas. Each mind is a virtual world of sending and receiving, and each one attracts other minds that are similar to it. The sad ones prefer the saddened; the ignorant ones gather together; criminal minds share in the same subject; and good ones establish mutual ties of work and accomplishment. Here we have the intuitive phenomenon, which is common to all individuals to a greater or lesser intensity, not only on the constructive plane, but also in the circle of less elevated expressions. Hence, we have been observing an elderly sister and her adult son who have completely adapted to being exploited by their discarnate acquaintances caught up in ignorance and infirmity, and they have thus established a perfect exchange of lower vibrations. Transformed into effective hosts as far as their psychophysical potential will allow, they speak under the direct influence of their unfortunate vampires. Also under our analysis we have a young woman who just turned sixteen in her new existence. Her inclinations, however, are quite different. She is able to receive our thoughts and translate them into edifying language. She is not involved in the technical work of mediumship per se, but rather in the blessed work of spiritualization."

And nodding to the young woman surrounded by a wonderful aura of light, he added:

"She continues to maintain her physical vessel in the same state of purity in which she received it from the benefactors who prepared her for her current incarnation. She has not yet been drawn to the plane of stronger emotions and her potential for reception in the intuitive realm remains clear and malleable. Her cells are still completely free of toxic influences; so far, her vocal organs have not been corrupted by slander, rebelliousness and hypocrisy; her centers of sensitivity have not yet suffered deviations; her nervous system enjoys an enviable harmony, and her heart, enveloped in good sentiments, communes with the beauty of eternal truths through a sincere and consoling faith. Furthermore, since she does not have any very serious debts from her past – a condition that frees her from contact with perverse spirits moving about in the darkness – she can reflect our innermost thoughts accurately. Since she is living much more by the spirit in her present state, all we need is a magnetic exchange in order for her to translate our essential ideas."

"Does that mean that this young woman is pure enough to continue enjoying such facilities throughout her whole lifetime?" I asked.

Alexandre smiled and remarked:

"Not to that extent. She still retains the benefits that she brought from the spirit realm, and the cards of happiness are still in her hands in order for her to attract the best advantages in the game of life, but it will be up to her to win or lose in the future. Her conscience is free to choose."

"So," I continued, "wouldn't it be difficult for all individuals to prepare themselves to receive influence from the higher planes?"

"Not at all," he clarified. "Within the spirit of service and balance, all righteous souls can commune perfectly with divine messengers and receive their programs involving work and enlightenment, regardless of the mediumistic technique that is presently being developed in the world. Nobody is privileged within creation; rather, there are faithful workers who are justly compensated wherever they are."

Strongly impressed by his remarks, I felt that my thoughts had become lost in a sea of new and blessed conclusions.

6
Prayer

After leaving his mother and sister, the young man headed home.

We followed close behind. It pained me to see him as a victim flanked by the two dark shapes.

The observations regarding psychic microbiology had impressed me strongly.

I knew all about the circulatory alterations that caused embolism, heart attacks and gangrene. As a doctor, I had treated countless cases of infection involving arthritis and myositis, gastric ulcers and miliar abscesses. I had carefully examined the manifestations of cancer and malignant tumors in complicated pathological processes. I had seen multiple microbial expressions in the treatment of leprosy, syphilis and tuberculosis. In my position as a defender of life, I would often spend many days in a duel with death, feeling the uselessness of my professional techniques in fighting strange viruses that hastened bodily destruction in their scorn of my efforts. However, as a doctor, in the majority of cases in which I was able to count on the marvelous intervention of nature, I believed that I knew several ways to fight health problems. When the diagnosis was diphtheria, I did not hesitate to employ Roux serum, and I knew how effective a tracheotomy was in the case of croup. In cases of congestion, I always remembered to increase circulation. With eczema, of course I remembered starch baths, bismuth creams, arsenic and sulfur-based medicines. Upon confirming edema, I remembered veratrin, calomel, caffeine and theobromine after analyzing the symptoms in detail. In dealing with cancer, I performed surgery if radiation proved ineffective. For all types of symptoms, I knew how to use regimens and diets, different types of applications, quarantines and interventions, but ... what about this case?

A different type of patient was walking ahead of us. His diagnosis was different. It was outside my knowledge of symptoms and my old ways of healing. Nevertheless, he was a patient in a very serious condition. We had seen the dark parasites; we had observed his inner despair due to the incessant siege. Was there no remedy for him? Might he be forsaken, and was he more unfortunate than the physically sick? What to do to alleviate his terrible sufferings manifesting themselves in tormenting and ongoing distress? I had helped disturbed and suffering spirits by relieving their atrocious afflictions. I was well aware of the constant efforts of our spirit colony to diminish the suffering of low order discarnates; but in this case, thanks to the magnetic approach of Alexandre, the great and generous instructor accompanying me, I was now observing an incarnate individual held prey to a unique form of vice. How to administer the assistance that was so crucial?

And of course, new ideas quickly began to surface. Could similar microbial manifestations follow discarnates? Could they attack the soul apart from the flesh? While I was going through inexpressible torment in the lower zones[8], I had obviously been a victim of the same cruel influences. So, where was the healing medicine? Where was the relief for such afflictions?

Displaying paternal interest, Alexandre came to my rescue:

"These inner questions, Andre, are very helpful to your soul. You have begun to observe the manifestations of vampirism, which are not limited to the environs of the incarnate. Almost all suffering in the lower zones owes its piteous origin to such vampirism. Individuals who have strayed from the truth and the good while trodding the long path of evolution join one another in order to continue their magnetic exchanges of a lower nature. Criminals of all sorts, the weak-willed, the character-impaired, the voluntarily ill, the stubborn and recalcitrant of all situations and times make up communities of sufferers and penitents of the same level, who drag themselves, heavy as lead, around the regions invisible to human sight. They all secrete hateful energies and create horrible shapes because all mental matter is covered in a pliable and exteriorizing power."

"But," I objected, "I feel that the medical field is much larger after the death of the body."

"Absolutely," replied Alexandre calmly, "when we understand the extent of moral qualities in all the events of life."

"Even so," I offered, "these new discoveries in the microbial field have filled me with horror. What can we do against vampirism? How can we fight these degrading mental forces? In the world we have specialized clinics, surgical techniques and antidotes used in various healing methods. What about here?"

Alexandre smiled thoughtfully and after a longer pause he said:

"As we can see, Andre, the ancient treatments in temples, the importance of faith in medical procedures in times past,

[8] A. Luiz's experiences in the lower zones, or the Umbral, are described in his book *Nosso Lar*, also translated into English and available through this publisher. – Tr.

and the notion that diabolical entities cause the strangest diseases in humans were not completely without reason. There can be no doubt that, as far as incarnate spirits are concerned, mental expressions depend on the balance of the body, just as good and perfect music depends on a trustworthy instrument. Medical science will reach sublime heights the day it discovers within the transient body the shadow of the eternal soul. Each physical cell is the instrument of a certain mental vibration. We are all heirs of our Father, who creates, preserves, perfects, transforms or destroys, and each day, with our potential as generators of latent energies, we are creating, renewing, improving or destroying something. I can understand the surprise of your reasoning as it faces the new landscape unfolding to your sight. The struggle for perfection is immense. As for the systematic fight against vampirism in the many illnesses of the soul, here too, on the plane of our activities, we have no lack of cleansing and healing processes of an outward nature; however, on examining the subject in its essence, we have been compelled to realize that each of God's children must be his or her own physician, and until this truth is fully accepted and its principles are applied, the individual will be subjected to unending imbalances."

Understanding my surprise, Alexandre nodded at the young man, who was about to enter his home after his short walk, and said:

"Against vampirism there are a number of methods of spiritual medication, which we can develop in different ways; but in order to give you a practical demonstration, let's visit our friend's home. There you will see the most powerful antidote."

Curious, I noticed that the unfortunate spirits now seemed to be terribly upset. Something was keeping them from following their victim inside.

"Of course," my kind companion pointed out, "you already know that prayer sets up vibratory borders."

Yes, I had already witnessed this.

"Here," he continued, "lives a sister who has been fortunate enough to cultivate fervent and righteous prayer."

We went inside. And while our friend was preparing to retire, Alexandre explained the reason for the sublime peace within those humble walls.

"A home," he said, "is not only an abode for bodies; above all, it is an abode for souls. The domestic sanctuary inhabited by persons who love prayer and uplifting sentiments becomes a sublime field for the most beautiful spiritual flowerings and harvests. Our friend has not yet balanced himself on the true foundations of life after the extreme oscillations and frivolous experiences of his early youth; however, his partner, a young Christian woman, has guaranteed his house's tranquility with her presence due to the abundant and continuous emission of purifying and luminous energies that nurture her spirit."

I was eminently surprised. In fact, the tranquility inside the home was great and comforting. In every corner and on each individual object there were vibrations of inalterable peace.

The young man entered the modest bedroom, looking forward to his nighttime rest.

Alexandre paternally took my right hand and went to the door – which had been closed without a sound – and knocked lightly as if we were before a sanctuary that should not be entered without religious respect.

A very young woman, whom I immediately perceived to be our friend's wife, having disengaged from her physical body during sleep, answered the door and greeted the instructor warmly. After greeting me upon Alexandre's introduction, she exclaimed happily:

"I thank God for the opportunity of praying together. Please come in. I wish to make our home a living temple of Our Lord."

We entered the private quarters and I could hardly contain my surprise.

At that very moment, the young man was getting in bed with obvious care not to awaken his sleeping wife.

I contemplated the beautiful and sanctifying scene. The bed was surrounded with an intense luminosity. I noticed the very subtle threads of magnetic energy linking the soul of our noble friend to her physical form as it lay there peacefully.

"Forgive me," she said kindly, gazing at my instructor. "I need to attend to my immediate duties."

"Please, go ahead, Cecilia," said the instructor with the tenderness of a father who blesses. "We dropped by only to visit you."

Cecilia kissed his hands and pleaded:

"Don't forget to leave your blessings with us."

Alexandre smiled silently and remained in deep thought for a few minutes.

While he was focused inwardly, I observed the tender scene: The wife, detached from her body, sat at the head of the bed, and at the same time, the young man, who seemed to be fixing his pillows, laid his head on her spirit lap. While stroking his hair, Cecilia lifted her eyes to the Most High in fervent prayer. Sublime light surrounded her completely and I could tune in to her innermost thoughts as I listened to her request for enlightenment for her partner, whom she seemed to love without bounds. Moved by the beauty of her pleas, I was surprised to see that her heart had become a blazing focal point of light, from which countless shining particles were emitted, projecting onto her husband's body and soul with the swiftness of tiny rays. The radiant particles entered his body in every direction, especially the sexual area, where I had seen such great psychic anomalies. The particles concentrated en masse there, destroying the tiny, horrible dark forms of the devouring vampirism. But the deadly elements did not remain inactive. They fought desperately with the agents of light. As if he had reached an oasis, the young man lost his expression of anguished fatigue. He seemed calmer and gradually stronger and happier as time progressed. With his essential energies restored, he slowly embraced his loving wife as she remained maternally at his side, and he joyfully fell asleep.

The intimate scene was incredibly beautiful.

I was readying myself to ask for explanations when the instructor gently asked me to leave.

Once outside the room, he spoke to me paternally:

"You have seen enough. Now you can draw your own conclusions."

"Yes," I replied. "I am very surprised by what I have seen, but I would love to hear your clarifying thoughts."

"Have no doubt," the instructor continued, "prayer is the most effective antidote for vampirism. Prayer is neither a mechanical movement of the lips nor a record of easy repetition by the mind. It is vibration, energy and power. The person who mobilizes his or her own energies in prayer performs deeds of indescribable significance. This type of psychic state unveils unknown powers, reveals our divine origin and puts us in contact with higher sources. In this act, spirits in any form can emit rays of astonishing power."

After a short pause, Alexandre declared, making the lesson more forceful:

"And you should be aware of the fact that the lower life forms of earth feed almost exclusively on rays. Every minute, billions of cosmic rays originating from stars and planets at very great distances from the earth descend upon humans' brows, not to mention the solar, heat and light rays that earthly science is only now beginning to discover. Gamma rays from radium, which incessantly disintegrates in the soil, as well as those of various expressions emitted by water and metals, reach the inhabitants of earth through their feet and exert a considerable influence. And in the horizontal direction, human beings experience the action of magnetic rays sent out by plants, animals and their fellow human beings."

Wonder had silenced me, but my instructor continued after a short pause:

"And what about the emanations of a psychic nature that surround humanity, originating from the colonies of discarnate beings that surround the earth? Every second, Andre, each one of us receives trillions of rays of all types, and we emit our own energies that are peculiar to us and which leave to act on the plane of life, sometimes in regions very far from us. In this circle of continuous exchange, the divine rays emitted by sanctifying prayer are converted into high level factors of effective and definitive cooperation in the healing of the body, the renewal of the soul and the enlightenment of the conscience. All elevated prayer is a source of creative and vivifying magnetism, and anybody who cultivates prayer with the proper balance of sentiment gradually becomes a radiating focal point of divine energies."

The instructor's explanations reached deep into my being. Wishing to check another detail of the sublime experience, I asked:

"Will the wife's efforts alone be enough to reestablish our ailing friend's psychic equilibrium?"

Alexandre smiled and answered:

"Cecilia's assistance is valuable for her partner, but her ability to send out divine emissions belongs to her alone as the incorruptible fruit of her individual efforts. For him it means an "added mercy" that he will attach permanently to the heritage of his personality through his own work. Receiving the assistance of the good does not mean that the beneficiary himself is good. Our friend needs to devote himself fervently to making good use of the blessings he receives, because all outside help can be interrupted and each of God's children is the heir of sublime potential and must act as his or her own physician."

7
Spiritual Help

"Do you need to return to your activities now?" Alexandre asked when we were back on the street.

"No, I still have some time," I answered.

My interest in continuing the lesson was enormous. Alexandre possessed vast medical experience; my knowledge was very pale in comparison to his.

"Later today, I have a meeting for the instruction of incarnate brothers and sisters," he continued, "and we would be pleased if you could attend."

"And why wouldn't I? I can't let this learning opportunity slip by."

We left the house.

The troubled spirits were still milling around outside the door as if waiting for a chance to go in.

As Alexandre continued his uplifting lesson, we walked almost step by step, just as we did when we were living on the earth.

It was early dawn. There was an enormous number of discarnate passers-by. Most of them were of a lower nature and wore dark clothing, but every now and then we were met by luminous groups hurrying along, fulfilling tasks that were obviously very important.

"There are always urgent tasks to do when helping our earthbound brothers and sisters," my instructor said kindly, "and most of the time our aid is more effective at night, when direct sunlight doesn't decompose certain resources of our cooperation..."

He had not finished when a pleasant elderly woman unexpectedly approached us.

"Justina, my sister, may the Lord bless you!" Alexandre greeted her.

With a look of great trouble in her eyes, his spirit friend replied with affectionate respect and explained:

"Alexandre, I have come looking for you because I am in urgent need of your help. Please forgive me."

And before the instructor could ask about what was troubling her, the woman continued:

"My son Antonio isn't doing well at all..."

Now it was Alexandre who interrupted her:

"I can guess what's going on. When I visited him last month, I noticed his circulatory problems."

"Yes, yes," continued the worried mother. "Antonio is living in a circle of highly undisciplined thoughts, despite his good heart. Tonight he took so many unfounded worries to bed, so much unnecessary anxiety, that his mental creations have turned into real torture. I tried to help him with my meager abilities, but unfortunately his inner imbalance is so great that all my assistance was useless, and his brain is at risk of a fatal stroke."

Sensing the gravity of the moment, she added sadly:

"Oh Alexandre, I know very well that we must subject our wishes to God's will, but my son still needs a few more days on earth. I think that in two months I will indirectly obtain for him the solution to all the problems that have affected his family's peace. Your authority could help us! Your Christ-centered heart is in a state such that you could do this good for us!"

Realizing the urgency of the matter, Alexandre exclaimed:

"Let's go! We have no time to lose!"

A few moments later, we entered the comfortable residence. The afflicted elderly woman took us to a large bedroom where her son, the head of the family, was lying on white sheets. He looked as if he was on his deathbed.

Antonio seemed to be close to seventy and was displaying all the signs of advanced arteriosclerosis.

The situation now became profoundly instructive for me; I had just entered a valuable realm of new observations.

I could clearly identify the pre-agonic phase in all its physical-spiritual expressions. The confused, unconscious soul was barely moving. It was almost completely outside and next to the motionless body, which was having a hard time breathing.

As Alexandre was leaning over him paternally, I could see that we were looking at a very serious case of thrombosis in one of the arteries that irrigated the motor cortex of the brain – a stroke was imminent. Another few instants and the victim would discarnate.

Alexandre concentrated all his attention on the patient, touched his perispiritual brain and said with serene authority:

"Antonio, stay awake! You must help us to help you!"

Partially disconnected from his body, the dying man opened his eyes outside his physical envelope, displaying vague signs of awareness. The instructor continued:

"You have been harmed by your own thoughts because of an unjustifiable conflict. Your excessive worries have created elements of cerebral disorganization. Strengthen your desire to gain control over your physical cells while we get ready to help you. This moment is decisive for your needs."

The patient did not answer, but I could tell that Antonio understood the warning at the core of the powers of consciousness, putting himself in a good enough state to cooperate on his own behalf.

Next, Alexandre began complex magnetic procedures on the inanimate body, administering new energies to the spine. After a few moments, he placed his right hand over the liver, and then held it for a time on the physical brain at the point of the motor area. He called me over and said:

"Andre, please help us out by praying. I will call for some of our brothers and sisters on duty tonight to help us."

And after thinking for a few seconds he remarked:

"Brother Francisco's group can't be far away."

Having said this, Alexandre concentrated intensely.

Not a minute later, a small team of eight spirits – four brothers and four sisters – came into the room in reverent silence.

We all quickly said hello and the instructor respectfully addressed the spirit who seemed to be in charge.

"Francisco, what we need here are emanations from some of our incarnate friends whose physical vehicles are in well-balanced repose at this moment."

And as the new brother was carefully observing the dying man, Alexandre added:

"As you can see, this is a very serious case. We need to be very careful in our choice of a fluid donor."

Francisco thought for a moment and suggested:

"Our friend Afonso might be quite helpful. While I go for him, our group will help your healing action by emitting energies of magnetic help through prayer."

Francisco left immediately.

The elderly woman approached Alexandre and said respectfully:

"If there is a need for fluids from incarnates, maybe we could get it from my granddaughters. They're asleep in the next room."

"No," answered Alexandre kindly, "they would not be suitable at this time. We need somebody who is sufficiently balanced in the mental field."

The worried mother stepped aside, wiping her eyes.

In response to the instructor's kind gesture, I drew nearer to take a closer look at the patient, although I maintained an inner attitude of prayer.

"Antonio has been a widower for twenty years," Alexandre explained, "and he is on the verge of returning to us in the spirit world. However, he still needs a few more days in the physical realm so that he can duly resolve some serious problems before he leaves. The Lord will grant us the pleasure of helping to temporarily restore his strength."

And either because I was focusing my attention on the group of spirits who were praying silently, or because he wanted to enlighten me further, the instructor explained:

"This is Brother Francisco's group. It is one of the countless service groups that lend us their cooperation. Many fellow spirits dedicate themselves to work of this kind, particularly at night, when our assistance activities can be more intense."

A veritable world of questions inundated my mind, aimed at solving the problems of the moment; however, understanding the seriousness of the case at hand, I decided to remain silent.

It was not long before Francisco returned with the incarnate friend Alexandre had referred to earlier.

There was no time for greetings. Taking his right hand, the instructor led him immediately to the head of the dying man's bed, telling him with affectionate authority:

"Afonso, we haven't a second to lose. Put both your hands on the patient's forehead and pray."

Afonso did not flinch. Giving me the impression of being a veteran at this type of assistance, he seemed totally unconcerned with the rest of us; he concentrated solely on his task.

That was when I saw Alexandre functioning as a true magnetizer. Recalling my old medical work regarding extreme cases involving blood transfusion, I could clearly recognize his efforts in transferring invigorating fluids from Afonso to Antonio's dying body.

As a disciple trying to improve my analytical faculties in light of such a valuable lesson, I noticed that the patient's appearance was gradually changing. As the instructor moved his hands over Antonio's brain, the patient started to show increasing signs of improvement. Deeply astonished, I could see his perispiritual form slowly reuniting with his physical one, each harmoniously integrating cell by cell with the other as if they were in a process of readjustment.

After a quarter of an hour – according to my calculations – the arduous magnetic intervention ended. Alexandre called to the old lady and pointed out:

"Justina, the clot has been reabsorbed and we were able to help the artery with our resources, but Antonio will have at most another five months to live. If you asked for this assistance to help him resolve urgent matters, don't squander the opportunity, because the repairs we have just made will not last more than one hundred fifty days. And don't forget to warn him via intuition about the care he should take of himself with respect to his excessive worrying, particularly at night. That is when the most serious circulatory upheavals occur due to the carelessness of many people who use the sacred hours of physical rest to create cruel phantoms in the living domains of thought. If our friend ignores his need for self-correction, he might discarnate before the five months are up. Complete caution is imperative."

Very touched, the mother thanked him in tears of happiness.

Alexandre asked the incarnate "helper" to remove his hands from the patient's forehead, and that is when I saw something unexpected. With his organic functions now reintegrated with as much harmony as was possible, Antonio opened his eyes as if he were drunk and began yelling:

"Help! Help! ... Help me for the love of God! I'm dying! I'm dying!"

Some young women dressed in white came running, surprised and trembling, and we realized that the anxious father's caring and sensitive daughters had come to assist him.

"Daddy! Daddy!" They cried. "What's the matter?"

"I'm dying!" The sick man clamored in a pungent voice. "Call the doctor ... Hurry!"

"But what are you feeling, Daddy?" one of them asked, weeping convulsively.

"I feel like I'm dying; my head's dizzy; I can't think."

A great bustle of incarnates passed by us in indescribable confusion, tripping over each other without the faintest awareness of our presence.

Alexandre asked Brother Francisco to furnish instructions to Afonso so that Afonso could go home. Alexandre then prepared to leave, but because of the surprise that the alarming behavior of the young women had caused me, he smiled and said:

"Usually, when our incarnate friends call out in tears for help, our work of assistance is finished. Let's go."

The semi-lucid patient was still restless as the telephone dial clicked for an immediate visit by the doctor.

The elderly woman said goodbye to us with great emotion, remaining at the patient's side, devotedly and humbly watching over him.

Back on the street, I asked my instructor for a closer conversation with Brother Francisco, who had kindly accompanied us.

Alexandre, affable as usual, granted my wish.

"Our small team," explained the head of the group, addressing me cordially, "is one of the countless assistance groups that work in the physical realm. There are thousands of us spirit workers serving in such a capacity. We are linked to various more-evolved regions in the spirit world."

"Does your group come from our colony?" I asked.

"Yes. Our activities are interlinked with the duties of several instructors from Nosso Lar[9]."

"And are there specialized duties for each of such groups?"

"Certainly. Ours, for instance," Francisco kindly pointed out, "is devoted to comforting the seriously ill and dying. Normally, the struggles faced by the sick are harder at night. During the day, the sun's rays destroy a large part of the inferior mental creations of the precariously ill. But that is not the case at night, when the moon's magnetism favors creations of all types, good or bad. Consequently, we must be vigilant. Very few in the circle of our incarnate brothers and sisters know the extent of our assistance. They are in a field of vibrations very different from ours, and they neither understand nor perceive our help. But that doesn't matter. Other benefactors, much more evolved

---

9 See the book entitled *Nosso Lar* (Brazilian Spiritist Federation, 2018). – Tr.

than those of which we are directly aware, devotedly watch over us and inspire us in the arena of our common duties without our being able to see their forms of expression in the work pertaining to the divine plan."

And perhaps because I was smiling in admiration of his ideal of serene and sanctifying selflessness, Francisco smiled and added:

"Yes, my friend, to demand understanding and results from individuals and situations that are not yet able to give them would be more cruel than the request for immediate reward."

This was the convincing truth. Brother Francisco reasoned with the highest logic. Those who help someone, but who are interested in recognition or reward, almost always have their eyes closed to the divine and invisible assistance they receive from the Most High. They demand that others notice their status as benefactors, but never remember that wise and caring friends offer them the best help from the higher planes without asking them for the least bit of personal gratitude.

"There are many brothers and sisters," Francisco continued, interrupting my inner reflections, "who, because of their affinity, meet up after the death of the body for tasks of fraternal help after they have reached the first rungs on the ladder of purification. From what I have been able to ascertain, such work on behalf of men and women is amongst the most effective and worthwhile. As long as they are enjoying excellent physical health, incarnates rarely understand the afflictions of the desperately ill and dying. However, since discarnates have a clearer perspective, we know that truly sublime spiritual accomplishments are possible in such cases in just a few days, even after many years of futile efforts on the physical plane. On their deathbed, people are gentler and more humane. One could say that relentless disease weakens the lowest instincts and attenuates the strongest flames of the lower passions; it de-animalizes the soul, opening up around it blessed openings through which the light of the infinite penetrates. Pain slowly tears down the heavy walls of indifference, crystallized selfishness and excessive pride. Then, greater understanding becomes possible. Admirable lessons bless those who perceive the greatness of the divine inheritance, even if only slightly. Their heroism is enhanced and living messages of love and wisdom will be inscribed on their hearts forever. In the dark night of dying, the dawn of life eternal begins to shine. And within its indistinct light, our principles are easily accepted; sensitivity shows sublime characteristics and immortal light casts sources of infinite power into the recesses of the spirit."

Francisco paused at length and then concluded:

"This is how we are able to carry out an effective work of assistance, bringing new worth to the realm of fraternity and real goodness. Haven't you ever noticed the unexpected patience of the seriously ill, the calmness of certain incurable patients and the supreme resignation of the majority of the dying? Often incomprehensible to the incarnates who surround such individuals, these uplifting occurrences comprise the fruitful efforts of our itinerant assistance groups."

Francisco had spoken sublime truths. In fact, the serenity of desperately infirm people and the unexplainable resignation of the irreligious dying could have no other origin. Divine goodness is infinite and everywhere there are always generous manifestations of God's paternal providence, comforting the sad, calming the desperate, helping the ignorant and blessing the unfortunate.

8
On the Plane of Dreams

After a few minutes of delightful conversation, Brother Francisco asked Alexandre about the objectives of the night's meeting.

"Yes," Alexandre explained affably, "we will do some work of basic instruction for our friends concerning problems encountered in mediumship and psychism, but without going into specific detail."

"If you would allow me," Francisco continued, "I would like to bring along some collaborators who frequently work with us. We would be very happy to see them take advantage of their time of physical sleep."

"Certainly. Tonight's work is meant to prepare our still-incarnate coworkers. We will be at your disposal and will be happy to welcome your helpers."

Moved, Francisco thanked him and asked:

"Can we make the arrangements?"

"Immediately," said the instructor without hesitating. "Bring your friends to the chosen place."

The group of "first aiders" went on their way, leaving me with a world of new thoughts.

According to what I had heard earlier, Alexandre would address a small gathering of students that evening. As soon as we were alone, he explained kindly:

"Our core of incarnate students has become quite large; however, they are lacking in certain qualities essential for functioning at their full potential. In light of that, it is imperative that we endow these friends with knowledge that is more constructive."

And since he thought it would be useful to supply me with personal information for my own clarification, he added politely:

"In light of such need, I have established a course of methodical education in order to improve the situation. Not everybody knows how to employ the hours of physical sleep to acquire such qualities, but if a few brave farmers don't actually go out to sow some seeds in order to raise a good crop, the rural community will never have a plentiful yield.

And smiling, he added:

"There are over three hundred members at our study center, but only thirty-two have been able to break the webs of the lowest physiological sensations in order to assimilate our instruction. And there are nights in which even some of these break their commitments by answering to worldly seductions; hence, the overall attendance is even smaller. In compensation, on the other hand, every now and then we enjoy the unexpected attendance of other coworkers, as is the case tonight due to Brother Francisco's idea to bring some friends."

"Do the brothers and sisters who attend have total recall of the work and study they've shared in, and the remarks they've heard?" I asked curiously.

Alexandre thought for a moment and considered:

"Later on, experience will show you how reduced sensorial capacity can be. The eternal person has total recall and will inwardly retain all the teachings, intensifying and valuing them according to his or her own evolutionary state. As a slave to necessary limitations, the physical human being cannot go so far, however. Due to the pressures of the struggles to which the spirit has been called, the physical brain is an apparatus of reduced potential, and it depends a great deal on the enlightenment of its owner regarding the retention of certain divine blessings. Consequently, Andre, the storage of such memories in the temporary book of the brain cells differs widely amongst disciples, and varies from soul to soul. Nevertheless, I must add that the benefit remains in the memory of everyone of goodwill, even if during their waking state they are unsure about their origin. The classes at the level of the one you will witness tonight convey messages of unimaginable practical usefulness. When students wake up after attending them, they experience relief, rest and hope, as well as the acquisition of new educational values. It is true that they cannot recall the details, but they will have retained the essence, feeling reinvigorated in a way they cannot explain, not only enabling them to recommence their daily struggle in the physical body, but also to benefit their neighbor and to successfully combat their own imperfections. Their thoughts become clearer, their sentiments more uplifted and their prayers more respectful and productive, thereby enriching their daily observations and endeavors."

"It's too bad," I said, taking advantage of a longer pause, "that all members of the group cannot attend classes of this nature in great numbers. There would be extraordinary significance in the act of gathering over three hundred individuals for the same sanctifying purpose, in which they could receive together the sublime blessings of enlightenment."

"Undoubtedly," Alexandre replied with his usual optimism. "However, we cannot force anybody. Every step represents an ascent and every ascent requires a climbing effort. If our friends do not employ their own strength, if they disregard their own divine rights by forgetting or sometimes loathing the sacred duties the Father has entrusted to them, how can we step in and do it for them if one's divine and eternal self-actualization is a primordial law?"

His remark was profound and indisputable.

At that moment, we came face to face with a large building, impressive because of its modest but well-lit lines.

"Now let's get to work!" Alexandre ordered decisively.

"But," I objected, "won't the classes be held at the group headquarters where the duties under your responsibility are carried out?"

"If the work," he replied kindly, "were meant solely for spirits free of their physical bodies, we could carry out our endeavors there with greater success, but in this case we must accommodate our still-incarnate brothers and sisters, who come to us in very special conditions, and we need to take advantage of the magnetic resources of our friends who are also still struggling on earth."

And when we arrived at the entryway, where a large number of fellow spirits from our realm were coming and going, the instructor explained:

"This is a fine Spiritist institution dedicated to serving the needy, the downhearted and the suffering. The sacred spirit of the evangelical family is alive in this place of Christian love, which Spiritism built with the aid of a venerable missionary of Christ. We can carry out our work here more efficiently with regards to what it is meant for."

"How interesting the fact is," I pointed out, "that we need domestic environments for instructing our incarnate fellow spirits!"

"Yes." Alexandre commented with much wisdom. "You mustn't forget that great lessons by the Master himself were given in family settings. The first visible institution of Christianity was Simon Peter's humble home in Capernaum. One of our Lord's first manifestations in the presence of people was the multiplication of family joys at a wedding party in the comfort of the home. Jesus often visited the homes of confessed sinners, switching on new lights in their hearts. The last meeting with the disciples took place in a home setting. The first center for Christian service in Jerusalem was in the simple house of Peter, by then an unshakable bastion of the new faith. Of course, every stone worship place that is guided worthily functions as a lighthouse in the darkness, pointing out the right path to the wayfarers of the world; but we cannot forget that the vital movement of ideas and achievements is based on the living church of the spirit in the heart of God's creatures. Unless people adhere to the belief that lies within them, every religious expression is reduced to mere outward ritual. That is why, Andre, that in the future of humankind the material churches of Christianity will become church-schools, church-orphanages and church-hospitals, where the leaders of the faith will not only convey words of interpretation, but where children will find support and instruction; the youth, the preparation needed for achievements worthy of character and sentiment; the sick, health-giving remedies; the ignorant, learning; the elderly, support and hope. Evangelical Spiritism is the great restorer of the loving and hardworking apostolic churches of the past. Its faithful followers will be valuable helpers in transforming theological ministries into schools of spirituality, and stone cathedrals into welcoming homes of Jesus."

I would have given anything to continue listening to my instructor's fascinating explanations, but at that moment, we crossed the threshold.

I noticed that it was 1:55 a.m.

By the large number of spirits that came hurriedly to meet us, I could see that there was a great interest in that night's instructive lecture. They were not only the students directly linked to Alexandre's activities, but also others brought there by loved ones from the spirit plane.

A small group of friends approached us with more familiarity, especially one who spoke to Alexandre in particular:

"Aren't they all here yet?" asked the instructor with caring interest after their first greetings.

I clearly perceived that he was referring to incarnate brothers and sisters who were supposed to attend as part of the group for which he was one of the spirit directors.

"We are missing only two," the spirit explained. "Vieira and Marcondes still haven't arrived."

"We need to get started," said Alexandre. "We have to finish the work by four at the latest."

And demonstrating particular concern as a friend, he added:

"I wonder if they had an accident. We'd better find out."

In his calm decisiveness – one his characteristics – he recommended to the assistant who had given him the information:

"Sertorio, while I go and finalize some arrangements for tonight's class, please find out what is going on."

Respectfully, the subordinate asked:

"How should I proceed if our brothers are under the influence of criminals?"

"In that case, leave them where they are," replied the instructor decidedly. "This is not the time for long conversations with those who deliberately tie themselves to the lower realms. Once our work is finished, you can arrange for the necessary resources."

The messenger was about to leave when the instructor, having noticed my great desire to accompany him, added:

"If you wish, Andre, you can go along and assist our emissary. Sertorio will enjoy your company."

Feeling very happy, I thanked him and greeted his helper, who replied with a warm smile.

We left.

It was crucial that we tend to Alexandre's request quickly; however, to satisfy my curiosity, Sertorio kindly explained:

"While incarnate on the earth, we are not fully aware of the work we do during physical sleep; nevertheless, such endeavors are indescribable and immense. If humans seriously appreciated the value of spiritual preparation in light of this sort of undertaking, they would certainly accomplish the most uplifting realizations in the psychic realms, even though still linked to their physical envelopes. Unfortunately, the majority unconsciously use their nighttime rest in search of frivolous or less worthy excitements. They lessen their own defenses, and certain impulses – largely repressed during the waking state – overflow in all directions due to the lack of a truly felt and practiced spiritual education."

Interested in a complete explanation, I asked:

"But is that the case with students of advanced courses in Spiritualism? Could students of a teacher of Alexandre's caliber be the victims of such behavior?"

"Why not?" replied Sertorio fraternally. "Have no doubts as to that possibility. How many preach the Truth, but do not inwardly adhere to it? How many repeat formulas of hope and peace, while desperate and prone to persecuting others at the bottom of their hearts? There are always many who are 'called' in all arenas of growth and self-improvement! The 'chosen', however, are always few and far between."

Completing his thought, and as if to guard himself from creating any false notion of individualism in God's work, Sertorio added:

"And we need to readjust our definition of the 'chosen'. Our fellow men and women thus classified are not particularly favored by divine grace, which is always the same source of blessings for all. We know that 'choice' in any type of constructive endeavor does not exclude 'quality', and if people do not bring higher qualities to the divine work, they should under no circumstance expect the distinction of being 'chosen'. We can infer, therefore, that God calls all his children to cooperate in his magnificent work, but it is only the devoted, the persistent, the hardworking and the faithful who build eternal qualities that make them worthy of great deeds. And by realizing that these qualities are the fruit of our own making, we must never forget that divine choice starts with each one's own efforts."

My companion's theory was indeed interesting and instructive, but by now we had reached a small building, in front of which Sertorio stopped and said:

"This is where Vieira lives. Let's see what's going on."

I followed him in silence.

In a few seconds, we were inside a comfortable bedroom, where an elderly man was asleep, making a very odd noise. We could clearly see his perispiritual body joined to the physical form, although they were partially disconnected from each other. Next to him stood a very peculiar spirit, dressed completely in black. I saw that our sleeping friend was under the influence of heartrending terror. Shrill cries came from his throat. He was choking in deep distress while the dark spirit made gestures that I was not able to understand.

Sertorio leaned close to me and remarked:

"Vieira is suffering a cruel nightmare."

And pointing to the strange spirit:

"I think that he himself has attracted this visitor who is scaring him."

Indeed, very gently, Sertorio began a conversation with the spirit:

"My friend, are you a relative of the man who is sleeping?"

"No, no. We are old acquaintances."

And very impatiently he added:

"While thoughtlessly talking with his family this evening, Vieira called me with reiterated memories and accused me of wrongs I didn't commit. Naturally, this upset me. Isn't what I have suffered since my death enough? Do I still have to listen to false witness by slanderous friends? I didn't expect such behavior from him, because of the bonds of affection that have joined our families over the years. Vieira has always been a person I trusted. Because of my surprise, I decided to wait for him when he went to sleep in order to give him the necessary explanations."

The strange visitor then stopped for a moment, smiled ironically and continued:

"However, from the moment I began to explain the situation of the past, informing him of the true reasons for my actions and decisions in the corporeal life so that he does not continue to slander my name – albeit unintentionally – Vieira took on this look of terror and seems like he doesn't want to listen to my truths."

Interested in new lessons, I drew nearer to the person, whose body was resting in a horizontal position, and I sensed his cold sweat soaking the sheets. He did not seem to rightly understand the help that had arrived. He stared at us with surprise and anxiety, his shrill moans growing louder.

Aware of Sertorio's silent disapproval, the visitor from the lower zones said to him:

"Do you believe that we should listen impassively to the taunts of thoughtlessness? Shouldn't an unfaithful friend, who uses the circumstances of death to slander and cause distress, be scolded and punished? If Vieira felt he was right to accuse me, unaware of certain details about the problems of my private life, isn't it only fair that he endure my explanations until I'm satisfied? Doesn't he know that the dead continue to live? Is he unaware of the fact that the memory of every friend should be held sacred? The nerve! I, myself, in my new condition as a discarnate being, have heard him giving long speeches on the respect we owe to one another ... So, don't you think I have a just motive for demanding a correct understanding?!"

Sertorio displayed his open-mindedness and remarked:

"Maybe you're right, my dear fellow. However, I think you should forgive your friend! How can we demand strictly correct behavior from others if we ourselves are not yet irreprehensible creatures? Let's be tolerant and charitable toward each other!"

And while the spirit began to ponder these words, Sertorio said to me discreetly:

"Vieira won't be able to come tonight."

I could not avoid the bad impression the scene was having on me, and perhaps because of my pleading look on behalf of our poor brother, who seemed ready to discarnate with fear, Alexandre's assistant continued:

"To forcefully remove this visitor, whose presence Vieira himself made possible, is not a task compatible with my present position. But we can help him by waking him up."

And without blinking, he shook the sleeping man vigorously, shouting his name loudly.

Vieira woke up, confused, half-asleep and very fatigued. He exclaimed, white as a sheet:

"Thank God I woke up! What a terrible nightmare! Could I actually have been struggling with old Barbosa's ghost? No! It couldn't be!"

He did not see us, nor was he aware of the dark spirit that had been there for God knows how long. And as we were leaving, I noticed he was still asking himself what he might have eaten for dinner, trying to find a reason for the cruel fright through physiological excuses. Far from examining his own conscience regarding the issues of slander and thoughtlessness, he sought to situate the lesson in his stomach in an effort to escape reality.

However, Sertorio did not allow me further reflections. Calling me to immediate duty, he added:

"Let's visit Marcondes. We have no time to lose."

Two minutes later, we entered another private apartment; however, the scene was now even more upsetting and embarrassing.

Marcondes was in fact there, partially disconnected from his physical body, which looked fine resting under laced covers. He was not under the influence of terror – like the first case – but displayed the relaxed posture characteristic of someone on opium. Next to him were three female entities in a compromising posture with mocking expressions on their faces.

Seeing us suddenly, Marcondes could not conceal his surprise, especially when he saw Sertorio, who was an old acquaintance. Ashamed, he got up and tried hard to offer some type of explanation:

"My friend," he started to say to Alexandre's assistant, "I know you have come looking for me ... I don't know how to explain this..."

But he was unable to continue and immersed his head in his hands as if he wished to hide from himself.

At this point of the embarrassing scene, I noticed that, beyond any shadow of a doubt, the visiting spirits were of the worst kind of all those I was aware of in the lower zones of darkness.

Perhaps annoyed at our friend's retreat as he showed himself sad and humiliated, they began raising a great racket, approaching us without the least respect.

"You can't take Marcondes from us!" said one of them emphatically. "After all, I have come from too far to just waste my time like this!"

"He himself called us for tonight," the second said insolently, "and he won't get away under any circumstances."

Sertorio listened calmly, demonstrating inner compassion.

The third spirit seemed to possess even baser instincts. She addressed us with a terrible look of sarcasm, and giving me to understand that this was not the first time Sertorio had come to this house for the same reasons and under the same circumstances, she said:

"You guys are nothing more than intruders. Marcondes is weak, letting himself be influenced by your presence. Nevertheless, we shall fight back. You will not snatch our favorite from us."

And with a burst of laughter, she pointed out ironically:

"We also have a course on pleasure. Marcondes will not leave."

Unlike myself, Sertorio was paying no attention to her. The words and expressions of that creature, however, began to anger me. Sertorio remained extremely kind. The victim himself remained humble and downcast. What was the reason for such insults? I was going to say something in order to clarify the situation in more precise terms when Sertorio stopped me:

"Contain yourself, Andre! One minute of giving in to the tempting provocations of the lower planes can cause us to lose a century."

And then, with enviable tranquility, he addressed Marcondes, asking without a tone of criticism:

"Marcondes, what shall I say on your behalf tonight, my friend?"

Marcondes answered, tearful and humiliated:

"Oh, Sertorio, how hard is to keep one's heart on the straight and narrow! Forgive me ... I don't know how this happened ... I can't explain myself!"

Sertorio, however, was not interested in nourishing regrets, and indicating that he wanted to make use of the rest of the time available, interrupted Marcondes:

"Yes, Marcondes. Everybody chooses the company they prefer. In the future, you will understand that we are your loyal friends and that we wish the best for you."

The women unleashed a new series of scornful remarks. Marcondes once again began to say how sorry he was, but Alexandre's messenger took my hand without hesitation and we returned to the street.

"Let's head back," he said decisively.

"What about this case?" I asked, "Aren't you going to wake him up?"

"No. In this case we can't. Marcondes must remain in that situation so that tomorrow the unpleasant memories will last longer, strengthening his repugnance toward evil."

"Then what should we do?" I asked, surprised.

"We will tell our instructor what is going on," answered Sertorio calmly. "That is what we have to do."

And summarizing the extensive considerations he could offer regarding the subject, he emphasized:

"For now, Andre, a higher duty is calling us on our journey toward God. However, when tonight's work is finished, I'll go back to see what can be done on behalf of our poor friends.

For now, we mustn't waste a minute. Alexandre's lectures are not aimed only at preparing our brothers and sisters who are still linked to their physical envelopes; they are also valuable to us, who need to enhance our abilities to successfully help our incarnate fellow spirits."

"Yes, I agree," I answered. "Nevertheless, Vieira's and Marcondes' situations have touched me deeply."

Sertorio interrupted me, concluding confidently:

"Uphold your sentiments, which are sacred. But do not lean toward morbid sentimentalism. Be assured that assistance will not be lacking for both of them at the right time; do not forget, though, that if they themselves shackled their hearts to that imprisonment, it is natural that they acquire some useful experience at the expense of their own disappointment."

9
Mediumship and Phenomena

A considerable number of incarnate spirits, temporarily freed from their physical bodies through sleep, had gathered in the vast hall. Next to the main table, where Alexandre was at the head, were seated the direct and permanent students of the generous and wise instructor. The rest were seated in successive tiers.

I calculated the audience of fellow spirits as being perhaps slightly over one hundred individuals, not counting the discarnates, who were arriving in much larger numbers. Besides Brother Francisco's group, which had brought the individuals under his care, other groups of a similar nature were in attendance with their students interested in new lessons.

I noticed something odd, however: only those learners working closely with Alexandre were allowed to express their doubts, requests and questions, not verbally, but transmitted to him beforehand, prior to the beginning of the lecture.

In reply to my curiosity, Sertorio kindly explained:

"There are many schools of this type for incarnates who are willing to make good use of their moments of physical sleep. It is natural that the permanent disciples of this or that sector should be given the right to ask the questions. As you can see, there is no favoritism; it is a matter of order, although the students who come only occasionally will in turn have other rights at the centers to which they belong."

Satisfied with this explanation, I asked:

"What is tonight's theme? Is there a pre-established program?"

"There is always an organized plan for this sort of activity," he answered. "But Alexandre improvises on the topics after he receives the questions and remarks of the usual attendees. He carefully examines the questions put forth by the majority and offers instructions so as to satisfy the issues of interest of a smaller number of interested parties as well."

"And can you tell me what the theme is that has been requested by the majority tonight?"

"I believe it refers to mediumship and to phenomena in general.

In a particularly kind gesture, my companion invited me to join the group of assistants of the devoted instructor, who was now standing at the podium to begin his instructive task.

His venerable and imposing figure stood out even more than on other occasions. Radiating the light that came from within, Alexandre had complete control over the meeting of workers and students, not by means of the absorbing magnetism of impassioned speakers, but by his simple kindness and unpretentious ascendancy.

With everyone's attention focused on him, Alexandre began his lecture with a prayer to the Lord, beseeching him for the gift of understanding his audience, and, in turn, of being understood by them. To me, such a prayer was touching and new; it was entirely spiritual and without a shred of personal individualism. Nevertheless, the more he tried to impersonalize himself, affirming that he was only an instrument of the Divine Will, the more outstanding he became in my eyes as a true exponent of wisdom, humility, prudence, loyalty, trust and light.

At the end of the touching prayer, he began by addressing the audience with firm and direct words:

"Brothers and sisters, in continuance of our work, tonight we will comment on your requests for guidance in mediumship, in view of the problems you are facing in your daily struggles and which you consider as impediments of a psychic-physiological nature. You long for worthwhile achievement in the realms of higher revelation and you dream of glorious conquests and sublime accomplishments; however, you must correct your mental posture in light of human life. How can one attempt to build without having laid a good foundation, or to achieve ends without addressing beginnings? Faith is not reduced to a simple heap of shining promises, and the sum of the anxieties that possess your hearts is not in any way indicative of spiritual accomplishment per se. The building of an inner kingdom with the divine light requires persistent and calm efforts. It will not be by words alone that you will erect temples of living faith. As is the case with any other ordinary project, the choice of materials and the effort for acquiring them, the previously structured plans, the necessary procedures, examination of sturdiness, demonstrations of balance, firmness of lines, harmony of the whole and care in the finishing are all essential."

Alexandre paused briefly, gazed at the audience attentively as if sending them energetic waves of creative magnetism, and then continued:

"Many brothers and sisters who would like to develop mediumistic perceptions are gathered here; however, they are expecting simple phenomenological manifestations, mistakenly believing that spiritual energies are limited to the simple mechanism of blind and fixed energies, without any effort of preparation, discipline and constructiveness. They ask for clairvoyance, clairaudience and the whole array of means of communication with the higher realms; however, have they learned to see, to hear and, above all, to serve in the realm of their daily work? Have they gained mastery over all the lower impulses in order to set out on the path toward the higher planes? Can a fetus walk and talk on the physical plane? Should we give a five-year-old child the rights to which a half-century-old adult is entitled? If human laws, still transitory and imperfect, set lines of demarcation for the inexperienced, would the unchangeable and eternal divine laws be at the mercy of the inordinate wishes of the individual? My friends! Of course, there are many mediumistic forms and processes at work in the world of matter in which you live! However, you must recognize the value of work before rest, accept duty without demands, perform the apparently little tasks before concerning yourselves with greater deeds, and put the Lord's designs above all individual concerns! It is imperative to avoid undue appropriations in the exchange with the invisible powers, and to guard yourselves against temporary fascination and both subtle and perverse obsession! Collectively, we are not two opposing races or two great armies strictly separated by the lines of life and death, but rather a great and infinite community of the living, separated from one another by the constraints of vibration, although we are almost always united in the same task of final redemption! Do not think that the death of the body sanctifies the being that used to inhabit it! If the ray of sunlight does not become contaminated upon contact with the swamp, likewise the rebellious patient continues to be ill if he or she merely changes dwellings. The physical body represents only a vessel used for a period of time, and a broken vessel does not mean the redemption or elevation of its temporary owner. We make use of this image to tell you that the inhabitant of the realm currently invisible to your eyes is a brother or sister who is not always of a higher order than you in terms of evolutionary circles. Discarnation does not mean sanctification. The fellow spirits who have preceded you into the other world are involved in a process of learning that is not much different from your own. The electrons and photons that comprise your physical body also comprise the vessels through which we spirits manifest according to other vibrational characteristics. It is necessary, therefore, that you pay attention to your inner possibilities, to the marvels of your potential divinity.

"In your overwhelming desire to interact with the invisible realm, you naturally hope that heavenly messengers are close at hand. You long for the revelation of divine truth, along with simple elements of serene certainty; however, in order for that to happen, it is crucial that you organize and develop your heavenly qualities as the heavenly beings you truly are. At each of your Spiritist centers, a whole army of Christ's workers labors in activities regarding spiritualization, calling you to enlightened sentiments, to active virtue, and to the higher realms of the inner life; however, your tendency to materialize all the expressions of the spirit is still very strong because you have neglected to spiritualize matter. You ask for light, while almost always remaining in darkness; you demand happiness, while sowing suffering; you request love, while encouraging separation; you search for faith, while doubting even yourselves.

"The possibility of bartering emotions with the invisible realms surrounding you in no way represents the spiritual achievement indispensable for the divine edification of each of us, because the problem of mediumistic glory does not entail being the instrument of certain Intelligences, but being a faithful instrument of the Divinity. In order for the incarnate soul to achieve such an accomplishment, it must develop its own divine principles. An acorn is potentially an oak tree. A handful of tiny seeds is tomorrow's wheat field. The insignificant avian embryo will in a few short days be a powerful bird covering great distances."

Alexandre was becoming increasingly more vibrant and striking. Delicate rays shimmering with brilliant light poured over his brow from above.

"Mediumship," he continued, enchanting our hearts, "is a 'means of communication', and Jesus himself tells us, 'I am the door ... if anyone enters through me, he will be saved, and will go in and out and find pasture!' By what incomprehensible impudence do you imagine you can carry out the sublime accomplishment without loving the Spirit of Truth, who is the Lord himself? Listen to me, my dear brothers and sisters! ... If you are resolved to enter divine service, there is no other way than through the Lord, who holds the infinite light of truth and the inexhaustible fount of life! There is no other gate to heavenly mediumship, to the access of the divine equilibrium you crave within the hidden sanctuary of your hearts! It is only through him, by living his sublime lessons, that you will reach the sacred freedom of entering the domains of spirituality and exiting them, winning the eternal bread that will satisfy your hunger forever. Without Christ, mediumship is simply a 'means of communication' and nothing more; a mere possibility of information like so many others, which can be possessed just as easily by those interested in causing trouble, thereby increasing the number of unfortunate captives. However, remember that divine law has never endorsed captivity and has never sanctioned slavery! Have you forgotten the divine words that declared, 'You are gods?'"

On uttering this last phrase, the instructor took on a much different appearance. It seemed that in the middle of his chest a sublime, slightly indigo light had appeared – a light that he sent out to all of us in rays of inexpressible joy. His hair resembled threads of sunlight with a sapphire-like sheen. His gaze had become more sublime and deeper. And many of us, both discarnate and incarnate, wept with gratitude and joy, touched by inexplicable emotion.

After a brief pause, the loving and wise teacher continued:

"My friends, your insistence on remaining in an animalized condition plays havoc with you! You are the spiritual halo of the earth, because you have been garlanded by the Lord of the Universe. The splendorous beam of reasoning illumines the sanctuary of your consciousnesses; the sublime invites you to the 'way beyond'; elder brothers and sisters are calling you to live with our Father; nevertheless, you willingly linger in the fauna of primitive irrationality. In the vibrational field of the human mind, the poison of ungrateful vipers, the instinct of famished wolves, the slyness of foxes, the bloodthirsty impulse of voracious tigers, the vanity and pride of lions can still be sensed. Do not believe that these attributes are simply characteristics of the mortal body. They are qualities that the spirit retains within itself, while forgetting its divine heritage. However, physical death catches people in the behavior they have cultivated. Their vibratory planes are modified, but their spiritual essence remains the same; that is the reason for the tangle of less evolved manifestations in the mediumistic areas of your activities. On many occasions, instead of cultivating the positive qualities of accomplishments with Jesus, you foster the petty interests of human circumstances in the temporary realms of the senses. Taken by enormous mistakes in the circles of mediumistic development, you believe that it is possible to overcome the heavy domain of dense vibrations – crystallized by the vices of many centuries – solely by the automatic movement of physical cells. Without any preparation, you attempt the crossing of the vibrational borders, invoking invisible powers of any nature for the training of your psychic abilities, like an inconsequential person who picks instructors at random from a crowd, forgetting that not all passers-by on a public street are in a position to benefit, supervise and teach him or her. If the simplest machines on earth require workers to undergo a preparatory course so that the production department is not affected either in quality or quantity, how can you expect sublime mediumship to be reduced to automatic work, to pure manifestation of physiological mechanisms, unaffected by education and responsibility? It is always possible to open up means of communication between you and the realms invisible to you, but do not forget that affinities are immutable laws that will connect and combine in the infinite realms of the spirit! Without the benefits of preparation, you will inevitably end up in the company of those who avoid the Lord's instructive processes; and without the blessings of responsibility, you will undoubtedly encounter irresponsible individuals. You might object by saying that phenomena are indispensable in the experimental arena of scientific accomplishment, and that the unusual must be called upon to promote new convictions; however, we are the first to acknowledge the fact that your paths on earth unfold in the midst of marvelous phenomena. Have you perchance solved the mystery of the combining of hydrogen and oxygen to form a drop of water? Have you explained all the secrets of how plants breathe? By what dispositions of nature does the poisonous hemlock that kills flourish next to the wheat that nourishes? What do you say about the thorny stem coming out the ground that offers a flower like a gracious cup of heavenly perfume? Have you solved all the biological questions regarding the physical forms that inhabit the planet in all the different species? What is your definition of a ray of sunlight? Have you ever seen the imaginary axis that keeps the world stable? If such types of phenomena of an ongoing character do not awaken slumbering souls, giving them a legitimate concept of the existence of God, how do you expect to destroy the millenary defiance of humans who demand premature displays of manifestations of evolved spirits? No, my friends! It is imperative that you abandon the clatter outside in order to begin the development of the divine faculties on the inside! The passion for phenomena can be as addictive and destructive for the soul as the alcohol that intoxicates and kills the centers of physical life! Your array of hypotheses, in most circumstances, is nothing more than a macabre dance of arguments that avoid the universal realities and postpone indefinitely the real edification of the spirit! We agree with you that experimentation is necessary; that intellectual research is the starting point for great evolutionary undertakings; that healthy curiosity is the mother of enterprising science; that each and every process of knowledge requires a field of observation and work just as educational material is indispensable for the simplest of schools. However, we must realize that the elements for learning should not be used by students as mere toys or entertainment. Furthermore, even if students become enlightened with respect to their lessons, one must realize that information is not everything, since educational instruction is only part of the learning experience. What about disciples who are always studying without ever learning to correctly put what they learn into practice? What about our fellow brothers and sisters, filled with wonderful words of light for others, who never enlighten themselves? To catalog qualities is not the same as living by them. To show the way to travelers does not imply direct and personal knowledge of the trip. There are excellent statisticians who have never visited the original sources of their information, and eminent geographers who rarely leave their homes. We refer to such images to make you realize that, even if it is possible to maintain these types of attitudes in the limited duration of the short existence on the earth, the same cannot be done in the infinite kingdom of the spirit life, in whose circles you have begun to take part from this time forth, despite your condition as creatures linked to the inferior vehicles of your bodies. Mediumship is not a quality of the transitory flesh, but an expression of the immortal spirit. Naturally, the optimum exchange between the two realms requires healthy conditions of the sacred vessel of physiological potential that the Lord has granted you for sanctification. Nevertheless, the body is an uplifting instrument in the hands of the artist, who must be divinely inspired. If you desire advanced development, then abandon the lower realms. If you intend to have exchanges with the wise, then grow in knowledge, value your experiences and increase the light of you reasoning! If you are hoping for the sublime company of saints, then sanctify yourselves in your daily struggles, because angelic entities do not remain secluded in celestial jubilation; they also work for the improvement of the world, awaiting your own rise to the angelic state! If you desire the presence of the good, then become good yourselves! Without affability and gentleness, without fraternal understanding and spiritually constructive attitudes, you will not be able to understand affable and friendly, evolved and constructive spirits. If it would not be reasonable to find Plato teaching advanced philosophy to primitive tribes, or Francis of Assisi cooperating with villains, it would also be inadmissible to presume the fraternization of enlightened and sanctified spirits with souls still strongly engrossed with the lowest and densest manifestations of corporeal existence. In your spiritualist activities, remember that you are not looking with some sectarian doctrine of individuals in transit on the planet! You are involved in a divine and worldwide movement for the liberation of consciences in a sublime revelation of the eternal life and immortal qualities for all persons of goodwill! Having accepted this principle, do not linger in the exclusive and presumptuous attitude of those who think they have found in mediumship merely a sixth sense! Mediumship is not a gift of the privileged; it is a quality common to all people and requires sincere goodwill in the realm of betterment. For now, it is indisputable that we need great stimulating undertakings, to which certain incarnates are called to bear witness in the field of collective enlightenment and in the dissemination of a positive and uplifting faith. But the future will reveal to us that service of this nature belongs to all individuals, for we are all immortal spirits. Do not harbor any doubt! Do not allow the vibrational pattern of the physical forces to extinguish the glorious light of the divine certainty of this moment, because all of us, my dear friends, are faced with our endless spirituality, renewing energies corrupted over the centuries, trodding the pathway to transformations that you cannot even imagine in the spheres of your present evolution! So, from today onward, let us uplift ourselves in the spirit of the Lord, who has invited us to the banquet of light! Let us uplift ourselves for the future, not in the sense of scorning the earth, but with the aim of improving our individual qualities so that we can be truly useful for its realizations yet to come! Let us truly love one another, fulfilling the evangelical precepts, and let us improve each day, uplifting ourselves toward our final redemption."

Ending the beautiful lecture of the evening, Alexandre concluded, after a lengthy pause, with the following emotional appeal:

"Let us all join together in the sacred commitment of true cooperation with Jesus!

"If human hands can change the geographical structure of the planet by opening up new roads, building magnificent cities and giving a new look to the waterways of the earth, let us intensify our spiritual efforts, renewing the millenary dispositions of animalized reasoning in the world; let us build solid pathways for true fraternity, solidifying the work of uplifting people's sentiments and thoughts, forming Christian foundations to sanctify the course of relationships among people!

"Do not foster the premature development of your psychic faculties! To see without understanding or to hear without discerning can cause considerable disasters to the heart. Seek, above all, to progress in virtue and to perfect your sentiments. Enhance your self-balance and the Lord will open up to you the door of new knowledge!

"If the desire to transform your neighbor torments your soul, remember that there are a thousand ways to help without imposing, and that only after the fruit is ripe will there be enough seeds to tend to the needs of other areas of sowing!

"Distance yourselves from an excess of words without deeds! I am not talking here only about the good deeds realized on the physical plane, but more particularly about the silent constructions of self-denial, about daily efforts to understand Jesus Christ, about the patience, hope and forgiveness that are expressed within the closed doors of the soul in the great country of our inner experiences!

"In all earthly endeavors, transform yourselves according to our Father's will! And in your endeavors of faith, do not try to get high order spirits to come down to you, but learn how to go up to them, aware of the fact that the paths of exchange are the same for all, and that it is more worthwhile to uplift the heart to receive the infinite good than to demand the sacrifice of benefactors!

"Never break the thread of light that connects us individually to the Divine Spirit! Do not allow selfishness and vanity, the lower appetites and the tyrannies of the 'self' to tarnish the faculty of reflecting the Divine Light. Remember that in our capacity of serving and in our work situations, we are to God what the precious gems of the earth are to the creative sun – the greater the purity of the stone, the greater its ability to reflect the sun's light!

"Put the demonstration of phenomena in your work on a secondary level, always remembering that the spirit is everything!"

Alexandre became quiet, in silent prayer. Surprised and moved, I noticed that the generous teacher underwent a transfiguration right there in front of our eyes. This was the first time after my return to the new plane that I witnessed such a remarkable event. His raiments turned white as snow; his brow emitted an intense light and his outstretched hands, brilliant rays; and when they struck us they seemed to fill us with a strange enchantment. I was overcome by deep emotion. Unable to define the cause of those divine vibrations, nearly all of us were weeping with joy, our hearts filled with unexpected rejoicing.

After a few moments of sublime ecstasy, I saw that Sertorio had understood my perplexity. It is true that I had witnessed prayers by high order spirits on many occasions, and that these prayers were always accompanied by the most beautiful phenomena of light; but never before had I observed such a transfiguration!

Gently touching my arm, my companion emphasized:

"All the powers of a higher nature have congregated around Alexandre at this moment, transforming him into an intermediary of blessing for us. That is why he is radiating and shining with such intensity."

I understood the beauty of the scene and the sublimity of the lesson.

After a few seconds, Alexandre resumed his usual appearance, offered a prayer of recognition to the Lord and joyfully closed the divine meeting.

10
Materialization

Due to my interest in the study of materialization phenomena, I did not hesitate to ask for Alexandre's eminent assistance and he kindly placed himself at my disposal.

"Our group," he stated kindly, "is not involved in that type of work specifically, but it will be no problem for us to resort to other friends who are. There are devoted workers at centers involved in such activities."

And because I was displaying my deep scientific curiosity, my supervisor continued:

"This work entails a big responsibility. Besides demanding the full potential of the mediumistic instrument, it is necessary to mobilize all the collaborative elements of the incarnates present at meetings intended for such a purpose. If there were a perfect overall understanding and respect for the gifts of life, and if we could rely on spontaneous moral qualities rightly consolidated in the collective mind, such manifestations would be as natural as could be, without any harm to the medium and assistants.

However, it is very rare to find incarnates who meet the spiritual conditions that this type of work requires. For this reason, due to the uncertainty of effective collaboration, materialization sessions entail a great risk to the medium's body and thus require a large number of coworkers from our realm."

"I understand," I broke in, taking advantage of the kind instructor's brief pause. "Many times, when enveloped in flesh, we are unable to conduct intellectual research!"

"That's exactly right!" exclaimed Alexandre benevolently. "If scientific investigation were accompanied by true sentiment, character and conscience, the accomplishments would be different, because the light of spirituality would be illuminating the way. But we are almost always beset by demands full of pretence, and thus failures are unavoidable."

The friendly instructor continued with a series of moral, sublime and edifying explanations, and I eagerly waited for the time when I could observe these prodigious activities performed by spirit workers, and which cause such great surprise to earth's researchers.

Courteous as always, Alexandre made all the necessary arrangements. Kind friends took it upon themselves to attend to my healthy curiosity and I was notified of all measures taken. On the appointed night, Alexandre gave me the pleasure of accompanying me to a residential home, where a different type of meeting was going to take place.

The meeting was due to begin at 9:00 p.m., but fifty minutes before that time we were both there in the private, welcoming and comfortable room where a large number of workers of our plane were coming and going.

The work was being supervised by Brother Calimerio, a spirit of a higher order than Alexandre. After receiving his warm welcome, Alexandre introduced me and said:

"I have come here in answer to my companion's thirst for knowledge. Andre wanted to learn about materialization work and I have taken the liberty of bringing him; however, we are not here as mere observers. If possible, we would like to work as well."

"Alexandre," answered Calimerio, very kindly, showing extremely fine manners, "the work belongs to all of us. Provide our new friend with everything that we can make available to him, and forgive me if I cannot assist you personally. It is my job to oversee tonight's work, but please make yourselves at home."

And fixing his very lucid eyes on me, he pointed out:

"To observe in order to do is divine work."

Respectfully, we went inside the home. I was astonished as I noticed the great difference in the environment. Unlike other meetings that I had attended, there was not a crowd of suffering spirits at the door. The private residence where the work was going to take place had been isolated by a large sixty-five-foot cordon of workers from our plane.

Noticing my surprise, Alexandre explained:

"It is vital that we take the utmost care so that mental emissions of a lower order do not affect the physical health of our incarnate coworkers or the purity of the substance required for the phenomenon to occur. That is why we must insulate the location of our activities and defend it against access by unworthy spirits by setting up vibrational barriers."

Noticing the extent of such precautions, I asked:

"If such care is necessary for our area of service, wouldn't the same hold true for the incarnates who are to be our assistants?"

Alexandre smiled, aware of the subtlety of my question, and answered:

"The whole danger of these endeavors lies in the lack of preparation by our incarnate friends, who, alleging scientific authority, usually avoid the most common principles of moral elevation. When they do not exercise due care on their part, failure can take on terrible characteristics, because our brothers and sisters who set the vibrational borders outside the room cannot prevent the entry of low order spirits who are completely integrated with their incarnate victims. There are obsessed persons who feel so comfortable in the company of their persecutors that they are like earthly mothers clinging to their children, entering places consecrated to certain services that are not proper for the infantile spirit. When unaware persons start the work under such conditions, the threats are truly disconcerting."

"So," I offered, "the victims of vampirism should not come here."

"Technically, they shouldn't," said the instructor, smiling, "especially because there are other centers where they can be helped; sometimes, however, fraternal charity calls for tolerance, even in environments such as this one."

And after a short pause, he emphasized:

"That is why meetings for the work of materialization are quite rare; homogeny here must be much more intense. Most of our activities are dedicated to efforts of Christian charity. In this environment, however, the work is limited to certain demonstrations related to spiritual knowledge. Nevertheless, people in general are not presently able to understand the divine essence of such demonstrations, and usually come to them placing reason above sentiment. Due to the expectations regarding the experiment, they often waste the opportunity to cooperate, and the results are negative. The day when they are able to come with enlightened hearts, however, they will receive joys equal to those that descended on Jesus' disciples, when, behind closed doors and in a sublime communion of love and faith, they received the visit of the Master – perfectly materialized after his resurrection – in a humble house in Jerusalem, as described in the Gospel narrative[10]."

Since Alexandre had become silent for a few instants, I increased my observations.

I was surprised to notice the efforts of twenty high order spirits who were stirring the ambient air. In their rhythmic gestures they looked like ancient priests as they performed magnetic operations for the cleansing of the room.

In answer to my inquisitive mind, Alexandre explained:

"These are not hierophants making conventional gestures. They are enlightened coworkers who are preparing the environment by ionizing the atmosphere and combining resources for electric and magnetic effects. Work at this level demands accelerated processes of materialization and dematerialization of energy. In the visual field of our incarnate friends, the manifesting spirits are almost always individuals closely tied to the earth and its sensory planes, but the true organizers of the work at hand are real, competent guides from the spirit realm who have vast knowledge and responsibility."

A few moments later a number of workers from our sphere arrived, bringing small apparatuses, which, due to the rays they were emitting in all directions, looked to me like small instruments of great electrical potency.

My curiosity knew no bounds.

"These friends," Alexandre explained, "are in charge of performing the condensation of oxygen throughout the house. The environment for the materialization of an entity from the plane invisible to human eyes calls for a high level of ozone; moreover, such an operation is crucial in order to exterminate all the larvae and microscopic residue of low order activity.

[10] Reference to Jn. 20:19. – Tr.

The relative 'ozonization' of the inner area is necessary as a bactericidal procedure."

And after a meaningful gesture, he added:

"The ectoplasm or neural energy that will be abundantly extracted from the medium cannot bear the intromission of certain microbial elements without dire consequences."

Soon thereafter, I was surprised to see the work performed by several spirits who had arrived from outside with a large quantity of luminous material.

"Those are resources from nature," the solicitous instructor informed me, "which these workers from our plane have gathered for the job. They consist of elements from plants and water and are of course invisible to human eyes, which are structured for a lower number of vibrations."

"Will they be used in this evening's work?" I asked.

"Yes," Alexandre clarified patiently, "they will be activated by the guides."

At that moment, incarnates familiarized with the meeting entered the room and took their usual seats.

A light conversation began among them, during which they commented on the work that had taken place on previous occasions.

Before long, the medium, an affable and friendly young woman, entered the room in the company of several spirits, among whom one of a more elevated status stood out, who seemed to be leading the group of workers. He exerted considerable control over the woman, who was connected to him by very thin threads of a magnetic nature.

Noticing my unappeasable curiosity, the supervisor explained:

"The mediumistic operator is Brother Alencar, who, like you, was a physician on earth. Calimerio is the one actually in charge of supervising the work in our sphere."

Noting my surprise, Alexandre reiterated:

"Alencar is the supervisor in charge of the mediumistic instrument for the materialization activities per se. Let's approach him."

Deeply moved, I was greeted by our new friend, who welcomed us warmly:

"The presence of both of you will be very useful to us," he said, gazing at my instructor in particular, "because we need coworkers to provide magnetic assistance to the medium's body."

"We are at your disposal" stated Alexandre happily. "We will take our place among your assistants."

Alencar thanked us with a gesture of true satisfaction.

Among the coworkers, there was one individual who was very dear to the instructor. It was Veronica, who had been an excellent nurse on earth, and who put me at ease with her friendly speech.

"Brother Alexandre," she said, after a short warm chat, "let's begin the magnetic assistance. We need to stimulate the digestive processes so that the mediumistic instrument may function without obstacles."

There was no opportunity for me to ask further questions. However, Alexandre gave me a meaningful look, inviting me to observe closely.

He, Veronica and another three of Alencar's direct assistants put their hands like a crown over the young woman's head, and I watched as their combined energies formed a vigorous magnetic flow that was projected over the medium's stomach and liver. These organs immediately began to vibrate in a new rhythm. The energy gradually concentrated over the solar plexus and spread throughout the entire autonomic nervous system, and I was astonished to see that the digestive chemical process had sped up. The glands of the stomach began to secrete greater quantities of pepsin and hydrochloric acid, rapidly transforming the alimentary bolus. I noticed the elevated production of digestive enzymes and saw the pancreas working hard to inject large doses of trypsin into the top part of the intestines, which resembled a great repository of acidophilic bacilli. I took the opportunity to study the liver, which seemed to be undergoing a special influence, and I noticed its status as an intermediary organ, not only with defined functions in the production of bile, but also with an important role in the nutritive phenomena related to the life of blood cells. The hepatic cells hastened to store up nutritional resources along the interlobular veins, which looked like little channels of light.

In just a few minutes, the stomach was entirely empty.

"Now," exclaimed Veronica obligingly, "let's prepare the nervous system for the release of the energies."

I watched the differentiation of the magnetic fluxes in light of this new operation. The assistants had withdrawn somewhat, and while Alexandre projected his personal energy over the brain area, Veronica and her colleagues spread their own resources over the whole central nervous system, each taking charge of a certain area of the cervical, thoracic, lumbar and sacral nerves.

The energies projected into the medium's body initiated an energetic and effective cleansing, and I was astonished to see the dark residues that were pulled from the vital centers.

Under the luminous emission coming from Alexandre's right hand, the young woman's brain took on a remarkable brilliance as if it were a crystalline mirror. The most important glands glowed like vigorous centers enlivened by sublime elements. Beneath the shower of spiritual rays directed over her, one could perceive the divine work of which the medium was the object, and which seemed to restore electrical equilibrium to all her organic cells.

With the task finished, Alexandre noticed my unconcealed curiosity and said:

"The mediumistic instrument has been submitted to magnetic operations meant to assist her body in the processes of nutrition, circulation, metabolism and protoplasmic action so that her physiological equilibrium is maintained regardless of any troublesome surprises."

Continuing my examination of the work in progress, I noticed that Veronica was now placing her right hand over the young woman's head, holding it for a while over the center of sensibility.

"Our sister Veronica," explained the affable instructor, "is applying magnetic passes[11] in preparation for the necessary disengagement of her spirit from her body."

At that moment, something strange happened in the sphere of our spiritual work. A large vibrational jolt was felt in the room. Two workers approached Alencar and one of them explained, alarmed:

"Mr. P... has just arrived, but his condition is undesirable."

"What's the matter?" Alencar asked without losing his composure.

"He has drunk a lot of alcohol and we need to take measures to insulate him."

Showing his displeasure, Alencar whispered as he headed for the entrance:

"This is very serious! We need to neutralize his influence right away."

Alexandre invited me to observe the case more closely. In view of the astonishment that had suddenly come over me, he explained:

[11] [Passes are] a transfusion of energy, altering the cellular field. ... In magnetic assistance, spiritual resources are blended between emission and reception, helping the individual in need to help him or herself. (A. Luiz, In the *Realms of Mediumship*, Brazilian Spiritist Federation, 2018, ch. 17) – Tr.

"In this type of phenomena, Andre, moral factors are a decisive organizational element. We are not looking at mechanisms of least effort, but rather the sacred manifestations of life, in which we cannot dispense with the higher objectives and vibratory attunement."

At that moment Mr. P... came through the door.

Appearing to be in an excellent mood, he did not look like a threat to the overall equilibrium, because he was not displaying any overt signs of drunkenness.

Nevertheless, following Alencar's instructions, several workers quickly surrounded him like nurses dealing with somebody gravely ill.

Unable to silence my impressions, I asked:

"What's the problem? This man seems calm and normal."

"Yes," explained Alexandre kindly, "but appearances aren't everything. In such a state, his breath emits poisons. In a different setting he might be treated charitably, but here, because of the specialized work to be performed, the ethylic elements he is exteriorizing through his nose, mouth and pores are highly damaging to our work. As you can see, there is a need for moral preparation for any procedure. An addiction of any type will harm the addict first of all, but it will also disturb others."

I remembered the effect of alcohol on the human body, but as soon as I thought about it, Alexandre quickly explained:

"You know that small doses of alcohol intensify the digestive process and promote diuresis, but in excess it is a destructive toxin. The emanations from the large amounts of sugarcane alcohol ingested by our brother are very harmful to the delicate elements of pliable matter that are going to be used in our efforts, and they are a serious danger to the exteriorized energies of the mediumistic instrument as well."

In fact, we could gradually perceive, although vaguely, the characteristic smell of alcoholic fermentation.

I noticed that Mr. P... was now surrounded by spirits involved in the activities at hand and was neutralized by their influence, just as debris is disposed of by hard-working bees in a busy hive.

The work progressed normally.

Amid wishes of success from the semi-confident incarnate companions, the medium was led into a small, improvised booth; a short prayer followed. It was apparent, however, that just like in other meetings, our earth-bound friends emitted silent requests, and the mental vibrations began to actively conflict with one another, complicating instead of helping the evening's work, which demanded a high level of harmony. By the gentle, weak glow of the red light that had replaced the stronger ordinary bulb, the luminous emissions of our incarnate friends' thoughts were noticeable. Actually, the small gathering did not possess the spirit of divine understanding for the work being carried out. No one considered the meaning of the event for earthly humankind. One who was eager for heavenly revelations could see that the meeting was profoundly dominated by the "self." While some voiced their demands, others were deciding which discarnate spirits ought to manifest in the materialization phenomena. Nevertheless, I tried to hold back my displeasure, because all the higher order workers in the room were behaving very calmly, treating the corporeal attendees with devoted care, just like learned individuals in the presence of children dear to their hearts.

Several spirit workers began to combine the magnetic radiations of our terrestrial audience in order to compile the materials that would assist in the endeavor, while Calimerio, projecting his transcendent supply of energies onto the medium, accomplished the medium's disengagement from her body, which took a few minutes to effect. Veronica and other helpers were supporting the young woman, who, although partially freed from her physical vehicle, was somewhat confused and worried next to her body, which was by now in a deep trance.

Next, I noticed that, under the action of the noble guide, neural energies began exteriorizing like an abundant flow of thick, milky mist.

Perceiving the vibrational disturbance in the atmosphere due to the unacceptable attitude of the incarnates present, Calimerio said to the mediumistic operator:

"Alencar, we need to quench the conflicting vibrations. Our friends still do not know how to lend us harmonious aid with their mental emissions. It would be better if they abstained from concentrating for now. Tell them to sing or to make music. Try to distract their uneducated attention."

But Alencar, who was seriously concerned about the many duties he had to perform at the moment, asked for Alexandre's help. Alexandre obliged immediately:

"Andre," he said seriously, "let's devise an ectoplasmic throat. We have no time to waste."

And remembering my inexperience, he added:

"There's no need to worry. All you have to do is help me visualize the anatomic details of the larynx."

I was confused, but my instructor offered:

"The medium's neural energies are a pliable matter that is highly sensitive to our mental creations."

Alexandre took a small portion of the milky effluvium that was coming particularly out of the mouth, nose and ears of the mediumistic instrument, and as if he were holding a small quantity of liquid plaster in his hands, he began to manipulate it, giving me the impression that he was completely unaware of his surroundings and that he was in full control of himself as he concentrated on the creation at hand.

Bit by bit before my astonished eyes, I saw a delicate phonation device take shape. Within the cartilaginous outline, sculpted to perfection from the ectoplasmic material, the tenuous threads of vocal cords were coming together, elastic and complete in the epiglottic cavity. When it was ready, Alexandre tried out a few sounds by moving the arytenoid cartilages.

A perfect throat had taken shape under the mental control and technical action of the instructor.

I was astonished to see that, through the small improvised device and with the help of the sounds of human voices stored in the room, our voices could be fully heard by all the incarnates present. Obviously pleased with the success of his work, Alexandre spoke through the artificial throat like someone using a human vocal instrument:

"Dear friends, may the peace of Jesus be with you! Help us by singing! Make music and stop thinking!"

Music was made in the room and I saw Brother Alencar, after linking deeply to the medium's body, begin to take shape right next to the medium, who was being supported by Calimerio and several other workers.

Gradually, using the exteriorized neural energies and various fluidic elements taken from inside the house in addition to various resources from nature, Alencar appeared perfectly materialized in front of the incarnates.

I was surprised as I realized that the medium was at the center of all the work. Extremely fine threads linked her to Alencar's form, and when we gently touched the medium's body, Alencar displayed obvious signs of concern, as did the young medium. The onlookers' uncontrolled and enthusiastic expressions in trying to greet the materialized messenger directly had a disagreeable repercussion on the intermediary's body.

Brother Alencar gave a short talk to our ecstatic earth-bound friends. However, what touched my heart were not the words exchanged between him and the onlookers, but rather the beauty of the phenomenon, the reality of the materialization. It lent great hope for the future of humankind regarding religious faith, the comforting philosophy of immortality and an ennobled science in the service of enlightened reasoning.

Alexandre said to me:

"Behold the grandeur of what is happening. The medium is fulfilling the role of a maternal entity while Alencar, under the positive influence of Calimerio, undergoes a temporary filial connection in regards to the mediumistic instrument. All forms that materialize are 'provisional children' of the intermediary's pliable energies. The person conversing with the incarnates is Alencar, but his envelope at this time is born from the medium's passive energies and the active energies of Calimerio, the highest order director of this meeting. If on our plane we put a strain on the medium, we will harm Alencar, who is under the process of materialization; if our earthly friends harm Alencar's temporary material form, they will severely injure the medium, causing disastrous and unpredictable consequences."

Perplexed by the phenomenon, I asked:

"But is such neural energy the property of only a few privileged individuals?"

"No," Alexandre replied. "All people possess it to a greater or lesser extent; however, one must understand that we have not yet reached a time when such materializations can be widespread. You know that this matter requires sanctification. Human beings will not be able to abuse the course of spiritual progress as they have been doing on the path of material evolution, where wonderful divine gifts are made into forces of destruction and misery. My friend, in this field of sublime realizations, to which we feel connected, ignorance, vanity and malicious intent act as agents to draw their own lines of limitation."

Impressed by the marvels I was witnessing, I noticed that, at Alencar's request and with Calimerio's generous cooperation, hands and flowers materialized as affectionate messages for those attending the meeting.

There was great joy amongst all, with the exception of Mr. P..., who showed signs of unexplainable discomfort while under the direct control of the several spirit workers neutralizing his harmful influence.

After wonderful minutes of effort and jubilation and with meaningful displays of gratitude toward God, the evening's work ended and we all helped out to ensure that the medium was completely reintegrated with her psycho-physical patrimony.

My heart was overflowing with happiness and hope; I had to admit, however, that, in comparison with the manifestations of service and the sublime blessings we had witnessed, the incarnates really did not understand very much. They were like light-hearted children, more interested in the rare spectacle than in wanting to consecrate themselves to divine service. Frankly, I was disappointed. So many celestial emissaries making such an effort for half a dozen people who seemed far removed from the purpose of serving the cause of the Truth and the Good!

I voiced my opinion to my devoted instructor, but Alexandre answered peacefully:

"What about Jesus? Do you think that he worked only for the Galileans who did not understand him? Do you think that he only taught at the temple in Jerusalem? No, my friend; you can be sure that all our actions, whether good or bad, are for all humankind. For the moment, our earth-bound friends do not understand us, nor have they grown into complete consecration to Jesus, but the sowing is alive and in time it will produce. Nothing is lost."

And smiling, he concluded after a long pause:

"It's true that as a doctor you were always interested in seeing the results of your work, but don't forget the silent effort of the farmers sowing the fields and remember that the seeds placed in Egyptian sarcophagi thousands of years ago have begun to produce wonderfully in the soil of the earth."

11
Intercession

One evening, after the talk Alexandre had dedicated to our incarnate collaborators, he was approached by two women who had been taken to that advanced course of enlightenment under very special circumstances because they were individuals who were still bound to their vessels of flesh. They had sought out the instructor while temporarily detached from their bodies during sleep.

The older woman was obviously the more advanced due to the light that surrounded her. She seemed to be well known and regarded by Alexandre, who welcomed her with undisguised displays of affection. The younger woman, however, was enveloped in darkness and had a tearful and distressed expression on her face.

"My dear friend!" exclaimed the more pleasant of the two, addressing the benevolent instructor after the initial greetings, "I'm bringing you my cousin Ester, who lost her husband in woeful circumstances."

And while the other woman silently dried her tears, deeply melancholic, the first one continued:

"Alexandre, I know the elevation and urgent nature of your work; nevertheless, I would dare to ask for your help in our earthly grief! If our plea is absurd, please forgive us with your insightful and kind heart! We are human women! So forgive us if we come knocking on your benevolent door to deal with our heartbreaking problems!"

"Etelvina, my friend," the instructor said tenderly, "everywhere, sincere affliction is worthy of help. If there is suffering in the flesh, it also exists here, where we find ourselves without our physical remains, and in all places we must be ready to offer true cooperation. So, please tell me what it is that you want and put yourselves at ease!"

Both women seemed relieved and began to speak calmly.

Satisfied, Etelvina introduced her companion, who began telling her sorrowful story. Twelve years ago she had married the second groom whom destiny had reserved for her; the first one, whom she had loved very much, had committed suicide under mysterious circumstances. At first she had been profoundly concerned about the situation of this first and much-loved husband, whose name was Noe. However, the devotion of Raul, the husband whom heaven had sent her after Noe, had managed to deliver her from her sadness and they built a loving marriage, filled with tender understanding. They had received three little ones from Divine Providence and were living in compete harmony. Although given to bouts of melancholy, Raul was dedicated and faithful. How many times she had wanted to soothe his hidden wounds, but to no avail! Her companion never really opened up to her! Nonetheless, life flowed happily and peacefully in the sanctuary of mutual understanding. Notwithstanding their dedication to their sacred domestic duties, hidden enemies appeared, robbing them of their happiness. Raul was inexplicably murdered. Anonymous friends picked up his body from the road, and brought the terrible surprise home to her. He had been shot in the heart with a handgun, which, although found next to his bloodless body, was not his. What mystery clothed the heinous crime? Many townspeople and the police were convinced that it was a suicide; hence, all criminal justice investigations had been suspended. However, her woman's intuition told her it had been murder. What motives would lead an honest and hardworking man to commit suicide for no reason? Why would Raul kill himself when everything was going so well for them as far as the future was concerned? Of course, their financial resources were not extensive, but they knew how to rightly balance domestic expenditures with their regular income. No, no. In her view, her companion had left the earth due to an evil crime. Because of her kindness, however, Ester did not want to place the blame on anybody, nor did she want vengeance; she only wanted to ease her broken heart. By means of Alexandre's intermediation, would it be possible for her to dream about her companion in order to obtain news directly from him, and to let him feel the tenderness they still nurtured for him at home? Because of her small children and an elderly aunt and uncle who depended on her, the anguished widow found herself in a terrible financial bind as a result of her unexpected widowhood. Nevertheless – she added tearfully – she was willing to work and dedicate herself to her little ones and to start her life over; but before doing so, she hoped for some comfort for her soul. She eagerly wanted to know what had happened and what her husband's situation was in order to resign herself to it.

And at the end of the long and heartfelt account, she concluded tearfully, addressing the instructor:

"Have pity, my generous friend! Can you tell me anything? What has become of Raul? Who could have murdered him? And why?"

The suffering widow seemed crazed with grief and had been overcome by the most disparaging questions; however, far from being displeased by her ill-timed questions, Alexandre assumed a fatherly attitude, and kindly taking her hands, he replied:

"Be calm and brave, my friend! It is not possible to explain things at this moment. It is imperative to investigate with care in order to solve the problem with due diligence. So go home and rest your oppressed mind ... There are troubles that are not solved by the power of the world's reasoning. It is indispensable to know the refuge of prayer, entrusting them to the Supreme Father. Lean on sincere faith, trust in Providence and we shall see what can be done regarding information and fraternal help. We will carefully examine the issue!"

Both women spun a few more sorrowful comments about what had happened, and then said goodbye with words of gratitude and comfort.

Alone with me once again and perhaps sensing my need for preparation and understanding, the instructor explained:

"Our incarnate friends often believe that we are simple fortune-tellers and that by the mere fact that we are now living outside the flesh we possess sublime gifts of divination. They forget that personal effort and genuine work comprise a law applicable to all evolutionary planes."

With a fatherly smile, he added:

"Nevertheless, we must remember that when we ourselves were on the earth and faced with the same circumstances, we would not have acted any differently."

The very next day I had some time available and Alexandre invited me to go with him to Ester's house. He would take the woman's home as the starting point for his investigation.

"What for?" I asked. "Wouldn't it be more practical to use our mental powers to evoke the discarnate husband directly? That way Raul could be heard without difficulty, and then we would know what to do to help the widow."

However, without scorning my idea, the instructor replied:

"Of course, that would be the easiest method, and in many cases we must use such resources; nonetheless, Andre, in order to be complete, intercessory work requires something from ourselves. By giving our sister Ester some of our time and abilities, we will acquire greater knowledge about the general situation and at the same time enrich the quality of our help. Those who do good are the first to benefit; those who turn on a light are the first to be illumined."

Indicating that he did not want to talk about it any more, Alexandre became silent, and as we set out, I was once more able to understand that, just as on the earth, the work of fraternal cooperation in the spirit realm demands effort, tolerance and diligence.

The poor widow's house was located on a modest street, and although relatively comfortable, it seemed to be inhabited by many spirits of an inferior nature. I noticed this without difficulty due to their comings and goings, even before we entered the home. We entered without these unfortunate discarnate spirits noticing our presence because of the low vibrational level that characterized their perception. It was painful, however, to look at the situation. The family, made up of the widow, three children and an elderly couple, sat around the dinner table in front of a very simple lunch. However, a phenomenon that I had never seen before marred my observations: six spirits enveloped in shadow joined them at the meal as if they were taking in nourishment by absorption.

"Oh my God!" I cried out, bewildered and addressing the instructor: "Is that real? Discarnates sitting at the table?"

Alexandre answered calmly:

"My friend, the pictures of mental degradation, ignorance and suffering in homes lacking a religious foundation are immense. Where there is no spiritual organization, there are no defenses for peace of mind. This is intuitive for all who value righteous thinking."

After a short pause, during which he gazed sympathetically at the scene, he continued:

"Those who discarnate in a state of excessive attachment to those whom they have left behind (who are also bound) almost always remain connected to the house, the former domestic situations and the family's vital fluids. They eat with their relatives and they sleep in the same rooms where they left their physical bodies."

"But do they really eat, enjoying the same flavors as before?" I asked, shocked to see the satisfaction of the spirits gathered there as they happily absorbed the emanations from the steaming plates.

Alexandre smiled and added:

"Are you so surprised at seeing them taking in food only by inhaling it? What about us? Are you perchance unaware of the fact that incarnate humans receive more than seventy percent of their normal nourishment through atmospheric elements collected by means of the respiratory channels? You know that substances cooked by fire undergo profound disintegration. Well, our brothers and sisters who are addicted to physiological sensations find in such disintegrated elements the same flavors they used to experience when in the flesh."

"Still," I considered, "it seems like it would be unpleasant to eat meals while having to keep the unavoidable company of strangers, especially those of the type we are looking at."

"But you mustn't forget," indicated the instructor, "that these are not unknown individuals. This is a group of relatives who are held here by the incarnates themselves because of their heavy vibrations of morbid attachment."

Alexandre thought for a moment and continued:

"Let's accept your hypothesis, however. Even if the domestic dinner table were surrounded by despicable entities without any blood ties, we would be left with the fact that souls gather together in obedience to their characteristic tendencies and the fact that each spirit keeps the company it prefers."

And wishing to provide me with solid bases for my learning, he pondered:

"The family table is always a receptacle for influences of an invisible nature. If individuals use it while thinking of the good, spirit workers close by come and take part in the blessed field of good thoughts. If the family remains on a higher plane, rendering worship to the higher experiences of life, the guides of spiritual enlightenment will come closer, casting onto the ground of constructive conversation the seeds of new ideas, which will then grow with the sublime beauty of spontaneity. However, by the same provisions of the law of affinity, slanderous conversation will attract invisible slanderers, while sarcasm will of course draw mocking and sarcastic spirits who will inspire undignified tales, opening up a vast room for frivolousness and perturbation."

Pointing to the group at the table, Alexandre added:

"In this case, these sad individuals have attracted their like-minded discarnate relatives; it is mutual vampirism. Listen to what they are saying."

I pricked up my ears and noticed that the conversation was in fact very woeful.

"I never thought I would have to suffer so much!" exclaimed Ester's old aunt, complaining bitterly. "Agostino and I worked so hard when we were younger! ... Now that we are old and lacking the resources to face life, we have to burden a poor widowed niece! What a dreadful fate!"

And while tears ran down her wax-like cheeks, the old man chimed in:

"That's for sure! For such a laborious and hard life, such a bitter reward! I never anticipated such a bleak old age!"

On hearing these statements, the spirits dressed in tunics of darkness seemed to become more touched and hugged the old couple fervently.

Although sad, the widow added resignedly:

"It's true that our trials have been cruel, but we should trust in God's goodness."

Alexandre concentrated all his attention on her, and I noticed that a peculiar disposition came over the widow's soul. With eyes shining as if she had perceived our outside spiritual influence, she vaguely remembered her dream from the previous night:

"Thanks to Providence, I woke up this morning feeling much more comforted. I dreamed that cousin Etelvina led me into the presence of a heavenly messenger who blessed my soul, alleviating the heavy grief of these last few days! Oh, how glad I would be if I could remember that dream of light!"

"Come on, Mommy, tell us!" exclaimed the little girl of about seven years of age, who had kept still until then.

The woman willingly went on:

"My child, I cannot begin to describe the wonderful feelings. I can't remember everything precisely, but I do remember that Jesus' emissary listened to me patiently, and then gave me words of encouragement and love. Rather than reproaching me, he welcomed me kindly, and displaying divine tolerance, he listened to all my complaints until the end like a selfless doctor. Of course, I got up this morning in a different mood. So, let's accept our situation, because God will help us. As soon as I'm totally recovered, I'll begin earning our daily bread with honest work. Let's have hope and faith."

In light of Ester's encouraging words, the children smiled at each other and the elderly couple stopped their bitter complaining.

I wanted to make myself visible to the unenlightened discarnate companions in the room so that I could speak with them and probe into their experiences, but Alexandre dissuaded me:

"It would be a waste of time," he said. "If you want to help them, come here another time, because the mental crystallizations of many years cannot be undone by the verbal explanations of only one day. Right now, we have a different objective. We need to gather information on Raul. Furthermore, if we used this time to listen to our discarnate brothers and sisters, we would soon realize that they are able to report only sorrowful grievances, and that would be of no use to us."

And showing little interest in the incarnates' conversation due to the crucial purpose of the moment, he considered:

"Let's look for one of the brothers who watch over this area. We need some initial information in order to structure our intercessory work right away."

Because Alexandre headed for other rooms, I too left the modest dinning room, although I wanted to continue my observations. However, the instructor had no time to waste.

After a few minutes, we were face to face with a humble though dignified looking spirit, whom Alexandre addressed cordially:

"My friend, are you an overseer on active shift?"

"Yes, at your service," he replied attentively.

In a few words, the instructor frankly explained to him what we wanted.

The overseer then explained himself. He had known Raul quite well and had helped him many times by giving him continuous spiritual assistance; however, neither he nor other friends had been able to prevent him from committing coldly calculated suicide.

"Suicide?" asked Alexandre, trying to obtain more complete details. "His widow thinks it was murder."

"Well," our new friend offered, "he knew how to disguise it carefully. He had been thinking about the unfortunate act for a long time, and on the final day he bought a gun to carry out his plan. Shooting an area close to his heart and handling the weapon in a way to avoid fingerprints, he then threw it away from him. That is how he was able to deceive his relatives, making them think that a grievous crime had been committed."

"And were you able to see him in the last moments of this tragedy?" asked Alexandre paternally.

"Yes," the other explained. "Some friends and I tried to help him, but in light of the fact that is was an intentional, coldly planned death, we were unable to remove him from the pool of blood in which he was immersed, held there by extremely heavy and anguishing vibrations. We were still working to help him, when a 'gang' of several dozen spirits approached, abusing the wretch and moving him easily due to the attunement of their wicked energies. As you can understand, we were unable to wrest him from the hands of those thieves of darkness as they took him with them."

The instructor seemed satisfied with this explanation, and when I realized that he was about to end the conversation, I dared to ask:

"But ... what was the reason for the suicide? Wouldn't it be interesting to hear what the overseer has to say about that?"

"No," explained Alexandre calmly. "We shall ask Raul himself."

We said goodbye, but a question was tormenting my mind. I could not hold it back for long, and addressing my generous guide, I asked:

"A 'gang'? What does that mean?"

Alexandre, who now seemed to be more worried, explained:

"The 'gang' he mentioned is a crowd of delinquent spirits dedicated to the practice of evil. Although their influence is limited due to the many defenses that surround groups of our incarnate brothers and sisters as well as our own spheres of action, they can cause a lot of trouble by concentrating the impulses of their collective energies."

Because of my great astonishment, the instructor added:

"Don't be so surprised, my friend. Physical death is not a miraculous immersion that instantly converts evil spirits into good ones, and ignorant spirits into wise ones. There are discarnates that cling to their home surroundings like ivy to a wall. Others – a lot of them in fact – rebel within the circles of ignorance proper to them and form so-called legions of darkness, which confronted even Jesus through various obsessed individuals. They organize themselves diabolically into criminal cooperatives, and woe to anyone who becomes one of their companions! Those who stumble and fall along the evolutionary pathway by disregarding divine opportunities are the suffering slaves of such transitory but terrible powers of darkness. They are in a bondage that can last a long, long time."

"But the regional overseer, as a guardian of this place," I inquired, surprised, "couldn't he have defended the unfortunate suicide?"

"If he had been the victim of murder, yes," answered the instructor, "because if they are true victims, humans emanate certain currents of magnetic energies that can put them in contact with missionaries of assistance. But in a premeditated suicide without the interference of concealed enemies – like the case at hand – the soul's imbalance is dreadful and brings about the total inability of the mind to tune into higher elements."

"But," I asked, astonished, "couldn't spirit guardians have helped him anyway?"

In a gesture of fraternal tolerance, Alexandre pointed out:

"Since inner freedom is the natural endowment of all children of creation, it would not be possible to rush to assist all those who fall into the abysses of suffering due to their own intentional actions, with full awareness of what they are doing. In such cases, pain works as a measure of assistance in the indispensable correction of the wrong. But ... what about the evil ones who seem happy to be that way? you will naturally ask. These are the wicked and hardened suffering spirits of all eras, who, despite realizing their own spiritual decadence, build up a dangerous coating of insensitivity around their hearts. Desperate and disillusioned, and harboring venomous anger, they plunge themselves into the dark tide of evil until a new ray of light arises in their conscience."

The topic presented an opportunity for invaluable explanations, but Alexandre made a gesture to indicate that he did not have any more time for words, and after a short pause, he added:

"Andre, Help me by praying for a few moments. Now that I have concrete information from the overseer, I need to mobilize my abilities of sight in order to find out the location of our unfortunate brother."

Notwithstanding the fact that I was praying, I noticed that Alexandre had fallen into a deep silence. A few moments later, he spoke again and stated as if he had come back from a surprising journey:

"We can proceed. Our poor semi-conscious brother is magnetized to a dangerous group of vampires in a nearby location."

He set out and I followed step by step in silence despite my great curiosity.

We were soon far from the suburban enclaves and found ourselves outside a large slaughterhouse.

My surprise knew no bounds as I observed the vigilant attitude assumed by my guide, who entered decisively through the large entrance door. From the vibrations filling the air, I realized that, in my new phase of spiritual experiences, this was one of the most unpleasant places I had ever come across. Following Alexandre very closely, I saw several groups of obviously low order spirits scattered throughout. In the area where the cattle were being slaughtered, I beheld a petrifying scene. A large number of discarnates in a dreadful state were lunging at the fresh, gushing blood as if they were trying to drink the liquid to quench their devouring thirst.

Alexandre noticed the dolorous bewilderment that had taken hold of me and explained serenely:

"Do you see, Andre? These wretched brothers and sisters cannot see us due to their deplorable state of brutishness and inferiority. They are sucking up the energies from the animals' blood plasma. They are famished spirits who warrant our compassion."

Few times in my life had I felt such repugnance. The saddest scenes I had witnessed until then in the lower zones had not stricken me with such dread. Discarnates in need of that type of nourishment? A slaughterhouse full of perverse spirits? What did it all mean? I recalled my limited knowledge of history, going back to the times when primitive peoples offered the blood of bulls and goats to supposed gods. Could it be that the horrendous scene taking place right here was the representation of ancient sacrifices on stone altars? I allowed my first impressions to set my mind afire to the point of feeling like my ideas were wandering in a whirlwind.

Alexandre, kind as always, explained warmly:

"Why are you feeling such dread, my friend? Come out of yourself; break the shell of personal interpretation and enter the broad arena of reasoning. When on earth, didn't we both patronize butcher shops? I recall that in my old home the slaughtering of pigs was a source of family contentment. A carcass of meat and fat meant abundance in the kitchen and comfort in the stomach. By the same token, these discarnates – as low-ordered as we once were – gather around the dead animals, whose steaming blood offers them strong vital elements. No doubt the scene is deplorable, but it is not up to us to pass judgment. Each thing, each being, each soul is in the evolutionary process appropriate to it. And if we have already gone through the lower stations and know how difficult it is to improve on the plane of elevation, we must try and keep a genuine willingness to help, mobilizing our best abilities in the service of our neighbor."

The warning had been highly useful. Alexandre's words pierced my soul as a teaching, correcting my mental attitude. I looked serenely at the scene before me, and noticing that I had recovered my equilibrium, Alexandre showed me a spirit in a deplorable state, similar to an automaton, wandering around amid the others. After gazing at his almost expressionless eyes, I noticed that his clothes were covered in blood.

"He's the suicide we're looking for," exclaimed my instructor with certainty.

"What?" I asked, astonished, "Why would the vampires need him?"

"These types of wretched spirits," explained Alexandre, "abuse defenseless newly-discarnate beings like poor Raul during the first days following their physical death by extracting life forces from them after exploiting their physical body."

I was shocked. I recalled ancient religious information on diabolical temptations, but the instructor, focusing firmly on his sacred mission of assistance, replied:

"Andre, don't be negatively impressed. Every person, whether incarnate or discarnate, who deviates from the straight and narrow path of the good, may become a dangerous spirit of evil. We have no time to lose. Let's act right now to help this poor fellow."

Following my helpful mentor, I approached the wretch. Alexandre placed his right hand over Raul's head and enveloped him in a vigorous magnetic influx. Within a few moments Raul was surrounded by light, which was immediately seen by the beings of darkness. I saw that most of them drew back, shrieking in terror. Upon seeing the luminosity that encircled the victim, they became ashen and frightened. One of the more courageous torturers said in a loud voice:

"Let's abandon this man to his fate. 'Powerful spirits' are interested in him. Let's let him go!"

As if they feared something I could not yet understand, the tormenters left in a hurry due to that blessed light coming down from the Higher Realms. My mind was overcome by painful inner questions. The scene was typical of those old legends of demons abandoning the souls imprisoned to their infernal purposes. The words "powerful spirits" had been pronounced with undisguised sarcasm. By the bright light that enveloped the suicide, they knew we were present, and although they fled in fear, they still shouted mockeries at us.

Little by little, the huge slaughterhouse became free of voracious vampires. Concluding the magnetic operation, Alexandre took the hand of our suffering friend, who still seemed stupefied by the malignant influence. Leading him outside in the direction of the fields, he told me kindly:

"Don't harbor their sarcastic words in your heart. Those unfortunate brothers and sisters deserve all our compassion. Let's get on with the matter at hand."

He suggested that I support our new friend, who seemed unaware of our assistance. After walking for a few minutes, we stopped under a large leafy tree and placed our weakened and stumbling brother on the fresh grass.

Impressed by his expressionless eyes, I asked the instructor for an explanation. He was not long in his friendly reply:

"The poor man has temporarily lost his memory. After the prolonged sucking away of his vital energies, his state is one of lamentable unconsciousness."

Because of my surprise, Alexandre added:

"What would you expect? Do you think that the law of least effort would prevail here? The magnetism of evil is also full of power, particularly for those who willingly fall into its tentacles."

Next, he leaned paternally over the unfortunate suicide and asked him:

"Bother Raul, how are you feeling?"

"I ... I...," mumbled the wretch as if he were immersed in a deep sleep, "I don't know ... I don't know anything."

"Do you remember your wife?"

"No..." answered the suicide vaguely.

The instructor got up and said to me:

"He is totally unconscious. We need to wake him up."

He told me to stand watch while he went in search of the necessary resources.

"Can't we wake him up ourselves?" I asked in surprise.

Alexandre smiled and offered:

"It is quite clear that you are not a veteran of 'intercessory' work. Have you forgotten that we are going to wake him up not only to his own awareness but also to suffering? We are going to break the shell of inferior magnetism enveloping Raul and he will come back to the awareness of his situation. He will feel the torment of his chest perforated by the bullet, and he will roar in anguish when he faces his dolorous afterlife condition, a situation that he himself created. In such cases, the first impressions are truly terrifying and a few hours have to pass before he can feel any relief at all. Since other duties await us, it will be appropriate to hand him over to the care of other friends."

His comments struck me deeply.

After twenty minutes, Alexandre returned accompanied by two brothers who were willing to take the wretch, and in a short while we were in a spiritual center for emergency first aid located on the earth itself. One could see that the organization only tended to emergency cases because the resources were obviously quite rudimentary.

Guessing my thoughts, Alexandre explained:

"We cannot put a full-service institution within the circle of antagonistic vibrations of earth's inhabitants, so the aid work here has undeniable deficiencies, of course. This place is a mobile hospital that depends on the devotion of a larger number of coworkers."

Once Raul was placed on a white-linen bed, Alexandre began to apply magnetic passes over his cerebral area. It was not long before the wretch let out a gasping and desperate shriek that pierced my heart.

"I'm dying! I'm dying!..." screamed Raul in supreme affliction, now trying to climb the walls. "I'm begging you to help me!"

And clutching his chest with his hands, he cried in a piercing voice:

"My heart is shattered! Help me! ... I don't want to die!"

Helpful nurses assisted him attentively, but the patient seemed overcome with terror. Crazed eyes in a mask of indefinable suffering, he continued shouting loudly as if he had just awoken from a terrible nightmare.

"Ester! Ester!" the wretch called out, remembering his devoted wife. "Come help me for God's sake! Help me! My children! ... My children!"

Alexandre came to him paternally and said:

"Raul, be patient and have faith in the Divine Power! Try to be brave and face the difficult situation that you have created for yourself, and do not call out the name of your dedicated wife, nor call for the beloved children whom you left in the old landscape of the world. The physical door of your home was shut along with your eyes. If you had cultivated Christian love and had taken advantage of the opportunities entrusted to you by the Lord, it would be easy in a time such as this to return to your loving home to see your loved ones, even if they could not register your presence. But now, my friend, it is too late ... you will have to await another opportunity of work and purification, because the one you had with the earthly name of Raul is over."

With immense dread stamped on his face, Raul answered:

"Then I'm dead? Can't I feel my heart pierced by pain? Aren't my clothes drenched in blood? Is this what death is like? That's crazy!"

Serenely, the kind instructor spoke again:

"Didn't you aim your gun at your own chest? Didn't you locate your heart in order to take your own life? Oh, my friend, people may fool one another, but no one can fool Divine Justice."

Displaying profound shame at realizing he had been found out, the suicide broke into tears and muttered:

"Ah! How wretched I am! A thousand times wretched!"

Alexandre did not speak to him again at that time. After lovingly handing him over to the care of the brothers and sisters responsible for the work of assistance, he said:

"Let's go, Andre! Our new friend is in a crisis whose peak will not be over for about another seventy hours. We'll return to see him later."

Back at my work, I anxiously awaited the moment of resuming my educational observations. The complexity of the "intercessory" work had impressed me. The simple prayers of a longing and dedicated wife had been the source of numerous activities for my guide and valuable lessons for me. How would Alexandre proceed in the end? What revelations would Raul have for us as individuals interested in his welfare? Would his wife be consoled in her widowhood?

With many questions on my mind, I waited for the right moment. After four days, the instructor invited me to return to the subject, which made me very happy because of the possibility of continuing to learn for my personal evolution.

We found Raul filled with pain; nevertheless, he was more composed and able to sustain an explanatory conversation. He complained about his open wound, his out-of-control heart, his acute suffering, and his great despondency. However, he knew that he was no longer in the physical realm, although such truth made him weep in anguish.

"Now settle down," said my instructor with indescribable kindness. "Your situation is difficult, but it could be much worse. There are suicides that remain attached to their corpses for an indeterminate time, watching it rot and feeling the attack of the voracious worms."

"Woe to me!" sighed the wretch, "because, besides being a suicide, I am also a criminal."

And displaying great trust in us, Raul told us his sad story, trying to justify his extreme act.

In his youth he had come from the country to the big city at the invitation of Noe, his childhood comrade. A devoted and true companion, this friend introduced him on a certain occasion to his dear fiancée, with whom he hoped to build a nest of domestic bliss in the future. Alas! From the day Raul saw Ester for the first time, he could not get her out of his mind. The young woman personified what he, Raul, held as the highest ideal for a happy marriage. In her presence, he felt the happiest of men. Her gaze nourished his heart, her ideas were a continuation of his own thoughts. But how could he make her feel his immense affection? Noe, his good friend from the past, became an obstacle that had to be removed. Ester would be incapable of betraying her commitment. Noe was too infinitely good and lovable to cause a break up. That is when the dreadful idea of a crime was born in Raul's mind. He would eliminate his rival. He would not surrender his happiness to anyone. His comrade would have to die. But how could he carry out the plan without problems with the police? Blinded by his violent passion, he began a detailed study on how to carry out his criminal objective. He found a clever formula for eliminating his dedicated and faithful companion. He started ingesting a well-known, terrible poison in very small doses, slowly increasing them until his body became accustomed to quantities that would be lethal for anyone else. When he reached the necessary level of resistance, he invited his friend for dinner and put the odious poison in a pleasant wine, which he himself drank without any danger. However, Noe was dead a few hours later and it looked like suicide to most. Raul kept the terrible secret forever, and after courting the mourning fiancée with kindness, he was able to generate her sympathy, which ended up in marriage. He had gotten what he wanted most: Ester belonged to him as his wife; children followed to enhance his life, but ... his conscience had been stricken beyond repair. In the most intimate scenes at home, he would see Noe on his mental screen, reproaching his conduct. His wife's kisses and his children's hugs could not keep the implacable vision away. Instead of decreasing, his remorse continued increasing. At work, when reading, at the dinner table, in the bedroom, the victim continued to stare at him in silence. At one point he had wanted to turn himself over to the justice of the world and confess the heinous crime; but he did not feel he had the right to grieve his wife, nor should he throw his children's future into turmoil. Society respected him, honoring his domestic life. Distinguished colleagues valued his company. How to reveal the truth in such circumstances? Despite loving his wife and children tenderly, he found himself exhausted at the end of prolonged spiritual endurance. He feared insanity, the mental institution and death while running from the need to confess the crime; but the need to do so grew nearer every day. At this point, the idea of suicide began to grow in his tormented mind. He could no longer resist. He would conceal the last act of his silent drama, just as he had hid the tragedy of the first. He bought a gun and waited. One day after work he took a detour on his way home and aimed the gun at his heart, careful to avoid leaving fingerprints. Having hit the target, he made a supreme effort to throw away the murderous weapon. He could not think about anything else but the indescribable torture in his strangled chest. As his eyes clouded over, he felt that some people were trying to help him, and soon a veritable unseen mob took him from that painful place ... From then on, a generalized weakness had overcome him completely. He felt imprisoned in a deep, anguishing sleep filled with cruel nightmares. He had finally recovered his self-awareness there in that simple room only after Alexandre had restored his prostrated energies.

Finishing his long and bitter confession, Raul felt his chest compressed and heavy tears streamed down his face.

Highly moved, I did not know what to say. That secret drama would have touched hearts of stone. Alexandre, however, displaying the greatness of his elevated realizations, remained composed and said:

"Raul, in the deepest abyss there is always room for hope. Do not allow yourself to be dominated by any idea that things will not work out. Think about renewed opportunities; meditate on God' greatness. Turn your remorse into the purpose of regeneration."

After a short pause as the wretch wept incessantly, the mentor continued:

"Truth is, your present ills cannot miraculously go away. We shall all reap according to what we have sown, and we, who have learned something today, have also gone through the lesson of starting all over again many times. Be calm and brave."

Next, Alexandre told him the reason behind our interest, explaining that our work of fraternal assistance had been set in motion through the prayers of his loving and forlorn wife. He gave him news about her, his young children and his elderly aunt and uncle; he told him about how much Ester missed him and how she longed to see him even if only for a fleeting moment during the sleep of her physical body.

Hearing this bit of information, the suicide became upset and remarked:

"Oh, no! I'm not worthy! My misery would only increase her grief!"

Nevertheless, the instructor patted his shoulder paternally and promised to intervene to solve the problem.

We left once again, and noticing my profound wonder, Alexandre offered:

"In the small drama we have been observing, my friend, you can now begin to imagine the extent and complexity of our tasks in 'intercessory' work. Our incarnate friends sometimes ask us for assistance, even though they are clueless as to what the real situation is. As far as human society is concerned, Raul was the victim of unknown criminals, whereas in reality he was only the victim of himself. According to his wife, he was the ideal husband, when in reality he was a criminal and a suicide."

I understood the moral difficulties in which we found ourselves in complying with the request that had led us to such a task; the instructor's words displayed nothing else. Understanding this fact, I dared to ask:

"Do you think that our sister Ester is prepared to face the reality of what we found out?"

Alexandre shook his head and replied:

"Only those who are completely free of passions are capable of facing the whole truth. Ester is a very good person, but she has yet to gain full control of herself. She does not possess her emotions; rather, her emotions possess her. In view of this, we cannot provide her with full knowledge of the matter. She is ready to be consoled, but not to hear the truth."

The instructor's statement shocked me – somewhat. How could we omit the details of the tragedy? Would that not be avoiding reality? Through what process could we comfort the longing wife if we hid from her the true account of what had actually happened?

Alexandre understood my queries, though, and remarked:

"What right would we have to upset the heart of a poor widow under the pretext of being truthful? Why would we taint the tranquil hopes of three adorable children, perhaps poisoning their destiny, just to show ourselves off as champions of reality? Would there be more joy in revealing the darkness of the crime than in uncovering the source of comfort? Andre, my brother, life asks us to be very discerning! Each word has its occasion, just as each revelation has its time! We cannot conceive of a form of assistance that crushes the supplicant. Ester's prayer must not become a vehicle of discouragement, and that is why not all receive from the Most High the work of assistance when they want it."

I registered the comment.

That day, Alexandre went with me to the authorities of the Ministry of Assistance to request the collaboration of one of the sisters that worked with the first aid teams in order to help Ester more effectively. Romualda, a dedicated and kind person, was chosen, and she accompanied us back to earth, receiving attentively the instructions of our esteemed instructor. Alexandre did not dwell on lengthy instructions. Romualda should prepare the widow spiritually so that she could visit her discarnate husband the next night. Then she should remain with Ester for two weeks, working to rebuild her psychic energies and helping in other ways so that she could reorganize her financial life by finding an honest and honorable job.

It was touching to see the care with which the delicate instructor set all the arrangements in motion.

At about the time set for the spouses to meet, we went to the mobile spiritual aid hospital, where the instructor personally took care of all the preparations. He recommended to Raul that he be in good spirits, insisting that he avoid even the smallest complaint and abstain from any gesture that could show impatience or affliction. Next, he ordered the open and bloody wound – highly visible in the dilacerated area of the perispiritual body – to be covered so that his wife would not perceive any feelings of suffering. Surprised by this lesson on appropriate behavior, Raul was happy to comply with all the instructions.

A few minutes later, Romualda entered with Ester, whose eyes showed anguish and expectation. Alexandre took her by the arm and guided her to her husband lying on a bed of white linens.

"Raul! Raul!" cried the forlorn widow, temporarily free of her physical body and rending my heart with the sorrowful tone of her voice.

Her distress was immense. She wanted to say more but could not. Her knees buckled and she ended up kneeling by her husband's bed, weeping. I noticed that his eyes were full of tears that did not fall. Alexandre gazed at him firmly, letting him know that he needed to be brave for the painful conversation to follow. Like a child who wants to meet his father's expectations, the suicide followed the generous guide's smallest gestures. And when Alexandre nodded to him, Raul took his tearful companion's right hand and said:

"Please don't cry anymore, Ester! Trust in God! Look after our little ones and help me with your faith! I'm doing just fine ... There's no reason for us to grieve! My dear, death is not the end. Accept our Father's will as I am trying to accept it ... our separation is only temporary ... I will never forget you! You will be in my heart wherever I go! I too miss your company, your dedication, but the Most High will teach us how to transform our longings into hope!"

The suicide's words, as well the gentle tone of his voice, surprised me. Raul displayed a potential for gentleness and psychological sensitivity that I had not seen before. That was when, by sharpening my visual perception, I noticed that very fine lines of light linked Alexandre's forehead to Raul's brain, and I understood that the instructor was providing him with a vigorous magnetic influx to support him during the difficult situation.

Listening to his consoling words, the widow seemed to regain some serenity and exclaimed tearfully:

"Raul, I know that we are now separated by the abyss of the grave! ... I know that I need to wait for the determination of divine providence to join you forever ... Listen! Help me while I'm on the earth enduring my unexpected and pain-filled widowhood! Get up and come home to provide my grief-stricken spirit with hope! Defend us from the evil ones ... don't leave me alone with our little ones, who need you so much ... ask God for such grace and come help us till the end!"

Although he was still lying on the bed, Raul stroked her hair tenderly and answered:

"Have courage and faith, Ester! Remember that there are those who suffer much more than we do, and resign yourself ... I'll get stronger and will continue working for us ... Just as you are hoping for my help, I'm hoping for your trust. The Lord doesn't entrust us with problems that we're not worthy of! Go home and be joyful! Don't be afraid of necessity; we will never lack the blessing of bread! Search for the joy of honest work and sow the good at every opportunity the world offers you! The practice of the good gives the body health and the spirit happiness! God is good and just and will bless our children so that they may be happy at your side ... Don't wait any longer! Go back confident! Be certain that I'm alive and that the death of the body is only a necessary transformation!"

Realizing that the meeting was coming to an end, the anxious wife displayed extreme curiosity and affliction, and looking at her companion through her tears, she asked:

"Raul, before I leave, tell me truthfully ... what happened? Who robbed you of your life?"

I noticed a terrible anguish in his eyes at the unexpected question. He perhaps wanted to confess the truth to shed light on his past experiences, but Alexandre's magnetic help came quickly. A flash of intense luminosity came from his right hand, which at this point of the conversation was held protectively over the suicide's head. His facial expression changed, and his composure and courage were reestablished. Calm once more, Raul said to his wife:

"Ester, the workings of Divine Justice are not readily available for us to surmise them ... you can be sure that we are being instructed every day and in everything that happens ... learn to seek ... God's will."

The poor widow wanted to prolong the conversation; through her suffering eyes one could guess her intense desire to continue to bask in the sublime consolations of the moment, but Alexandre took her arm and told her she needed to say goodbye. The tearful wife did not resist. Concentrating all her capacity for affection in her words, she said goodbye to the suicide and kissed his hands with infinite tenderness. Upon leaving the emergency spiritual hospital, the instructor entrusted her into Romualda's care and returned with me.

I was unable to hide my enormous wonder regarding this work of assistance.

Alexandre noticed my feelings and spoke with emotion:

"As you have seen, the work of assistance requires much effort and fraternal devotion. We cannot forget that Raul and Ester are two spiritually infirm individuals, and in that condition, they are in need of much understanding on our part. Fortunately, the widow is returning home filled with new courage, and Raul, having become aware of the extent of the care dedicated to him, and realizing how much he can help his incarnate companion, will hasten to develop new stimuli and energies in his heart."

However, impressed by the level of destruction suffered by his spirit body, I asked:

"What about the wound? How long will Raul have to endure such suffering?"

"Maybe for many years," answered the instructor in a grave tone. "But that will not stop him from working intensely in the arena of his conscience, making efforts to bring another opportunity closer in order to regenerate himself."

Other questions sprang up in my mind. Nevertheless, the instructor needed to leave to deal with other difficult duties in which I would not be able to accompany him.

I asked for permission to personally follow Romualda's work of assistance and received his generous approval. I wanted to know how far the distraught widow had been comforted, and to find out how she had benefited by the reunion that had been carried out as such a high concession.

The following day, I returned to the simple home right at lunch time. Romualda had been very busy. The inner environment had taken on a new appearance. The spirits seen there previously had not disappeared completely, but there were significantly fewer of them. Supporting her ward, the helpful sister greeted me warmly. She told me that the widow had awoken feeling much better, and that she, Romualda, had done everything possible to help her retain a full memory of the dream. As was only natural, the poor woman was not able to remember all the details; however, she had kept the most important impressions, enabling her to awaken her divine hope and restoring her good spirits. She suggested that I find out for myself the wonderful effects of Providence.

In fact, the widow's face had acquired a new look. With clear and shining eyes, she was telling the aunt, uncle and children about the sublime dream she had had last night. They were all ears, particularly the children, who seemed to share her inner joy.

Ester ended the story greatly moved. Then I noticed that the old aunt was mouthing a gesture of disbelief, asking her:

"Do you actually believe you visited Raul in the other world?"

"Why not?" replied the widow without blinking. "I still have the feeling of his hands on mine, and I know that God granted me such grace so that I could find my strength again to work. Today I woke up totally refreshed and happy! I can face the future with new hope! I will make an effort and I shall be victorious."

"Oh Mommy, how your words console us!" exclaimed one of the little ones with bright eyes. "How I wish I could have been with you to listen to Daddy in that wonderful dream!"

At that moment, the elderly man, who had been eating in silence, stated, as an excellent example of human disbelief:

"It's interesting to notice that although Raul was able to console your female heart, he wasn't able to clarify anything about the crime that sent him to his grave."

Ester was aware of the irony of the comment, and influenced by her benefactor close by, she readily replied:

"Uncle dear, sometimes we do not know how to be grateful for divine blessings. I remember this truth when I listen to reasoning such as yours. I feel ashamed when I recall having asked a similar question of poor Raul as he lay exhausted and pale on his bed. It was enough joy for me to have seen and heard him in a world that I cannot understand for now. I'm sure I visited him somewhere. What interest can we have in finding out who the criminals were if we are unable to raise his physical body? In our concerns about punishing the guilty, without considering our own wrongs, can we be so absurd as to wish to be more just than God himself?"

The uncle became quiet and thoughtful, and I noticed that the children were feeling immensely happy with their mother's reply.

Ester's heart had entered the lucid and sublime zone of living faith, absorbing peace, happiness and hope for a new life.

Upon saying goodbye, I congratulated Romualda on her fine work. The kind servant brought me up to par on her service plans. She would remain close by the widow, instilling her with courage and hope, and next week she planned on helping her find a well-paying job.

I marveled at hearing the plan, particularly with regards to the material help; however, Romualda very calmly added:

"When our earth-bound brothers and sisters are deserving, we can cooperate on their behalf with all the resources available as long as our help does not hinder their freedom of conscience."

I then asked her if she would accept my help on the day scheduled for the final tasks.

Romualda kindly agreed, and after a week she sent word to me regarding the conclusion of her work of assistance.

I returned to the widow's home in the company of the noble spirit worker, who suggested:

"Please help our friend here while I go and get the person appointed to assist her. I have already made all the necessary arrangements and we don't have any time to waste."

I remained there filled with curiosity, and after about three hours somebody knocked at the door. A distinguished lady, followed by Romualda, had come looking for Ester to offer her honest work in her sewing shop. The widow wept with emotion and joy. While surrounded by overall jubilation, she arranged certain details regarding the work. The assisting sister spoke to me contently:

"Now, brother Andre, we can go back in peace. The work entrusted to us has been completed, thanks to the Lord."

12
Preparing for New Life Experiences

Alexandre and I were ready to return to our spirit work headquarters, when the guide was approached by a high-order friend. He greeted me as well, showing great esteem and warmth.

"I will be brief," he told my instructor, who listened kindly. "I do not have time for a long explanation."

His facial expression changed and he asked:

"Do you remember our old friend Segismundo?"

"Of course," replied Alexandre. "We both owe him for significant favors in the past."

"Well," replied the visitor, "he is in urgent need of help. I realize that you are not a specialist in the work of reincarnation. However, I feel the need to ask for help from my friends."

Our new companion paused shortly and then continued:

"Do you remember that, despite great deeds of kindness in the past, our friend also committed many wrongs?"

"Yes, yes," replied the instructor, "his story is still very much alive in my memory."

"Segismundo is due to return to the stream of physical life," continued the other. "The situation demands it and we must not waste this opportunity to direct him toward the redemption he needs. He knows that Raquel, that poor woman he led astray at a time when we were all connected by strong ties of affection, and Adelino, the unfortunate husband that our brother murdered in a lamentable duel, have been back on the earth for quite some time now, and four years ago they reconnected through the bonds of matrimony. Everything has been readied for Segismundo to return to the company of his victim and enemy from the past in order to cleanse his soul. In compliance with the permission granted by our Superiors, he will be the couple's second child. However, we are having a hard time finding him. Unfortunately, Adelino, who will be his future father, repels him fervently as soon as he falls asleep[12], thereby working against our best efforts at bringing them together. In light of this, the preparatory work for this new physical experience has been very slow and unpleasant."

"And what about Segismundo?" my mentor asked worriedly. "What is his prevalent attitude?

Herculano, the messenger who was visiting us, informed us with fraternal interest:

"At first, he was encouraged with the best of hopes. However, now that his old rival has been sending him thoughts of hatred and jealousy, forgetting commitments made in the spirit world, he feels forlorn and not strong enough to redeem his former evil. At other times, his sadness fills him with profound

[12] " ... During sleep, the bonds that join [the spirit] to the body are loosened, and since the body does not need it while sleeping, the spirit travels though space and enters into a more direct relationship with other spirits. "(*The Spirits' Book*, nº 401.) – Tr.

rebelliousness, and in such a negative state he prevents himself from receiving our help."

The visitor paused for a moment and added in a pleading tone:

"Would you be willing to help us out with this difficult process of reincarnation? I remember your friendship with both of them. Maybe your affectionate intervention would convince Adelino."

"You can count on me," replied the instructor attentively. "I will do all I can so that this opportunity is not wasted."

As Herculano smiled with satisfaction, Alexandre concluded:

"Next week, I will be with you when you talk to Adelino in spirit to solve the problem of rapprochement. Let us trust in divine help."

Herculano thanked him and left deeply touched.

Alone with my devoted mentor and friend, I started to ponder the possibility of contributing to the case. I had never had the opportunity to follow a reincarnation process up close by studying spiritual ancestry in matters of embryology. Would it not be interesting for me to make use of this experience? With this in mind, I addressed the instructor, but without mentioning my intentions directly:

"I find today's request remarkable," I said. "When I was in the world, I would never have imagined the variety of tasks given to discarnate benefactors and missionaries. The extent of the work in our dimension would astonish any mortal."

"Without a doubt," Alexandre replied kindly. "The work unfolds in all directions. Herculano's request has brought into focus one of the most important problems of human happiness: that of fraternal rapprochement, reciprocal forgiveness and the sowing of love through the law of reincarnation."

Alexandre thought for a few moments and then continued:

"This is a typical case. Segismundo's life story is far too complex to be explained in just a few words. But it is enough to recall that he, Adelino and Raquel are the principal protagonists in a grievous tragedy that occurred at the time of my last pilgrimage on the earth. As the result of a fit of passion, Adelino became the victim of murder; Segismundo, of crime; and Raquel, of prostitution. Each one discarnated under intense vibrations of hatred and despair, and they suffered for many years in the lower zones. Later on, due to the intercession of redeemed friends, the former spouses returned to physical bodies in order to sanctify their emotional ties and to reunite with old adversaries. But as almost always happens, heroes in promises weaken when it comes time to fulfill them, because they become much more attached to their own desires than to the understanding of the Divine Will. Now in possession of the gift of physical life, Adelino refuses to forgive Segismundo, thereby wrongly repeating the ways of the past. Even before his former transgressor has had a chance to reincarnate, Adelino has shown that he is unwilling to assist. It is always the same old vicious circle: when he is outside the blessed opportunity of earthly work and is able to see the extent of his needs, Adelino commits himself to promises of fidelity and fulfillment, but as soon as he acquires the treasure of a physical body, he returns to spiritual hardness and disdain toward God's laws."

My mentor was silent for a few seconds and then remarked:

"Nevertheless, I will try to help them recall their commitments."

Realizing that this would be a priceless opportunity, I asked:

"Would it be possible for me to accompany you? I think I would learn a lot. Maybe I could acquire significant knowledge for serving my neighbor and also for my own personal benefit. I don't know how much longer I will be allowed to study in your company and I would value the enlightenment of such an opportunity."

Alexandre smiled compassionately and said:

"I have no objections. Nevertheless, I don't think that you should observe this work without some prior knowledge on the subject. In every case of truly useful spiritual edification, we cannot dispense with the foundations. I have good friends in Reincarnation Planning, a very important service here in our spirit colony and directly linked with the activities in the Ministry of Elucidation. If you spend a few days at that institution, you will get an approximate idea of our task by observing such work directly. A large percentage of reincarnations follow standardized formats for everybody in cases involving reincarnation for purely evolutionary purposes. However, another percentage does not follow the same plan. As the soul grows in learning and knowledge, and thus in responsibility, the individual reincarnation process becomes more complex – an exception to the general rule – as is logical. In light of this fact, the most elevated spirit colonies have special services for the reincarnation of their workers and missionaries."

These explanations were alluring and relevant, and aware of their importance for my spiritually poor mind, Alexandre continued:

"When I refer to workers, I do not mean those who are completely good and redeemed, but rather those who at present display a greater number of higher qualities, those who are on their way to complete victory over the denser conditions and expressions of life. Generally, as is our case, they are indebted spirits, but they possess goodwill, perseverance and sincerity, and this grants them the right to influence the factors of their reincarnation and thus to avoid the normal pattern to a certain extent. Of course, such alterations do not always result in pleasant conditions for the upcoming lifetime. The work of rectification holds enormous tasks."

Wanting to strongly impress the notion of responsibility on my mind, the instructor continued more seriously:

"The problem of failure is also a question of learning, and evil indicates a situation of imbalance that requires restoration and correction. Advancement gives us the power, but we spend a lot of time learning how to use this power harmoniously. Rationality offers a secure venue for our knowledge; however, Andre, almost all of us who toil on the earth spend centuries on our inner enlightenment, because it is not enough to acquire ideas and abilities; it is necessary to be responsible. Moreover, it is not right that we possess only the information arising from thought; we must also have the light that arises from love."

"And thus you have the successive struggles in repeated reincarnations of the soul!" I exclaimed, highly impressed.

"Yes," continued Alexandre. "We need the struggle that corrects, renews, restores and perfects. Reincarnation is the means, while divine education is the ends. That is why that, alongside the millions who evolve, there are millions who re-educate themselves in the realm of sentiment, because they already have some life values, but are lacking in others no less important."

Perceiving my difficulty in fully grasping his teaching, the instructor said:

"Although you were a physician on the earth, I believe you were not completely foreign to the studies of the Gospel."

"Yes, yes," I replied, "I have memories of it."

"Well then, Jesus himself left us food for thought regarding this matter when he said that if our hand or our eyes are a cause for scandal, they should be disposed of so that we can enter the temple of life. It is up to us to change that literal image into a simple interpretation of the spirit. If we have already failed many times in lifetimes of authority, riches, physical beauty or intelligence, it wouldn't be logical to receive another such opportunity in the work of rectification."

I clearly understood where Alexandre meant to go with his friendly explanations.

"It is for regulating this type of work in our spirit colony that we have Reincarnation Planning, for example, where you will have the opportunity to receive invaluable instruction."

And caring for my needs like a loving father, the next day the instructor introduced me to the impressive institution.

The busy service center was composed of several buildings and numerous appurtenances. Welcoming trees lined the extensive gardens, lending an enchanting aspect to the landscape. I soon realized that the institute was characterized by much activity. Single spirits or small groups were coming and going, their faces expressing significant concentration. They seemed totally unconcerned with our presence because they went by us either by themselves, engulfed in deep thought, or in friendly groups discretely holding serious and absorbing conversations, as far as I could tell. Many of these brothers and sisters that passed us by held little scrolls of a substance similar to parchment, and of which, until then, I did not have the slightest idea.

As usual, however, Alexandre came to my rescue:

"The spirits we see here are workers who are interested in future incarnations. Not all are directly connected with such a purpose, because a large number of them are involved in intercessory work, obtaining favors of this nature for close friends. The white scrolls they are carrying are little charts of organic forms prepared by guides on our plane who are specialists in biological knowledge on earthy existence. According to the level of advancement of the one who is reincarnating, and depending on the work that will be assigned to him or her while in the physical body, it is necessary to draw up a plan that is adequate for meeting his or her essential goals."

"What about the law of physiological heredity?" I asked.

"It works with inalienable control upon all evolving beings, but of course it is subject to the influence of those who attain qualities that are superior to the general environment. Furthermore, when individuals interested in new experiences in the physical realm are deserving of 'intercessory' services, the higher powers can impress certain modifications on matter from the embryological development onward if they determine that alterations are needed for the work of redemption."

At this point of the enlightening conversation, Alexandre invited me to go in.

We were soon in one of the large offices of the main building, where one of the instructor's many friends kindly came to wait on us.

Alexandre introduced me to Assistant Josino, who welcomed me with great kindness and noble manners. The instructor explained the reason for our visit. He wanted me to be allowed to visit the planning institution as many times as possible that week because I needed to acquire a well-founded understanding about the assistance work relating to reincarnational activities. Assistant Josino promised to do all he could. He said he would introduce me to his colleagues so that my knowledge would not lack any minutiae, and that he would expound his own experiences for my observation so that I would derive the most benefit from them; and finally, to the extent that he could, he would guide my drive to learn.

I felt great about it not only because of the warm welcome but also because of the educational environment. Not far from us, two extraordinary statues rested on luminous pedestals. One was the delicate representation of a male body and the other a female model. They were remarkably beautiful in their anatomical perfection not only in form but also in the details of their organs and the many glands. Electrical devices enabled both figures to pulsate with life and heat, exhibiting luminous effluvia just like the most highly evolved men and women in the physical realm.

Noticing my wonder, Alexandre smiled and said to Assistant Josino, with the intent of having me hear:

"Perhaps Andre is not sufficiently aware of our respect and gratitude for the terrestrial physical apparatus."

"Indeed," I added, "until now I was not aware that the physical body was the object of such interest amongst us. I didn't even know our colony had an institution such as this one."

"And why not, my friend?" intervened the Assistant warmly. "The physical body represents a blessing from our Eternal Father. It constitutes the magnificent work of the Divine Wisdom, and we are fortunate enough to contribute to its continuous improvement. How much do we owe the human machine for its millennia of service on behalf of our growth in the life eternal? We will never be able to realize the extent of such a debt."

And gazing at the models that astonished me, he stated:

"All our zeal in the work of reincarnation remains far from what we should do on behalf of improving the organic machine."

Although hesitant, I dared to ask:

"Do all centers of higher spirituality have sectors devoted to this type of work?"

Alexandre was the one to answer in his usual considerate manner:

"Such tasks are performed with infinite care in all colonies of higher spirituality. Assistance in the reincarnation of our fellow spirits expresses our recognition of the physical apparatus that has provided us with so many benefits throughout time."

I recalled, however, that my earthly father[13] had returned to the corporeal experience directly from the lower zones, and I asked:

---

[13] See "*Nosso Lar*". – (Spirit auth.)

"And those who reincarnate directly from the lower zones – do they receive the same generous help?"

Wishing to mark my question with the deepest sincerity, I added:

"My father during my last terrestrial journey returned to the physical realm a little while ago under very bitter circumstances..."

Alexandre interrupted me mid-sentence:

"We understand. If he was an individual of clear but unenlightened reasoning, he was in a fallen state after death, and he could not have returned to the blessed opportunity of the physical school without 'intercessory' work and strong aid from loving hearts on our plane. In that case, he would have received help from benefactors from higher up, who would have endorsed his promises regarding redemptive work. However, if he was an individual undergoing a purely evolutionary endeavor – a circumstance in which he would not have returned under bitter circumstances – he would have counted on the blessed assistance of the spirit workers who watch over the ordinary execution of reincarnational work."

In light of the instructor's explanations, I understood the differences and my mind was put at ease.

Either because the conversation had brought up a very sensitive human family issue, or because they wanted to leave me to my deepest thoughts in that large workroom, the instructor and Assistant Josino fell silent, compelling me to find new reasons for conversation for my learning experience.

I then started carefully observing the male and female models a short distance away.

Josino very kindly put his hand lightly on my shoulder and said:

"Move closer to these instructional models. You will benefit a lot by taking a closer look."

I could not contain my gratitude and left my two respectable friends to get closer to the figures displayed there. I stopped to contemplate the male model, whose lines were perfectly harmonious, much like ancient Hellenic art.

The model, made of a luminous substance, seemed to be the most perfect anatomical work I had ever studied. The motionless human figure appeared to be something divine.

I was astonished as I gazed at the minutiae. I had never observed the perfection of physiology in such detail. The entire muscular system was formed of glowing fibers. From the frontal to the annular ligament of the tarsus, threads of light symbolized the various areas of the overall musculature. Some fibers such as those in the orbicular area of the eyelids, the triangular area of the lips, the pectoralis major, the pectineus, and the thenar and hypothenar eminences up to the extensor of the fingers, were even shinier. From the examination of the surface I went on to make a deeper observation, identifying the marvelous characteristics of the representation of the lymphatic and blood circulation. Oh! The organs were all there, vibrating in obedience to electric devices for educational purposes. The venous blood vessels were displayed in grayish light, while the regions of arterial blood were of a scarlet color.

Amazed, I rendered a silent tribute of admiration to the Divine Wisdom that grants us the sublime earthly physical apparatus for our on-going spiritual growth.

I was impressed by the perfect formation of the vessels distributed around the coeliac trunk, as they resembled small rivers of light, and I could see, standing out in luminosity, the upper and lower venae cavae, the outer and inner jugulars, the axillary arteries and veins, the portal vein, the upper mesenteric and splenic arteries, the descending aorta, the iliac vessels and the ganglia of the groin.

Covering these organic marvels was the nervous system, resembling a radiant cloak made of the finest strands of fairylike light. The area of the brain looked like a very soft blue lamp, whose luminosity was linked directly to the cerebellum, descending through the spinal medulla to the sacral plexus, where the shining focal point took on a more intense expression, lessening thereafter in the great sciatic.

Next, I began my observation of the equally radiant female form, concentrating my analytical abilities on the endocrine system, laid out like a constellation among the organic pieces. From the pineal gland, situated between the cerebral hemispheres, to the procreative organs, the glands seemed to form a beautiful luminous system like tiny stars of life gathered together vertically like glittering antennae attracting the light coming from the Most High. Each gland displayed its specific form, its vibratory expressions and its particular characteristics. All the glands shone in different colors, although they all received in their own way the coloration of the pineal gland, which resembled a small bluish sun, maintaining in its field of magnetic attraction all the rest of them, from the pituitary gland to the area of the ovaries, and which, like our life-giving sun, guaranteed the cohesion and the movement of its great family of "planets and asteroids."

My amazement had no bounds.

Nonetheless, I must confess that my surprise was all the greater when I observed the shiny effluvia that emanated from the genital centers, which as a group resembled a miniscule sanctuary full of light.

As I addressed my instructor with a questioning look, his explanation was not long in coming:

"Usually, down on the earth," said Alexandre smiling and coming nearer, "there is generally still much ignorance regarding the divine mission of sex. However, for those of us who wish to value the opportunities to progress, earthly motherhood and fatherhood are sacred. The creative faculty is also divinity in men and women. For us, the maternal womb represents the blessed door to redemption; for a great number of people on the global sphere, the vision of heaven is a symbol of endless rest and bliss, while for many of us, the vision of earth means edifying and constructive work. However, we will not reach the promised land of the redemptive endeavor without the help of the associated creative forces of man and woman."

With renewed vision, I understood the sublime character of the sexual energies and compassionately remembered all the incarnates who were not yet able to build respect and understanding regarding the sacred procreative organs. My instructor, however, like a receiving antenna of all my mental emissions, warned me kindly:

"Please forget any expression of unconstructive memories. Those who offend sex by writing, acting or speaking are already very unfortunate on their own account."

I kept the lesson and blessed the new experience that had begun.

Alexandre said goodbye and left me at the large planning institution, where Assistant Josino, busy with the duties under his responsibilities, put me under the care of Manasses, a brother working with the information services of the institution. He greeted me warmly, surrounding me with kindness and care.

I immediately felt that my learning experience there was beginning with great benefit. Manasses was like a living book. His opinions and information entailed invaluable instruction.

As we drew nearer to the design and planning pavilions, where a large number of coworkers were drawing up plans for uncommon reincarnations, my new companion was approached by a friendly spirit who asked him for information. Manasses introduced us joyfully. This was a colleague, who, after fifteen years of working in aid activities, would be returning to the physical realm to repair wrongs of the past. The newcomer seemed hesitant. One could see his fear and indecision.

"Don't allow yourself to be dominated by negative feelings," Manasses said to him, trying to cheer him up. "The problem of rebirth is not so complicated. Of course, it does require courage and a good attitude."

"Nevertheless," replied the somewhat sad spirit, "I'm afraid of accumulating new debts instead of paying off the old ones. It's so difficult to be victorious in the corporeal experience because of the temporary memory loss that comes with incarnation."

"But it would be much more difficult to be victorious by being able to remember," Manasses replied immediately.

And with a smile, he added:

"If we possessed great virtues and wonderful achievements, we wouldn't have to recapitulate the lessons already experienced in the flesh. And if we only have wounds and wrongs to remember, then we should bless the forgetfulness that the Lord grants us temporarily."

The other tried to smile and objected:

"I understand your optimism; I wish I were like you. I will return, trusting in the fraternal help of all of you."

And changing his tone of voice, he asked:

"Can you tell me if my model is ready yet?"

"I think you can check it out tomorrow," replied Manasses in good spirits. "I have already observed the initial design and I congratulate you for accepting the loving suggestion of well-guided friends with regards to your limb deficiency. You certainly will have to battle big problems at the start of your new struggle, but being resolute will do you a lot of good."

"Yes," the other replied, somewhat comforted, "I will have to guard myself against certain temptations of a lower nature, and the defective leg will help me by focusing me on more important matters. It will be an antidote to vanity, a sentinel against the devastation of excessive self-centeredness."

"Very good!" answered Manasses, openly optimistic.

"And can you tell me the approximate amount of time granted to my future physical form?"

"At least seventy years," replied my new companion happily.

The other expressed appreciation while Manasses continued:

"Remember the blessing you have received, Silverio, and after taking possession of it on the physical plane, don't come back here before you are seventy. Take advantage of the opportunity. All your friends are expecting you to come back to our spirit colony in the glorious condition of a 'completer'."

With a ray of hope in his eyes, Silverio thanked him and left.

Manasses' last remarks aroused my curiosity further. I could not hold back the question wandering in my mind, so I asked frankly:

"My friend, what does 'completer' mean?"

He smiled indulgently and replied in good humor:

"It is the title that applies to those rare brothers and sisters who profited from all the constructive potential that their earthly body offered them. Generally, in returning to the physical realm, almost all of us miss significant opportunities while wasting our physiological energies. We wander around, doing something useful for ourselves and for others, but sometimes we waste fifty, sixty, seventy percent, and often even more, of our potential. On many occasions, we also have the aggravating circumstance of having used the sacred energies of life on unworthy activities that degrade our mind and harden our heart. However, those who use their physical machine as faithful workers will acquire significant rights in our realm. As loyal and productive workers, 'completers' are free to choose their future body when they return to the earth on missions of love and enlightenment, or they may receive an ennobled physical vessel for the continuation of their tasks on their way to higher circles of work."

This news represented a valuable revelation for me. There could be nothing more right than to grant the faithful servant full resources. And I recalled the unruly behaviors of all sorts to which human creatures yield in all countries, belief systems and situations, thereby complicating their evolutionary progress and creating enslaving ties by rooting themselves in the attachment to temporary situations of material existence, nourishing mistakes and fantasies, destroying the body and poisoning the soul. In an enraptured moment of wonder, I replied:

"Remembering the captivity of incarnate spirits in the sensorial realms, it is consoling to know that there is a reward for those very rare persons who live the sublime art of spiritual balance even while in the flesh."

"Yes," said Manasses with a look of approval. "As strange as it might seem, such exceptions do exist in the world. They frequently return here among the anonymous individuals, without signs from the earth advertising it, but with an immense reserve of higher spirituality."

And giving me the impression that he wanted to enlighten me regarding his own situation, he added:

"For many years now, I have been making an effort to achieve the condition of a 'completer'; but so far I have remained at the stage of preparation."

I understood that, like myself, Manasses was carrying the usual baggage of less-than-happy memories regarding his use of the earthly body in past lives, and I tried to change the direction of the conversation:

"Do you know of any 'completers' who have gone back to earth?" I asked.

"Yes."

"Surely," I continued, curiously, "they must have chosen flawless bodies."

My new companion changed his facial expression significantly and pointed out:

"Despite their merit, none of those whom I have seen leave chose flawless forms. They requested arrangements for a healthy existence, more concerned with the resistance, balance, durability and strength of the instrument that was to serve them. But they also asked for measures that would temporarily decrease their personal magnetism, avoiding a highly beautiful physical appearance and thereby concealing the beauty of their souls in order to guarantee the effectiveness of their tasks. They did this because, living under the rules of appearances when on earth, most people, if they were aware of their true status, would try to crush such missionaries of the good by means of the destructive vibrations of jealousy, spite, gratuitous antipathy and unwarranted quarrels. Consequently, conscious workers most often organize their task in less gracious external molds, escaping beforehand the influx of devastating passions from unbalanced souls."

I had understood the extent of the explanation and was pondering the greatness of the spiritual principles that govern human life, when Manasses, after a long pause, added:

"Just like children, young minds play with the fire of the emotions; however, mature spirits, particularly when they reach the status of 'completers', avoid any lifetime that might distract them from the pathway of fulfilling the Divine Will."

Next, at the invitation of my new friend, I went into one of the rooms dedicated to design work. Small screens showing parts of the human body were placed in an orderly fashion all around. I had the clear impression of being in a large center for anatomists surrounded by competent and hardworking assistants. There were drawings of limbs, tissues, glands, fibers and all types of organs and for all sorts of preferences.

"As you know," Manasses remarked thoughtfully, "in recapitulation work or specialized tasks down on the earth, reincarnation is never ordinary. That is why hundreds of technicians in matters of embryology and general biology work here so as to guide the future lives of all the brothers and sisters who are linked to us in a collective effort."

With feelings of spontaneous reverence, I contemplated the workers who were carefully bent over, designing the futures of so many spirits. How complex was the opportunity of being reborn! What intense activities it required from spirit benefactors! In response to my gesture of surprise, Manasses replied with a meaningful summary:

"You are aware of the fact that primitive or semi-primitive people use the always sacred resources of nature to build their homes in more simple and rudimentary formats, whereas people who have already reached a certain level of ideals and have developed higher faculties build their homes by drawing up blueprints beforehand."

Pointing to the very busy scene there, he added with a smile:

"The only thing different we are doing here is that we are dealing with plans for future houses of flesh. The human body happens to be the most important dwelling for us when are compelled to spend time on the earth. We cannot forget that the Divine Master himself called it the temple of the Lord."

Impressed, I carefully observed the work being carried out. We were ready to move on when a very respectable looking sister approached and greeted Manasses warmly. He answered kindly and introduced us:

"This is our sister Anacleto."

I said hello and felt drawn to her.

"She is one of our bravest workers," pointed out the Ministry of Communication worker.

The woman smiled, a bit embarrassed to have been the object of her companion's open opinion. Nevertheless, Manasses continued in his usual optimism:

"Anacleto is planning to return to the earth in a few days on a task of great self-sacrifice involving four spirits who have been struggling in the abysmal regions of the lower zones for over forty years."

"I don't see any self-sacrifice in it," intervened the woman, smiling. "I will only be fulfilling my duty."

And unsurprised and serene, she gazed at me and stated:

"Mothers who were unable to complete the work of love that the Father entrusted to them regarding their beloved children must be strong enough to recommence their imperfect work. That is my case. We should not mention sacrifice where there is only obligation."

I was interested in this modest and kind sister's story, and that is why I worked up the courage to ask her:

"Will you be returning soon then? At any rate, your resolution shows devotion and goodness. I cannot ignore the fact that my own mother also returned to the physical realm filled with sublime dedication."

I noticed that she held back the discrete tears that had filled her eyes, maybe touched by my sincere remark. She kindly offered me her right hand, and giving me the idea that she did not wish to continue with the matter, she said to me movingly:

"Thank you for your comforting words. If you ever remember me, please help me with your kind thoughts."

At this point in the brief conversation, Manasses asked:

"Have you received all the plans yet?"

"Yes," she answered, "not only those concerning my poor children, but also the ones relating to my own future personal form."

"Are you pleased?"

"Very!" she replied. "In our Father's law, justice is full of mercy and I am still a big debtor. "

Then she calmly and pleasantly said goodbye.

Manasses perceived my curiosity and explained:

"Anacleto is a living example of tenderness and devotion, but she will return to the struggles of the body in order to carry out certain corrections in her maternal heart. Due to her lack of foresight in the past, the four children that God entrusted to her failed dreadfully. As a mother, she harbored certain concepts of affection that did not correspond with reality. Her husband was an honest and hardworking man, and despite having plenty, he never forgot the duties that as a man of good character he owed society in general. He was known to display constructive energy at all times, but although very devoted to him, his wife thwarted his influence in the home by coupling her motherly love with the excesses of unreasonable tenderness. As an indirect result, those four souls could not find the necessary resources for their journeys of redemption. Three young men and a young woman, whose intellectual preparation demanded the most arduous sacrifices, soon succumbed to physical and morally degrading behavior under the pretext of tending to their social obligations. Their conduct was so troublesome that they lost their bodies very early and entered the Umbral in a very sad state. When Anacleto returned to the spirit world, she understood the problem and decided to work hard not only for her own reincarnation but also for that of her children, who will follow her in their own purifying trials on the earth."

"How long did it take her to obtain this concession?" I asked, highly impressed.

"Over thirty years."

"I can only imagine her future sacrifices!" I exclaimed.

"Yes," explained Manasses, "her life will be very hard because two of the young men will be returning as paralytics and the other one will be mentally disabled. And to help her in her premature widowhood, she will only have the daughter, who will have her own pressing need for rectification.

As I was about to express my great surprise on the mechanisms of reincarnational work, another sister approached us looking for Manasses.

After affectionate greetings, she kindly addressed my new friend:

"I am looking for your kind intervention to modify my plan."

And opening a small chart displaying a perfectly drawn woman's body, she pointed out:

"Take a good look at my plan for the endocrinal system. I know that my friends have done me a favor by planning it very harmoniously up to the last detail, but I would like some changes."

"How so?" asked Manasses, surprised.

The newcomer indicated the points on the plan where the neck was and said:

"I have been advised by benefactors here that I should avoid re-entering the earth with flawless bodily lines. If I do avoid it, I might have a better chance of success in the task I'm planning; I would be grateful if the thyroid and the parathyroid glands were not so perfectly outlined. As you know, Manasses, my task will not be easy. I need to recapture a large spiritual heritage. I must avoid any possibility of failure and perfect physical harmony would get in the way of my goals."

My new companion gave me an expressive look and said to her:

"You're right. Physical seductiveness is a real danger, not only for those who radiate its influence but also for those who are subject to it."

"I would prefer an unattractive body," she replied. "I'm not interested in a body like Venus; I'm interested in the redemption of my spirit for eternity."

Manasses promised to put in a good word for her, and as soon as he said goodbye to her, he started showing me the most interesting representations of organs of the human body.

Deeply impressed, I was admiring the numerous diagrams that were aligned in perfect order, demonstrating the spiritual care that precedes the work of reincarnation, when my friend stated:

"Human medicine will be much different in the future, when science can grasp the extent and complexity of mental factors in the arena of illnesses of the physical body. Very rarely are the problems not directly related to a direct psychological cause. All organs are subject to moral ascendancy. Excessive preoccupation with pathological symptoms increases illnesses; powerful emotions can heal the body or destroy it. If this can happen in the sphere of normal activities of physical struggle, imagine the broad field of observation that the spirit plane offers us as thousands of discarnate souls are transferred to it on a daily basis in pitiful states of mental instability. Physicians of the future will know about these truths and will not limit their professional practice to simply furnishing technical diagnoses. They will be guided much more in their healing work to spiritual measures, where Christian love has a greater role."

However, wishing to continue with his explanations regarding reincarnation-related work, Manasses took a small diagram, and showing me the principal lines he pointed out:

"Here is the plan for the future reincarnation of a friend of mine. Do you see some dark spots from the descending colon to the sigmoid loop? This indicates that he will suffer from a large ulcer in this area as soon as he becomes an adult. Nevertheless, he has chosen it."

And because I had a look of extreme curiosity, Manasses explained:

"Over one hundred years ago, this friend committed a terrible crime by stabbing a poor man to death; as often happens, soon after the murder the discarnate victim became strongly attached to him, and from the seed of crime planted in an instant by that unfortunate murderer, terrible results have been reaped for many years. As you well know, mutual hatred causes a strong magnetization, and freed from the flesh the victim began avenging himself daily by killing the perpetrator slowly through systematic attacks of deadly thought. Finally, in addition to the natural remorse that the situation had imposed upon him, when the murderer discarnated, his perispiritual body was in a lamentable state. He repented of the crime, endured much in the purgatorial realms and after long, purifying suffering he approached his victim, benefiting him with laudable services of rescue and penitence. He developed morally, became friends with many benefactors, won the affection of various groups on our plane, and obtained precious intercessions. Nevertheless ... the debt remains. Love, however, has transformed the character of the redress. When he returns to the earth, our friend will not have to die in a bloody way, but wherever he may be during this time of complete healing in the flesh that he previously scorned, he will carry his own wound within him, day by day winning the needed renewal. He will experience sorrow because of his persistent physical suffering and will struggle incessantly from the appearance of the ulcer until the day of his final payment in the physiological body; however, if he can remain faithful to his new commitments, he will achieve full liberation in the future."

While I was giving the plan all my attention, Manasses continued:

"As we can see, justice is always served, but as soon as a spirit is willing to be transformed in the Lord, the harshness of the redemptive process is mitigated. Peter himself reminded us many centuries ago that 'love covers a multitude of sins'."

Impressed, I examined the educational plan, and because I could not find the right words to express my wonder, I remained silent, deeply moved.

Understanding my inner state, my companion continued:

"The plans for future bodies in our work department are countless, and from most of them you can conclude that all who are infirm in the flesh are souls undergoing the huge work of inner conquest. Nobody betrays God's will in the process of evolution without having to undergo serious reparatory work, and all those who attempt to deceive nature – the rightful stage for the divine laws – end up deceiving themselves instead. Life is a perfect symphony. When we try to play out of tune with regards to the notes we should be playing to make it sound its absolute best, we are compelled to stop and undertake the hard work of recomposing the broken harmony."

I remained at that worthy institution for a few more days, realizing that human existence is not an accidental act, and that in the realm of divine order, justice performs its ministry everyday, obeying the highest designs that order the gift of life to be ministered "to each one according to his deeds."

13
Reincarnation

I felt happy and touched by Alexandre's invitation to join him on his visit to Adelino and Raquel's home, where Segismundo's reincarnation would be taking place.

A profound contentment flowed from my spirit because this was going to be the first time I would receive direct knowledge on the phenomenon of reincarnation. Ever since my early years of medical study, I had been fascinated by biogenetic laws. However, I had never had the opportunity to expand my observations and experiences. In the spirit colony to which God's Providence and the generous intercession of friends had led me, I had often received lessons regarding the subject. Nevertheless, until now I had never seen up close the process of a discarnate spirit's plunge into the realm of dense matter.

In light of this, I accompanied my solicitous guide with pleasant and anxious expectations.

Alexandre very kindly explained to me that in a past life he had received many favors from the persons involved in this case of reincarnation and that he felt happy for having the opportunity to be useful to them. He commented on the difficulties of the work of spiritual liberation and praised the law of goodness, which calls all the children of creation to fraternal cooperation and 'intercessory' service.

After comforting and instructive conversation, we reached Adelino's home, delightfully set in a picturesque suburban location like a graceful nest surrounded by clumps of vegetation.

It was approximately 6:00 p.m.

I was very surprised to see Herculano waiting for us in the doorway; the instructor, however, told me that he had advised him of our visit, asking him to bring Segismundo along for the forthcoming work.

Our companion greeted us affectionately and addressed my instructor:

"Segismundo has come with me and is waiting inside."

"That's excellent," said Alexandre good-naturedly. "I will dedicate tonight to our friends. Let's see what can be done."

We went in.

The couple, Adelino and Raquel, were having their meal in the company of a little one, whom I guessed to be their first born. Not far away, a spirit was resting in an easy chair. When he saw us come in, he immediately rose to greet my instructor in particular. Alexandre embraced him affectionately.

Herculano was standing next to me and explained discreetly:

"That's Segismundo."

I watched as the spirit, weeping convulsively, embraced Alexandre. The instructor held him like a father, and after listening to him for a few minutes, said to him compassionately:

"Compose yourself, my friend! Who doesn't have their struggles, problems and pain? And since we are all indebted to one another, shouldn't it be a reason for happiness and jubilation to receive the sublime chance for redemption and repayment? No need for tears! Our brother and sister are having dinner. We mustn't disturb them by emitting magnetic energies of despair."

And helping Segismundo back to the big armchair as if he were weak and sickly, Alexandre continued:

"Be brave. This is going to be a divine opportunity for your spiritual future. We will get everything ready; don't worry."

"Nonetheless, my friend," said Segismundo in tears, "I foresee great obstacles."

And he added in a humble tone:

"I realize that I was a great criminal, and I intend to redeem my old wrongdoings. But despite the promises he made in the spirit world for his present life, Adelino has failed to forgive me for my past errors."

Moved, Alexandre listened, smiled paternally and retorted:

"Segismundo, why poison your heart? Why don't you forgive him instead?! Don't complicate your situation by harboring unjustifiable downheartedness. Raise your energy level, my friend! Put yourself in the situation of your former adversary, a victim of your thoughtless act in the past! Wouldn't you perhaps have the same difficulties? Be calm and prudent; don't miss out on the blessed opportunity of having to tolerate something sentimentally unpleasant in order to repair the past and meet the needs of the present. Come on, get your balance! The moment is one of gratitude to God and harmony with your neighbors!"

Segismundo wiped his eyes, made an effort to smile and murmured:

"You're right."

Herculano had been watching him compassionately and entered the conversation:

"He has been very depressed and downhearted."

"That's natural," replied Alexandre decisively, "because in such circumstances, individuals experience certain imbalances due to the necessity of returning to the flesh. Segismundo, however, has been taking the phenomenon too far by increasing his sufferings with unjustified expectations and worries."

Holding his gaze on the couple as they sat at the table, he said affectionately:

"Let's observe Adelino and Raquel. Let's see what assistance they might need."

We silently followed him.

The head of the family was in a taciturn mood, speaking with his wife only in monosyllables. One could see that his wife was making an effort, but he remained almost gloomy.

"Didn't you close the deal you were hoping for?" asked the woman, attempting an affectionate conversation.

"No," he replied dryly.

"But aren't you still interested in it?"

"Yes."

"Will you be traveling next week if the deal isn't closed by Sunday?"

"Maybe."

Somewhat disappointed, the wife kept silent for a while and then said:

"What's the company's excuse for the delay?"

The husband looked at her coldly and replied laconically:

"None."

At this point, Alexandre made a significant gesture with his head and said to us worriedly:

"Adelino's spiritual condition is very bad because the sublime love of domestic bliss dies when spouses lose the pleasure of talking to each other. In this state of mind he cannot be at all useful for what we hope to accomplish."

Alexandre walked around the small family and said:

"I will try to awaken the sensitive fibers of his heart in order to prepare him suitably so that he can listen to us tonight."

Having said that, the devoted guide approached the child, a handsome little boy about three years old, and placed his right hand over his heart. I saw the little one smile with a new twinkle in his blue eyes and say with a tone of infinite tenderness:

"Mommy, why is Daddy sad?"

The head of the house looked up in surprise, while the woman replied emotionally:

"I don't know, little Joao. He must be worried about his business."

"What is 'business', Mommy?" replied the innocent child.

"It involves the struggles of life."

The little boy looked at his mother carefully and asked:

"Does business make Daddy happy?"

"Yes, it does," replied the woman smiling.

"Then why is he sad at home?"

The father was extremely touched as he followed the dialogue, while the tender mother patiently explained:

"In the daily struggles of his job, your father needs to be content with everyone and can't offend anyone. So, what seems like sadness to you is only tiredness from work. When he comes home he brings a lot of worries with him. Even though your father has to be friendly and pleasant toward everybody in order not to hurt anybody, the same doesn't apply here, where he can think about the problems that concern him the most. This is his home, my son, where he has the right not to hide his innermost worries."

The child listened carefully, dividing his loving look between his mother and father, and then replied:

"Too bad, huh, Mommy?"

The head of the small family, touched in the innermost fibers of his soul by the tenderness of his son and the sincere humility of his wife, felt that the dark clouds of his thoughts had given way to the serenity of comforting relief. Suddenly transformed, he smiled and said to the little one in a different tone of voice:

"What are you talking about, little Joao? I don't feel sad. In fact, I'm very happy, just like on the last day of our trip to the mountains! Your mother has explained very well what is going on. When your father is quiet, it doesn't mean he's disheartened. Sometimes we need to be quiet in order to think better."

The wife smiled broadly at noticing her husband's sudden change. On his part the little boy could not disguise the joy on his infant face, and as soon as his father had finished his loving explanations, still surrounded by the good instructor's magnetic radiations, he asked Adelino:

"Daddy, why don't you pray with me at night?"

The father exchanged significant looks with his wife and said to the little one:

"I've been very busy at night, but I will come back earlier today to join you in your prayers."

And smiling with fatherly joy he added:

"Do you know how to pray by yourself?"

The little one replied with satisfaction:

"Mommy teaches me every night to pray for you. Do you want to see?"

And putting down his fork, he instinctively looked upward with his hands folded and recited:

"Dear God, please watch over Daddy on the pathways of life. Give him health, peace-of-mind and courage in his daily struggles! Amen!"

The father, who had been so resistant and rude at first, displayed eyes filled with tears. Touched in his innermost fibers, he gazed tenderly at his son and said softly:

"You're very grown up. Today, little Joao, I too shall pray."

Now with an unburdened soul, Adelino looked at his companion, feeling proud that he had her devotion, and added:

"Little Joao's words did me a lot of good. My heart has been sad and heavy. I myself couldn't define my state of spirit exactly ... For quite a few days now, my nights have been restless, full of afflictions and nightmares! I have been dreaming that somebody approaches me as a powerful enemy. Sometimes, I thank God in the morning when I wake up because I feel better at having to face the deceiving faces of humans than having to fight all night long in cruel dreams."

Surprised, his wife remarked lovingly:

"I think that you should take some time off."

Moved by his wife's kindness, Adelino continued:

"I have been afraid of myself! As soon as I settle into bed, I instinctively feel a shadow closing in on me. I fall asleep under incredible anxiety and the nightmare begins without my being able to consciously explain anything."

"Are the dreams always the same?" asked the wife attentively.

"Always," he replied with emotion. "I can see a man approaching, holding out his hands like a common beggar asking for help; but when I gaze into his face, inexplicable terror seizes my spirit ... I have the feeling that he wants to murder me from behind ... On certain occasions, I try to reach out to him, overcoming my feelings of dread; but I always end up running away in a mixture of hatred and repugnance! Oh! What long and terrible nightmares!"

And changing his tone of voice he added:

"I believe I'm suffering from a great nervous agitation, but I can't put my finger on the cause."

"Why don't you go see a doctor?" asked the wife affectionately.

The husband thought for a few moments, as if his spirit were wandering through distant memories. And then, fixing his shining eyes on his companion, he said:

"Perhaps I will not have to resort to doctors. Maybe our little boy is right ... The heavy struggles of the world have driven me to forget my faith in God. How long ago did I stop praying?"

With tearful and thoughtful eyes, he continued:

"When I was a boy, my mother taught me to pray. Bowing to the will of the Most High, I would feel the Divine Goodness in everything, and I would kneel trustingly at my loving mother's feet, beseeching blessings from heaven ... Then came the emotions of the senses, the battles with evil people, and the difficult experiences of having to compete for my daily bread ... Since then, I have lost my innocent belief, which I feel the need to regain."

Moved, his wife wiped her eyes. It had been many years since she had seen her husband show such emotion. Touched, she got up and said tenderly:

"Come home earlier today so we can all pray together."

And trying to impress notes of joy on the conversation, she called their little one and added:

"Daddy will pray with us later, Joao."

The little boy's face lit up with indefinable happiness. He gazed lovingly at his mother and said:

"I'll say all the prayers I already know, Mommy."

After eating and experiencing a different mood, Adelino said goodbye with a kindness that Herculano classified as unusual.

Returning the child to his mother's care, a very happy Alexandre said:

"Fortunately, our preparatory work now looks very promising. We have gained much in just a few minutes."

On my part, immense surprise had seized my spirit. Why were they being so careful? Could not Alexandre and the other, equally-evolved spirit benefactors organize all the work regarding Segismundo's reincarnation? Were they not masters of great power over all obstacles?

But giving me to understand that he wanted to reply to my inner inquiry, the instructor spoke to Herculano kindly:

"We must not, nor can we make anybody do anything, and we need Adelino to be in a good mood for the work ahead."

Next he began to talk to Segismundo regarding his mental conduct, advising him to prepare himself with all the resources within him to succeed in his forthcoming life. Other spirit friends of the individuals linked to the events unfolding between the two worlds also arrived at the house, increasing the happiness of fraternal camaraderie. The instructor's presence appeared to be an incentive for overall cheerfulness. Alexandre knew how to conduct high-level conversation and communicated his valuable optimism to all. We were talking about the difficulties of reincarnation due to the vibrational conflicts caused by people's lack of understanding, when the head of the house returned home, looking to foster the sweet emotions of that day.

Pleasantly surprised, his wife and little one greeted him wholeheartedly, engaging in renewed comforting and edifying conversation. They enjoyed more than an hour of good reading and an excellent exchange of ideas, with Adelino looking forward to regaining his inner serenity through better spiritual communion with his little family.

When the dedicated mother reminded her little one that it was time for bed, little Joao remembered his father's promise and asked:

"Daddy, do you know what we should do before we pray?"

Adelino smiled and asked him to explain.

With surprising liveliness, the boy went on:

"Mommy says that we should call God's messengers to assist us."

"Alright," replied his good-natured father, "call them for us."

The boy said some words of invitation with his hands folded, and then the three of them went into the bedroom.

Alexandre seemed very pleased with the spontaneous memory of the little boy and said:

"We have been invited to take part in their prayers. Let's accompany them."

Our group was joined by three of Raquel's spirit friends, who had been called by Herculano's dedication in order to help in the solution of the matter.

The scene inside the bedroom was very moving. The little boy was on his knees reciting the Lord's Prayer with childlike emotion. Adelino and his wife followed the prayer attentively. For our part, we continued to silently observe and collaborate in that spiritual endeavor with the best energies of our sentiments.

I noticed that the wife was surrounded by an intense luminosity, which, originating from her heart, enveloped her husband and her child in gentle radiations. Deeply touched, Adelino shed a furtive tear when his son, finishing the prayers brief in words but great in spiritually, tenderly kissed his hands.

Moments later, all got under the covers, happy and peaceful.

At that point Alexandre spoke:

"Now, my friends, let us join together in prayer. We need to have a serious conversation with Adelino regarding the situation."

The instructor asked aloud for divine protection for the couple; we followed in deep silence. The vibrations of our thought in prayer came together like bits of a luminous substance to form a whole, which poured over the marital bed as subtle currents of reinvigorating and regenerating magnetic energies.

It was then that I saw Raquel leave her physical body among luminous radiations, seemingly unaware of what was happening. Unconcerned and happy, she embraced one of the spirits who was with us, an elderly lady whom Alexandre had introduced to us a little earlier as Raquel's maternal grandmother. The discarnate old lady invited her granddaughter to pray with her, to which Raquel agreed with visible joy.

However, Adelino's wife seemed only to be aware of the presence of the loving old lady. She looked at us indifferently as if we were not even there. Thinking this was strange, I asked my instructor to explain. Alexandre was forthcoming, despite the delicate nature of the work at hand:

"Don't be so surprised. Each one of us must be able to see only that which gives us genuine benefit. Furthermore, it wouldn't be right to increase our friend's perception in order for her to accompany us in tonight's task. She will help us with her prayers, but she will not have to closely follow the explanations required by her husband's condition. Those who do what they can receive the salary of peace. Raquel has been doing all she can for the success of the duties that brought her into the world. Therefore, she should not be warned or disturbed. Let's focus on Segismundo and Adelino."

Satisfied with his explanations and impressed with the Divine Justice manifested in the smallest details of our spiritual activities, I noticed that Adelino's companion was in fervent prayer not too far from us.

At that moment, Raquel's husband initiated the laborious withdrawal from his physical body. Unlike his wife, he was not surrounded by a radiant aura and seemed to move around with great difficulty. As Adelino gazed around the room fearfully and worriedly, Alexandre remarked:

"Are you observing the lesson? Notice the peculiarities of spirit life. Adelino and Raquel are spirits who have been associated through many lives in common, sharing the same cup of earth's sorrows and happiness. At the moment, their bodies lie next to each other in the same bed; however, each lives on a different mental plane, as it is very difficult to reunite souls in domestic bonds if they are of the same sphere. Raquel, outside her vessel of flesh, can see her grandma, to whom she is linked on the same level of elevation. Adelino, on the other hand, can see only Segismundo, to whom he is magnetized by the forces of hatred that he has thoughtlessly allowed to develop once more in his heart."

The instructor's words were interrupted by a piercing shriek. Filled with dread, Adelino recognized the presence of his old enemy and made a futile attempt to run away. He moved with great difficulty, anxiously trying to return to his physical body like a terrified child looking for refuge; Alexandre, however, approached him with loving authority and extended his hands, which were emitting large sparks of light. Contained by these magnetic rays, Adelino started to shake as if he saw something else besides the figure of his former enemy. Due to Alexandre's energetic magnetic emissions, he was gradually able to see our venerable guide, and tuning in directly to his thoughts, he fell on his knees, weeping convulsively. I observed Adelino's thoughts at that touching moment and noticed that he connected the radiant vision to his son's prayers. He could see the strange figure of Segismundo and the resplendent presence of Alexandre, and he was making a great effort to recall something from the distant past that his memory could not grasp precisely. He evidently imagined that our mentor was an emissary from heaven sent to save him from the cruel nightmares; blinded by the intense light, he wept on his knees between fear and joy, imploring peace and protection.

The kind instructor addressed him with the serenity of a loving and experienced father, and helping him up, he exclaimed:

"Adelino, receive the peace that we have brought you in the name of the Lord!"

And holding him close, he continued:

"What are you afraid of, my brother?"

Looking up tearfully and pointing to Segismundo, he asserted sadly:

"Messenger of God, free me from this unfortunate nightmare! If you have come as a result of my innocent son's prayers, please help me for pity's sake!"

And pointing to the poor friend, he continued:

"That ghost has been driving me crazy! I feel sick and miserable!"

Alexandre looked at him firmly and asked:

"Is this how you welcome our more unfortunate brothers? Is this how you behave in the face of the supreme design? What have you done with your notions of human sympathy? Why do you run from those who are down on their luck? It is always very easy to love our friends, to admire good people and understand intelligent ones, to defend our relatives, to praise the objects of our affection, to watch over those who love us, to praise the righteous and exalt famous heroes. But if we inwardly admire ourselves for such things, we must realize that they represent work already accomplished in our process of evolution. But people like us, my friend, have not yet attained final redemption. That is why the tempest is our benefactor, difficulty our master, and an adversary an effective instructor. Change the vibrations of your thoughts! Welcome with charity the beggar that knocks on your door if you have not yet acquired enough light to receive him with the love that Jesus taught us!"

Impressed at hearing these words expressed with paternal tenderness, Adelino wept profusely and looked Segismundo in the eye. As if approving this new attitude, Alexandre remarked:

"Look at this poor man asking you for help! Look at his state of humiliation and need. Put yourself in his shoes and think about it! Wouldn't the indifference of others hurt you? Wouldn't your soul be torn by their cruelty? Would you like it if somebody called you a ghost just because you showed yourself to be suffering? Adelino, my friend, open the doors of your heart to those who have come searching for you in the name of the Almighty Father."

Like a fearful child, Adelino turned to the kind mentor and said:

"Oh! Messenger of Heaven, I'm afraid, so afraid! ... There's something between this man of shadow and me that compels me to profound aversion! I think that he wants to rob me of my life, to destroy my happy home, to poison my heart forever!"

I realized that Segismundo's presence had awakened memories of the dark past in the reincarnated Adelino. Adelino, the victim of the past, was unable to surmise the facts, but at the emotional level he sensed the imprecise memories of the event, filling him with pain-filled anxiety.

After a short pause, Alexandre continued:

"You must not allow negative and destructive energies to find their way into the inner realm of your soul. It is always possible to transform evil into good when an individual firmly decides to faithfully serve the Lord. Consider the great truths of life eternal, my friend! Even if this brother were to come looking for you as an adversary; even if he sought you out as a fierce enemy, you should open to him your fraternal spirit! All reconciliation is difficult when we are unversed in the practice of love, but without human reconciliation our glorious integration with the Divinity would never be possible!"

And because Raquel's husband was weeping copiously, the instructor remarked:

"Do not weep! Calm your heart and take advantage of this sacred opportunity!"

Adelino wiped his tears and asked humbly:

"Please help me for the love of God!"

Sensing his profound sincerity, Alexandre invited Segismundo closer. He got up, stumbling and worried.

Assisting the former victim, Alexandre introduced him to the former murderer:

"This is our friend Segismundo, who needs your help in his work of redemption. Extend your fraternal hand to him and help him in the name of Jesus!"

Adelino did not hesitate, and despite his great inner effort, visible to our spiritual perception, he shook the hand of his former adversary, profoundly moved.

"Forgive me, brother!" exclaimed Segismundo, infinitely humble. "The Lord will reward you for the good you have done me!"

Adelino looked him in the eye as if to dissipate the last shadows of misunderstanding, and replied:

"I am at your disposal ... I shall be your friend!"

The former murderer bowed respectfully and kissed Adelino's hands. Segismundo's willing act had won him over. That suffering and sad spirit who reverently and affectionately kissed his hands could not be evil. That is when I saw a peculiar phenomenon. Adelino's perispiritual body seemed to rid itself of heavy clouds, which began tearing from top to bottom, revealing its luminous nature. Highly delicate radiations now surrounded it, allowing its elevated and noble condition to shine through.

Next to me, Herculano said in a discrete voice:

"Adelino's forgiveness was sincere. The thick darkness of hatred has been effectively dissipated. God be praised!"

Alexandre embraced the two reconciled souls and once again counseled them with fraternal remarks full of wisdom and tenderness. As he prepared to leave with us, he recommended that Raquel's husband rest from the struggle. I noticed that, encouraged by their spirit friends, husband and wife returned to their physical bodies in order to exchange their impressions regarding the events, which they would put in the realm of dreams, according to each one's mental colorations.

As we left, Alexandre, quite pleased, commented paternally:

"With Jesus' help, the task has been successfully accomplished."

And looking at Segismundo, he added:

"I think you can start your definite reincarnation process next week. We will follow it carefully. Don't worry about a thing."

While Segismundo smiled, resigned and confident, the instructor turned to Herculano, explaining:

"I have already seen the diagram of our friend's future physical body. I got a close look at the images of the heart disease he will suffer as an adult as a consequence of the wrong he committed in the past. Segismundo will experience large disturbances in his cardiac nerves[14], particularly those regulating the cardiac tonus. However" – and he concentrated all his attention on Herculano – "you must help him realize that truly redemptive trials lead the incarnate soul into dangerous and difficult situations in the recapitulation of its experiences; nevertheless, these situations do not compel it toward new spiritual failures when we are imbued with true goodwill in our work of advancement. The dedicated learner may gain much time and virtue if he or she actually tries to understand the lessons and put them into practice. Divine Justice has never been carried out without love. And when sincere faithfulness to the Lord is alive in the human heart, there is always room for the 'added mercy' that Jesus referred to in his ministry."

---

[14] Our deepest gratitude to Dr. Sonia Doi of the U.S. Spiritist Medical Association for her help with some of the medical terms in this book, especially in chaps. 13 and 14. – Tr.

Alexandre then invited me to join him as he said goodbye to the others, emphasizing:

"We will see you again on the day of Segismundo's initial linking to physical matter. On that occasion, I will need to cooperate with our 'Constructors', whom I have asked to show me the chromosomal diagrams regarding Segismundo's reincarnation."

He left.

I could not curb the questions that were flogging my mind, distressed by a strange curiosity due to the extreme care that had been taken so that Adelino and Segismundo could reconcile with each other before their reunion in the flesh. Would it not be better to arrange for the reincarnation of the spirit-in-need without any further delay? Why such a display of affection toward Raquel's husband since he should feel happy at being able to take part in this sublime deed of redemption? Did we not have enough power to break down any resistance?

Alexandre listened to me patiently, displayed a fatherly smile and replied:

"Your surprise is natural. You still aren't accustomed to the work of assistance or organization on this side of life."

After a small pause, he continued:

"Each individual, like each spirit, is a self-contained world, and every mind is like a sky ... Sun rays and beneficial rains descend from the firmament on behalf of the planet; however, at the moment of the attrition of the atmospheric elements, destructive lightning also come down from this same sky. So it is with the human mind. The balancing and restorative energies for the trillions of cells of the physical organism originate from it, but when it is disturbed, it emits magnetic rays of a highly destructive power for the communities of cells that serve it. Adelino's bitter thoughts were destroying the genetic substance, poisoning the chromatin within its own seminal sac. He could have answered the call of nature and engaged in sexual union, but he would not have been able to achieve the sacred objectives of creation. The deplorable condition of his inner life was destroying the germ cells as they were born, and even though he did not destroy them altogether, he poisoned the genes' characteristics, making our actions very difficult ... In the case of Segismundo, linked to Adelino in an active process of redemption, we cannot deny Adelino our loving and fraternal assistance. Hence the need for this intense work to awaken his sentiments. Only love provides life, happiness and balance. Having changed his inner disposition, Adelino from now on will emit magnetic energies that will protect the elements destined for the lofty service of procreation."

The instructor's words could not have been more logical. I was now beginning to understand the meaning of the sublime work that had taken place in order for Raquel's husband to become gentler and more humane. Since I could not find the right words to express my amazement, Alexandre smiled and pointed out after a long pause:

"As you have seen, around here there are no miracles for the practice of least effort. And when we teach everywhere the need for the practice of love, we are not advocating mere principles of a religious essence, but are heeding the real imperatives of life itself."

In the course of the explanations related to Segismundo's interesting case, the kind instructor had touched on subjects that were of great importance to me. He had mentioned sexual union and had designated procreation as its sacred objective. Would this not be the right moment to hear more of what he had to say on this sensitive subject? I bombarded him with eager questions. Alexandre was not surprised and listened to my questions with imperturbable serenity. Once I stopped to hear what he had to say, he kindly answered:

"Sex has been so demeaned by the majority of reincarnate people that for now it is very difficult for us to enlighten human thinking on this issue. It is enough to say that the sexual union between most men and women is still too close to the way it is expressed among irrational animals. In the chapter of relations of this kind, there is much criminal thoughtlessness and systematic indifference toward the divine laws. On that level, any comment on our part would not be reasonable. It is the domain of half-brutes, where many admirable minds prefer to remain in lower currents of evolution. It is also undeniable that it is there that the work of self-denying Constructor Spirits occurs as they collaborate in the basic formation of bodies destined to serve the spirits that reincarnate in the denser realms. However, we must remember that the work in such realms is carried out en masse with characteristics of primitive mechanisms. Love on those lower planes is like gold lost in a large quantity of ore, demanding great efforts and laborious processes to reveal itself to the experts. But among those humans, who in fact are proceeding toward their elevation, the sexual union is much different. It entails the sublime exchange of perispiritual energies, symbolizing divine nourishment for the mind and heart, and creative power not only for children of the flesh but also for generous deeds and achievements of the soul for life eternal."

Alexandre paused briefly, smiled paternally and continued:

"Remember, Andre, that I referred to the sacred objectives of creation and not just the work of procreation, which can be accomplished by those who love, without being the exclusive object of marriage. The spirit who hates or places itself in a negative attitude before God's Law cannot create higher life anywhere."

I realized that the problem was very difficult to explain, but as if he wanted to clarify all my doubts, the dedicated instructor continued after a short interruption:

"It is necessary to shift the concept of sex, refraining from locating it solely in certain organs of the transitory human body. Let's view sex as an active or passive quality, a soul's agent or recipient factor. When we reach such an understanding, we realize that all sexual manifestation evolves with the individual. As long as we are immersing ourselves in the marsh of heavy and poisonous vibrations, we can only experience sensations in that realm. As we progress on the pathway of equilibrium, we gather material from valuable experiences and opportunities for correction, strength, knowledge, happiness and power. As we harmonize with the supreme laws, we find enlightenment and revelation, while high order spirits garner the comprehension of the Divinity. If we would replace the words 'sexual union' with 'union of qualities', we would see that all of universal life is based on this divine phenomenon, whose cause resides in God himself, the Father Creator of all things and all beings."

Alexandre's words opened up new horizons to my thought. The obscure aspects of the issue were becoming clearer in my mind. Giving me to understand that the breaks in the conversation were meant to give me time to think about it, the benevolent instructor continued after a long pause:

"This 'union of qualities' between heavenly bodies is known as the planetary magnetism of attraction; between souls it is called love, and between chemical elements it is known as affinity. Therefore, it would not be possible to reduce this fundamental of universal life by circumscribing it to the simple activities of certain organs of the physical body. Fatherhood and motherhood are sublime duties; however, they do not represent the only divine work in the realm of infinite creation. The disciple who produces in the field of Virtue, Science or Art employs the same principles of exchange but on different planes, because for such a disciple the exchange of qualities occurs in higher spheres. There are physical and psychic fertilizations. The former require the arrangements of the physical form in order to temporarily meet the demands of life in the sector of necessary life experiences. The latter, however, are independent of the prison of limitations and occur within the resplendent domains of the soul in a marvelous process of eternity. When we refer to the love of the Omnipotent One, when we thirst for the Divinity, our spirits, eager for the Eternal Fertilizing Principle, are looking for nothing other than this exchange of qualities with the sublime spheres of the universe."

Alexandre paused at length, as if he himself was enraptured by such concepts. I, in turn, was completely spellbound. I had never heard such profound thinking regarding the definition of sex in the life of the universe.

"It too bad," he continued gravely, "that most of our incarnate brothers and sisters have scorned the creative faculties of sex and have relegated them to the vortex of inferior pleasures. But penny by penny, they will all pay what they owe to this sacred gift, through whose door they have received the grace to work and learn on the earth. Every creative act is full of the sacred emotions of the Divinity, and it is precisely these sublime emotions of the soul's participation in the creative powers of nature that humans take carelessly to the realms of abuse and addiction. They try to drag the light down into the darkness and convert the sexual act, deeply venerable in all its characteristics, into a degraded passion as deplorable as drunkenness or drug use. Nevertheless, Andre, without any mortal eyes seeing their rectifying anguish, the unfortunate souls who have fallen into this abyss will be severely punished by divine nature."

At this point of the enlightening explanation, and sensing that my respectable friend was about to pause again, I dared to ask:

"But isn't the use of sex a law of nature in the physical realm?"

Alexandre smiled benevolently and answered:

"No one is contesting this aspect of sexual expression in the corporeal sphere, but all natural laws in the human experience – as everywhere else – must be exerted on the basis of the universal law of order and the good. Those who avoid the good are faced with crime; those who avoid order fall into imbalance. Thus, sexual unions that take place far from these sublime imperatives become the generating causes of suffering and perturbation. Furthermore, we must not forget that sex in human existence can be one of the instruments of love, without love itself being sex. For this reason, men and women, whose souls are breaking free from the prisons of the physical form, gradually escape the absolute domain of carnal sensations. For them the physical sexual union stops being an imposition because they learn to exchange the divine qualities of the soul between themselves, mutually nurturing each other through magnetic exchanges no less valuable for the Infinite Creation, generating spiritual accomplishments for a glorious eternity without any need for cellular attrition. For this type of person, the comforting and sublime union is not limited to the emotions of a few minutes, but comprises the integration of a soul with another for an entire lifetime in the realm of Higher Spirituality. As for the effects of physical presence, most of the time a look, a word, a simple gesture of affection and understanding is enough for them to receive the creative magnetism from their loved one's heart in order to garner the strength and encouragement to accomplish the most difficult edifying tasks."

Alexandre gave his explanation a little pause and then, shaking his head meaningfully, he remarked:

"There is no creation without fertilization. Physical forms are the result of physical unions. Spiritual constructions originate from spiritual unions. The universe is God's child. Sex, therefore, as an active or passive quality of principles and beings, is a cosmic manifestation expressed in every evolutionary circle until we arrive at Perfect Harmony, where those qualities become balanced in the bosom of the Divinity."

I did not dare break the silence that followed. The venerable instructor was deeply engulfed in thought and did not return to the subject, perhaps wanting to urge me to meditate more deeply on the subject.

I anxiously awaited the time to return to my observations of Segismundo's case. This study was truly fascinating, and for that reason I was justifiably happy when I received Alexandre's invitation to return to Adelino's home. The kind instructor stated that it was necessary to visit the couple and our reincarnating friend the day before the first link with organic matter.

When we arrived at the family home, we found Herculano and Segismundo in the company of different spirits. Alexandre informed me that they were the 'Constructor Spirits', who were going to assist in the formation of our friend's fetus.

As before, the domestic nest was bathed in the late afternoon sunlight and the family was seated at the table for their meal. However, Adelino displayed a different spiritual disposition. He was now surrounded by a clear environment of optimism, kindness and joy. My kindly instructor was very pleased with the new situation and began examining the chromosomal diagrams with the help of the Constructors. I tried unsuccessfully to decipher those peculiar characters, which resembled tiny arabesques.

Alexandre, as kind and benevolent as always, pointed out:

"This is a study that is beyond your understanding for the time being. I'm examining the geography of the genes in the chromosomes so that I can determine how far we will be able to work with magnetic resources on behalf of our friend Segismundo in the organization of the hereditary properties."

I acceded and began observing Segismundo, who seemed exhausted and disheartened. He had trouble sitting up. Assisted by the devoted Herculano, he struggled to talk to us as he lay on a bed, completely prostrated.

He seemed pleased with my fraternal sympathy, and while the others were studying his situation, I had a brief conversation with him. It once more reminded me of the stressful state of those who are at the threshold of a new earthly experience.

"I felt more cheerful for awhile," he said sadly, "but my energies are dwindling now ... I feel weak and unable to do things ... While I was fighting for my future father's spiritual transformation, I felt more confident and composed ... but now ... that I have obtained the gift of returning to the earthly struggle, I'm afraid of new failures."

"Don't worry," I answered, trying to comfort him. "The opportunity for your redemption is one of the best. Furthermore, you will have many friends following you closely to help you be successful in your new life."

Segismundo tried to smile and remarked:

"Yes, I know ... Along with all the other brothers who are assisting me now, Herculano will be diligently and faithfully following me ... I'm sure of it. But with our current spiritual enlightenment, rebirth in the flesh represents a very serious factor in our process of advancement ... God help me if I fail again!"

I was offering him words of courage and good cheer when my instructor, having finished examining the diagrams, came over to us and said with affectionate authority:

"Segismundo, it's unbelievable that you are weakening just as you've come to the culminating moment of your present achievements. Recover your faith and restore your hope, for you cannot enter the realm of matter in the same way as our ignorant and unfortunate brothers and sisters who have to be almost completely unconscious in order to enter the sanctuary of the maternal womb once again. Help us out with your trust in our work for your own good. Put your creative imagination to work. Visualize the initial moments of the fetal condition by forming the appropriate model in your mind. You will find the most efficient assistance in Raquel's noble motherhood and will receive unwavering collaboration from us; however, remember that your own personal efforts at adaptation and acceptance will be very important in order for you to be victorious in this upcoming opportunity. Don't waste your time on anxious, pain-filled and apprehensive expectations. Raise the level of your mental energies."

Segismundo listened respectfully to the warning. I noticed that Alexandre's comforting words had a wonderful effect on him. He suddenly felt better and made an effort to slough off his burden of needless worries.

Impressed by the esteemed mentor's explanation, I did not hesitate to ask him another question.

"So," I asked, deeply interested, "are there spirits who reincarnate unaware of what they are doing?"

"Certainly," he answered politely, "just as there are thousands who discarnate daily on the earth without the least idea of what is happening to them. Only enlightened souls have a real understanding of the true situation facing them at the time of the death of the body. The same applies here. The majority of those returning to corporeal life on earth are magnetized by spirit benefactors who have organized their new redemptive tasks, and they are led to the maternal temple of flesh like sleeping children. The initial stage, which generally is their onus in the formation of the fetus, is then executed by the mind of the mother and by the friends from our plane who assist them. Countless spirits reincarnate on earth under these conditions, taken there by higher authorities from our sphere of action according to the specific needs of certain incarnate souls, homes and groups."

The explanation could not have been more logical, and once more I admired my loving friend's gift for clarity and simplicity.

We stayed a little longer in that welcoming little home, and after having comforted Segismundo's spirit and saying goodbye at almost midnight, Alexandre spoke to Herculano and the Constructors in the following terms:

"We will return tomorrow night for the initial connection and hand our reincarnating brother over to our friends."

One of the Constructor Spirits, who seemed to be the head of the group, embraced him movingly and said:

"We are counting on your assistance for the chromatin splitting in the mother's uterus."

"Gladly!" he replied in good humor.

Returning to other tasks, I could not stop the flow of new ideas that Segismundo's reincarnation had awakened in me. How would help be rendered in those circumstances? Would Raquel be aware of our collaboration? How would the couple interpret the actions on our plane if they became aware of the extent of our involvement? Alexandre interrupted my inner questioning and added, as if he had been listening to my thoughts:

"In cases like this one, Andre, our help is rendered with the same sanctity that characterizes the assistance of a responsible and honest physician in assisting common labor and delivery. The fetal modeling and the development of the embryo obey natural physical laws, as occurs in the organization of forms in the other kingdoms of nature; however, in all cases, the elements of help from the spirit plane coexist with these laws in accordance with evolutionary or redemptive plans. Our assistance, therefore, in this type of procedure, is one of the most common tasks."

I understood the full meaning of the explanation, set my mind at ease and waited for the following day.

However, as the day wore on, my curiosity began needling me again. At what time would we be going to Adelino's house? Without any improper objective, I was concerned about the moment of Segismundo's first connection to matter. Would Alexandre be acting at the time of the sexual union or would the phenomenon obey different determinations? The instructor smiled silently, aware of my mental anguish. The hours followed one after the other, and noticing my impatience, Alexandre kindly explained:

"Our presence is not necessary at the moment of cellular union. Such moments of the conjugal bed are sublime and inviolable in well-founded homes. You know that fertilization of the maternal egg only takes place a few hours after intercourse. The male element undergoes a long trip before reaching its objective."

And smiling, he added:

"We have time."

I understood how sensitive his explanations were, but hungry for more information on the matter, I asked:

"In your opinion, are all sexual unions inviolable?"

"Not all of them," replied the instructor, attentively. "Don't forget that I said 'well-founded homes'. All incarnates who build their conjugal nest on righteousness win the presence of respectful witnesses, who guarantee the privacy of their most intimate acts, consolidating their vibrational borders and defending them against undignified forces. They base their work on the elevated thoughts they find in the couple's home environment. However, the same does not happen in homes where couples choose the company of lower order spiritual witnesses from the lower zones.

The wife who is unfaithful to the noble principles of married life, and the husband who links his home to prostitution, cannot expect their intimate acts to be crowned with veneration and sanctity; these acts are shared by the perverse witnesses they have chosen. They become the unwitting victims of twisted groups that share in their physiological emotions, inducing them to the most sorrowful vices. Even if these unfortunate couples are temporarily at the height of human social positions, they cannot conceal their miserable inner condition, as they anxiously look for dissipating pleasures while dominated by an outlandish and uncontrollable sensuality."

Alexandre's remarkable answer surprised me. I now fully understood that each one of us is the subject of our own choice of situation wherever we might be. Nevertheless, a new question came into my mind and I tried to air it in order to clarify my reasoning.

"I understand the magnitude of your explanations," I said respectfully. "But considering the danger of certain debasing attitudes by people who have taken on the responsibility of establishing a home, what would the situation be, for example, for a faithful and devoted wife who has a disloyal husband prone to sexual adventures? Would the noble and virtuous woman be at the mercy of the criminal witnesses that the man has chosen?"

"No!" He said, vehemently. "Evil cannot disturb what is genuinely good. In such cases, the wife will ensure the domestic environment, although doing so will demand real self-denial and heavy sacrifice on her part. The act that requires her noble presence is sacred, even if her companion has otherwise put himself at a level lower than that of the brute. In such cases, however, the improvident husband will slowly become blind to virtue, and sometimes can turn into a complete slave of the perverse spirits whom he has taken as his usual companions, and they are present on all his pathways and activities outside the family sanctuary. At such point it is very difficult to keep him from falling into the fatal abysses of crime and darkness."

"Oh, my God!" I exclaimed, "How much work there is waiting for brave souls! How much ignorance to overcome!"

"You have put it well," added the instructor seriously, "because, in fact, most conjugal tragedies continue beyond the grave, creating dreadful hells for those who lived them in the physical realm. It is very painful to observe the extent of the crimes perpetrated during corporeal existence, and God help those who lack the foresight to try to overcome their lower passions in time! Their awakening will be utter misery!"

I fell silent, and thoughtfully, Alexandre also went into a deep silence, which gave me an idea of his admirable ability to concentrate.

It was around 10:00 p.m. when we set out for Raquel's home.

The little family had just gone to bed.

Herculano and the others greeted us with great displays of affection.

The head of the Constructors addressed my instructor:

"We have been waiting for your collaboration in order to start our magnetic work on the patient."

We entered the small room where Segismundo was resting. He was still distressed, with a sad and vague look in his eyes.

I could not hold back a question:

"Why is Segismundo suffering so much?" I asked Alexandre discretely.

"For some time now, particularly since last week, he has been undergoing the process of direct fluidic connection with his future parents. Herculano is in charge of helping him with it. As this connection intensifies, he begins to lose the points of contact he consolidated in our sphere through the assimilation of the elements of our plane. Such a process is necessary so that the perispiritual body can regain its characteristic plasticity, and, at the stage he finds himself, this causes him suffering."

This remark was new to me so I continued:

"But isn't Segismundo's perispirit the same one he brought back with him when he discarnated the last time?"

"Yes," agreed the instructor, "it is essentially the same; however, with the passing of time and in light of a new diet and new habits in a very different environment, he has incorporated certain elements from our circles of life that he will need to discharge in order to successfully enter the stream of life in the flesh. The struggles between the primordial fluidic connections and the resulting emotions wear down the resistances of this type, with the emphasis that tonight we will finish the rest of our work, mobilizing our magnetic resources on his behalf."

"Oh!" I exclaimed, "Isn't that something akin to physical death on the earth?"

Alexandre smiled and acquiesced:

"Obviously, as long as we regard the death of the physical body as a simple abandonment of atomic earthly envelopes."

I realized that it was not the time for long dissertations on the matter, and seeing that Alexandre had begun to focus his attention on the Constructors, I asked no further questions.

Followed by his friends, Alexandre approached Segismundo and asked cheerfully:

"Well? Are you feeling stronger?"

And patting his face, he added:

"You should be happy: the decisive moment has arrived. All of our expressions of thanksgiving to God are insignificant in light of the new opportunity that has been given to you."

"Yes..." said Segismundo, gasping. "I am grateful ... don't forget me ... the help I need."

Looking anxiously at Alexandre, he remarked uneasily:

"I'm scared ... I'm really scared."

Alexandre sat down next to him like a father and said tenderly:

"Don't harbor the monster of fear in your heart. This is a time for confidence and courage. Look, Segismundo! If something is concerning you, share it with us; tell us all about your inner struggles! Open up your soul, dear friend! Remember that the moment of your final passage from one plane to another is drawing nigh. It is crucial for you to keep your thoughts pure, clean of any debris!"

Segismundo shed some tears and spoke with difficulty:

"You know that I undertook a small assistance project on the outskirts of our spirit colony ... It was authorized by our Superiors and ... and even though it is coming along nicely ... I feel that it is not finished yet and that I am still largely responsible for it ... I don't know if I have done the right thing ... asking to return to earth right now before having finished up my work there ... however ... I realized that in order to move on ... I had to reconcile myself with my own conscience by seeking out my former adversaries ... in order to redeem my wrongs ..."

And while Alexandre and the other friends listened in silence, Segismundo continued:

"That is why ... I was so insistent about my return ... How could I lead others to a full spiritual conversion ... in accord with Christ's teachings ... without having paid my own debts? How could I teach suffering brothers and sisters ... if I myself was suffering ... from painful wounds due to my cruel past? But now ... that this difficult new start is at hand ... I'm tortured by the fear of failing again ... When Raquel and Adelino went back ... they promised me their fraternal help, and I'm sure ... that they will be two benefactors for me ... but ... I'm afflicted by worries and anxieties before the unknown future."

Taking advantage of a pause, Alexandre spoke frankly and optimistically:

"There's no point in worrying so much, my friend! Let go of your endeavors on our plane. All our works, when carried out in accordance with the divine laws, are self-sustaining and wait for us at any time for the harvest of the delicious fruits of life eternal. Only evil is condemned to destruction and only error requires the laborious process of rectification. Therefore, be serenely happy. Your insistence on the current return to the earthy plane was well thought out. Redemption from the wrongs of the past will grant your spirit a new and more brilliant light. Stick to your purpose. The greatest joy of a faithful student is to take advantage of his school, to receive its sublime teachings, and to reap its benefits. So, Segismundo, your bliss in returning to the earth now is enormous. Cleanse your mind in the living water of trust in God, and forge ahead. You can't take anything into your new life except the divine heritage that you have already acquired with your efforts for life eternal, comprised of the noble ideas and inner enlightenment that your spirit has acquired. Don't hold yourself back with memories of outward aspects of our activities on this plane. To persist in such a state could have very serious consequences because your inadaptation could disturb the fetal development and cause the premature death of your new physical vessel during infancy. Don't get caught up in childish fears. It's true that you have debts to pay, but who doesn't? We will never redress them if we are forlorn and downcast. It is essential that we create new hopes."

Segismundo gestured in agreement and made an effort to smile, showing that he was less downhearted.

"Don't disturb your valuable work of this moment. Remember the blessings we have received and don't be afraid!"

As Alexandre became silent I noticed that Segismundo, under strong emotion, did not have the strength to continue the conversation. However, I saw him take Alexandre's right hand with infinite effort, kissing it respectfully as a token of his gratitude.

I pondered the enormous amount of help we all receive when returning to the physical realm. Those devoted benefactors had been helping Segismundo since day one, and even now, facing the possibility that he might change his mind, they were willing to console him in his sorrows, cheering him up for his success.

The Constructor Spirits began the work of magnetizing his perispiritual body, in which they were amply assisted by the efforts of the selfless instructor, who remained dedicated and steadfast in every aspect of the process.

Without being able to make myself immediately understood by the ordinary reader, I must say, nevertheless, that "something" from Segismundo's form was being eliminated. Almost imperceptibly, as the magnetic operations were intensified, he became paler. His gaze seemed to penetrate other realms. He was becoming distant, less lucid.

At a certain point, Alexandre spoke to him with authority:

"Segismundo, help us! Keep your objectives clear and your thought steady!"

I had the impression that Segismundo was trying hard to obey.

"Now," Alexandre continued, "tune in to the pre-infancy form with us. Visualize your return to the maternal refuge of earthly flesh! Remember the fetal format; make yourself smaller! Imagine your need to be a child again in order to learn to be a man!"

I realized that Segismundo needed to contribute a great amount of personal cooperation for assured success. I was surprised to see that under the magnetic influx from Alexandre and the Constructors, Segismundo's perispiritual form was shrinking.

The operation was neither quick nor easy. I could see the efforts everybody was making to accomplish the necessary reduction.

Segismundo seemed less and less conscious. He did not look at us with the same lucidity and his replies to our tender questions were incomplete.

Finally, I was greatly astonished to see that our friend's form resembled that of a child.

The phenomenon astounded me and I could not contain the questions that were welling up inside. Seeing that Alexandre and the Constructors were getting ready for a short break before entering the bedroom, I approached the esteemed instructor, who instantly perceived my curiosity.

He received me politely as always and said:

"I know. You continue to be pressed by your thirst for understanding."

I smiled sheepishly, but cheered up and asked:

"How is what I have seen possible? I didn't realize that rebirth entailed such complex procedures in the spirit world!"

"Ennobling work takes place everywhere," added Alexandre intentionally. "A heaven of idleness is perhaps the greatest illusion of the theological principles that have obscured the divine meaning of true religion."

He paused, made an impressive gesture, and continued:

"As for your feeling of astonishment, there's no reason for it. Normal discarnation imposes no less change on the physical body. For earth-bound humans, terminal illnesses are in a certain way a prolonged reducing process that finally releases the soul, untangling it from its physiological ties. There are people who become barely recognizable after a few weeks in bed. And we must remember that the physical body is very far from the plasticity of the perispiritual body, which is highly sensitive to magnetic influence."

The explanation could not have been more logical.

"But is what we have seen with Segismundo the general rule for all cases?" I asked.

"Not at all," the instructor replied kindly. "The processes of reincarnation, as well as those of physical death, differ infinitely from one person to the next, and I don't think there are two that are exactly the same. The degrees of ease and obstacles depend on numerous factors that are often related to the conscious state of the person who is returning to the physical plane or departing from it. There are high order spirits who barely require any help from us at all when they return to the denser sphere on a mission of service and enlightenment. On the other hand, some of our other brothers and sisters coming from the lower zones need much more complex help than Segismundo has required."

"But shouldn't reincarnation involve only those who show themselves to be prepared?" I asked curiously.

"We mustn't forget that reincarnation is the repeated course of necessary lessons," refuted my enlightened teacher. "Earth is a divine school, and love, through 'intercessory' activities, sends millions of students back to the school of the flesh every day."

Alexandre paused for a few moments, and then continued:

"Segismundo's reincarnation is following the more common guidelines. It is symbolic of the majority of such reincarnations because our brother belongs to the huge 'average class' of spirits that inhabit the physical realms, and who are neither exceedingly good nor consciously evil. But I must add that the return to the earth of certain spirits from the lower zones requires hard and patient work from the workers of our plane. Such beings compel us to processes that will take you a long time to understand."

Alexandre's explanations touched me deeply and satisfied my penchant for intellectual understanding; however, new questions were arising in my thirsty mind, so out of an intense and authentic curiosity, I asked respectfully:

"Is the assistance that we have witnessed available to everyone? This is a home with good foundations, as you yourself have affirmed. But ... what if we were in a typical house of carnal debauchery? What if we were faced with criminal passions and unbalanced perversions?"

The instructor thought deeply and replied:

"Andre, a diamond lost in the mud for a while is still a diamond. The same applies to fatherhood or motherhood, which in themselves are always divine. Everywhere, assistance is offered from the higher spheres as long as the work involves God's will. However, we must remember that under such circumstances the work of assistance is truly a sacrifice. The adversarial and rebellious vibrations of uncontrolled passions arising from unbalanced souls compromise our best efforts. Therefore, many times in these places of irresponsibility and vice, in order to extend our assistance in obedience to our ministry, we must first battle against monstrous spirit entities. They dominate the lives of men and women who recklessly choose the dangerous road of emotional instability on which such ignorant and unbalanced spirits travel. In such cases, our collaboration cannot always be perfect because the parents themselves have demeaned the greatness of the mandate that has been entrusted to them and have opened the doors of their sacred potentialities to the merciless monsters of darkness that persecute the children born to them. Certain heroic souls choose to enter their corporeal existence in this way in order to strengthen themselves in supreme resistance against evil from their very first days in the womb. However, we must remember that it is necessary to be very strong in faith and courage in order not to succumb. In rebirths of this type, most spirits fulfill the beneficial plan of corrective expiation. Many fail, but there are always many who garner the best spiritual profits in their experiences for life eternal."

Alexandre had commented on the subject with inspiring beauty. I had begun to understand the origin of certain teratological[15] phenomena and of certain congenital malformations that on the earth cause severe chest pain. Alexandre's explanations were directing me to a new and fascinating area of study: rectifying and obligatory trials.

Alexandre invited the Constructors to join him and Herculano in examining the chromosomal diagrams. I followed their work with interest, although I was completely lacking in the ability to ascertain with precision the meticulous drawings under our eyes.

Due to the lack of elements for an analogical comparison, it is impossible for me to describe certain determinations reached by that small group of spirit authorities, but I can say that after they had finished the technical part per se of their conversation, my instructor was happy to add:

"Except for the arterial tube in the structure that will dilate to form the heart, everything will go well. All the genes in this area will function with complete normality."

After a short pause, he emphasized:

"The limbs and organs will be excellent, and if our friend knows how to take advantage of future opportunities, he will probably be able to restore the control of the circulatory system if he remains in enlightening service for a blessed period of terrestrial work. His success will depend on his own efforts."

And turning to the Constructors, he spoke to them kindly:

"Friends, Herculano will remain at Segismundo's side for seven years in his new reincarnation, at which time the

[15] Teratology is "the science or study of monstrosities or abnormal formations in organisms." (*Random House Webster's College Dictionary*, 1991) – Tr.

reincarnational process will have been completed. After that period, his work as a friend and guide will be eased, for he will follow our brother at a distance. I know that our devoted companion will take all possible measures to ensure a harmonious fetal development, whether by helping Segismundo or by defending Raquel against any malevolent attacks. However, I ask you to be very attentive to the initial formation of the thymus gland, which, as you know, is crucial for the child from the time of its life in the womb. We need the glandular system to be in perfect balance until the bone marrow forms to produce the red blood cells. The various diagrams of chromosomal arrangements will facilitate this."

Some of the Constructors began to observe the diagrams more closely.

While my eyes focused on those microscopic characters, allowing for a close examination of the egg cell, I approached my instructor, and sensing him more accessible to my questions, I asked:

"These charts display the geography of the genes distributed in the chromosomes. Is the law of inheritance then unlimited? At rebirth, will the individual receive the full imprint of his or her parent's characteristics? Are illnesses or criminal tendencies entirely transmissible?"

"No, Andre," observed my supervisor in a serious tone of voice, "what we have here is a natural physical phenomenon. In its densest form, the newborn's organism derives from the bodies of the parents, which give it life and create its characteristics through their own blood; however, in this imperative of the divine law in the process of the reproduction of physical forms, we should not see a denial of the principles of spiritual freedom inherent in the order of Infinite Creation. That is why human beings inherit tendencies and not qualities. Tendencies surround persons being reborn from the very first days of their life not only in their transitory body but also in the general environment into which they have been called to live in order to advance. Qualities are the result of the incarnate soul's individual endeavor at defending, educating and improving itself in the blessed arena of new experiences. If the reincarnated spirit is inclined toward inferior tendencies, it will develop them when it finds them again in the scenario of human experience, thereby wasting valuable time and a sublime opportunity to evolve. On the other hand, if a soul returns to the world and remains willing to work for self-growth, it will overcome any ignoble demands from its body or the environment, and will triumph over adverse conditions and obtain victories of the highest significance for eternal life. Therefore, no one of sound mind can complain of destructive forces or overpowering circumstances regarding the environment where he or she was reborn. We will always have the light of inner freedom inside showing us the way upward. Practicing to ascend spiritually, we will always improve. That is the law."

In light of Alexandre's previous explanations concerning the importance of Herculano's assistance to the reincarnated Segismundo until age seven, I tried to get some information on the matter. I apologized to Alexandre, but I could not resist asking a couple of sensitive questions: Why such caution regarding the future newborn's blood? Would the reincarnation process really be completed only after the first seven years of his human existence?

As always, the noble mentor listened to me obligingly, smiled like a loving father, and answered kindly:

"You are aware that the human body has its vegetative activities per se, but you may not yet know that the perispiritual body, which gives form to the cellular elements, is strongly rooted in the blood. In the fetal organization, the blood elements are a gift from the mother's body. Soon after rebirth, a period of a different assimilation of organic energies takes place, where the reincarnated 'self' rehearses the consolidation of its new experiences. In this new cycle of physical life, it is only at age seven that it can begin to preside on its own over the blood formation process, which is the basic element for the equilibrium of the perispiritual body or preexistent form. Blood, therefore, can be regarded as the divine fluid that underpins our activities on the physical plane, and through its continual flow within the physiological organism, it furnishes us with a symbol of the eternal movement of the sublime energies of the Infinite Creation. When its circulation is hindered, imbalance or illness results, and if obstacles completely impede its flow, then the body's vital tonus is extinguished on the physical plane, followed by death with the immediate withdrawal of the soul."

Strongly impressed by my friend's revelation, I remarked:

"Oh! How great people's responsibility is concerning their material body!"

"How right you are," added the instructor, "when you refer with such admiration to this sovereign duty of the reincarnated spirit. Without tending to the grave responsibilities in the preservation of his or her physical vessel, no individual will be able to achieve spiritual progress. The spirit is reborn in the flesh to cultivate divine qualities in its nature, but how can it fulfill such requirement if it destroys the organic apparatus, the fundamental platform for the work to be done? You mentioned the law of heredity a while ago. The terrestrial body is also a patrimony inherited over millennia and humankind has been perfecting it down through time. Plasma, a sublime composition created when the divine influx infused seawater in primitive times, is the primordial foundation of physiological organizations. When returning to the planet, we must make use of this inheritance that has evolved to some degree in the human body."

I was surprised by these explanations, and after a short pause, Alexandre continued:

"As you well know, this is why that, while we move around in the physical realm, we are in fact marine creatures breathing on dry land. We cannot do without salt in our diet. Our physiological organism is essentially comprised of sixty-percent saline, whose composition is almost identical to that of seawater with its sodium, calcium and potassium. In the physiological realm of a reincarnated person the taste of salt can be found in the blood, sweat, tears and other secretions. The corpuscles acclimated to warm seas would live comfortably in the organic fluids. We could make some truly surprising analogies in this respect."

I did not know what to say in response to such remarks, and because of my silence, Alexandre continued after a significant pause:

"As you can see, when we are reborn we receive a sacred inheritance with the body, which we need to preserve by perfecting it. Our physical energies should evolve the same as our souls. If we have been offered this vessel of service for new elevating experiences, we need to give back through our efforts in labor and education involving the body, thus extending our assistance with the light of our respect and spiritual balance. In the future, humankind will understand that its cells are not only bits of flesh but companions in evolution, deserving of recognition and effective assistance. Until we understand this harmony in the organic kingdom, it is pointless to search for peace."

The wise and magnanimous instructor's brilliant discourse suggested sublime questions, but he reminded me of the work underway and ended his explanations for now.

It was 2:00 a.m.

We were now surrounded by not only Alexandre and the Constructors but also by several spirit friends of the family.

Gathering all the spirits together, Alexandre, as the highest figure of the meeting, spoke gravely:

"And now, my brothers and sisters, let us enter the bedroom so that the joy of spiritual union may take place."

Placing Segismundo in the arms of the spirit who had been Raquel's loving mother, he emphasized:

"Let it be you, dear sister, who carries the sacred deposit. The filial heart that is waiting for us will feel renewed happiness in contact with your tenderness. Raquel is well-deserving of such joy."

And turning back to the others, he explained:

"We will now proceed with the initial direct act of linking Segismundo with organic matter. Moreover, I expect you to visit our reincarnating brother repeatedly, particularly during the gestation of his future body. You are fully aware of the value of caring collaboration in this work. Only those who have sown much affection can receive the help of many friends, and Segismundo ought to receive such reward due to his noble sentiments and elevated work with all of us over these past few years, in which he dedicated himself to great works of beneficence and fraternity."

Soon thereafter, we entered the couple's bedroom; the intimate setting was divinely beautiful. On the wooden bed between soft linen sheets two bodies were resting, motionless in the blessing of sleep; however, Adelino and Raquel were waiting for us in spirit, aware of the greatness of the moment. On waking up in the dense sphere of struggle and learning, their physical brains would not retain a perfect memory of the spiritual scene in which they themselves were the main characters; but the event would be engraved forever in their eternal memories.

The home's invisible friends – fellow spirits from our plane – had filled the bedroom with flowers of light. They had obtained permission to enter Segismundo's future birthplace at midnight for the loving purpose of decorating the pathways of his new beginning.

Over a hundred friends were there to pay him loving homage.

Alexandre walked ahead of us, affectionately greeting the couple who were temporarily outside their physical vessels.

Next, those present extended their harmonious greetings, filling the expectant spouses' hearts with celestial comfort.

The scene was beautiful and moving.

Two spirits next to me commented fraternally:

"It is always painful to return to the flesh after experiencing the regions of divine light; however, Christian love is so sacred that, even in those circumstances, sublime is the happiness of those who practice it."

"Yes," replied the other, "Segismundo has fought hard for redemption, and in that struggle he has been a devoted servant to all of us. He is well-deserving of the joy of this moment."

At this point, I noticed that the spirit who had been invited to hold the reincarnating being was standing a short distance from Raquel between the Constructor Spirits.

I was thinking about this, when somebody touched me slightly to get my attention.

It was Alexandre, smiling paternally and explaining:

"Let's leave our friends for a few minutes in the soft contentment of their affections. We will begin work at the suitable time."

Perplexed by so many new things going on, I had not had the chance to coordinate my thoughts in light of the many issues that had come up that night; hence the questions spinning around in my mind. The instructor perceived this and that is perhaps why he seemed more patient.

Taking advantage of the moment, I nodded toward Segismundo, curled up in the welcoming arms that were holding him, and asked:

"Will our reincarnating brother eventually look like he did when he was living amongst us? Since his instructions are based on the pre-existent perispiritual form, will he have the same height and mannerisms that characterized him in our sphere?"

Alexandre answered without hesitation:

"Take your time and think it through, Andre! We have talked about the pre-existent form, that is, the typical configuration model, or more appropriately, the 'human uniform'. The anatomical details and contours will take shape in accordance with the principles of equilibrium and the law of heredity. Our friend Segismundo's physical form will depend on the father's and mother's chromosomes. To that primordial factor, however, you must add the influence of Raquel's mental molds, Segismundo's own actions and the assistance of the Constructor Spirits, who will act as workers of divine nature, invisible to earthly eyes, as well as the affectionate help of the spirit friends who will constantly visit Segismundo during the months of his new body's formation. Take all those factors into consideration and you will have an idea of the meaning of the physical temple that he will own as a gift from the Higher Authority of God in order for him to benefit from the blessed opportunity to redeem the past and enlighten his future in time and space. Some physiologists on earth assert that human life is solely the result of biological encounters, forgetting that this apparent encounter of organic forces is no more than the advanced application of the law of spiritual cooperation."

"So then," I insisted, "will Segismundo eventually have a physical form that we would not recognize?"

The instructor was quick to clarify:

"If we were directly linked to his case, we would have all the information regarding the future in this particular, but our collaboration in this event is temporary and does not have any major significance over time. However, Segismundo's guides in the higher spheres will watch over the plan that has been traced out for his benefit. Notice that I said benefit and not destiny. Many people confuse a constructive plan with fatalism. Both Segismundo and our brother Herculano have the information we are talking about, because nobody enters a school for a more or less long period without a specific purpose and without knowing the rules that he or she should obey."

At this point, the generous mentor paused for a moment and then continued:

"The anatomical contours of the physical form – disfigured or perfect, short or tall, beautiful or homely – are part of the educational rules. In general, systematic reincarnation is always a laborious course of work against pre-existent moral defects that show up in present lessons and conflicts. In the majority of cases, imperfect anatomical details, adverse circumstances and hostile environments are the best places of learning and redemption for those who are reborn. For that reason the diagram of useful trials is drawn up beforehand, much like a student's workbook at a regular school. In view of this, the diagram corresponding to Segismundo has been duly drawn up, taking into consideration the physiological cooperation of his parents, the domestic backdrop and the fraternal assistance that will be given to him by countless friends from this side. So, imagine our friend returning to a school – earth – and in doing so fulfilling a purpose: to acquire new qualities. In order to do this, he will have to submit to the rules of the school, renouncing up to a point the great freedom he used to enjoy in our environment."

"But then couldn't we call such a trial a 'fixed destiny'?" I asked.

Alexandre responded patiently:

"Don't fall into the error assumed by many people. That would imply an obligatory form of spiritual conduct. Of course, individuals are reborn with a relative independence and are sometimes subjected to certain harsher conditions for educational purposes, but such imperative never suppresses the free impulse of the soul in its aim toward advancement, stagnation or fall into lower conditions. There is a plan of spiritually edifying tasks to be fulfilled by spirits who reincarnate, where their guides set the approximate quota of eternal qualities that they are prone to acquire during their transitory existence. The spirit who is returning to the physical realm can either improve this quota and surpass its superiors' predictions by means of its own intensive effort or it can fall short and go further into debt to its neighbor, scorning the holy opportunities that had been granted to it."

Alexandre stopped, perhaps considering the amount of time spent on our conversation, and as if needing to end the talk, he remarked:

"Every plan that is drawn up in the higher spheres has the good and ascension as its basic objectives, and every soul that reincarnates, even one that finds itself in apparent desperate conditions, has resources to continue to improve."

Soon thereafter, the instructor invited me to come closer to the couple.

Alexandre reminded us that time was pressing and that we should deliver the sacred deposit to the joyful couple.

Through the mentor that was leading them, the Constructors asked Alexandre to say the prayer for that act of trust, and a deep silence fell on everybody.

The instructor was about to begin his prayer, when Raquel approached him and asked humbly:

"My dearest friend, if possible, I would like to receive my new son while on my knees!"

Alexandre agreed with a smile. Between the kneeling Raquel and Adelino, who, like us, remained standing, he began to pray, extremely moved, extending his generous hands toward heaven:

"Father of Love and Wisdom, bless the children of Your Terrestrial Home, who in this moment are about to share with you the divine creative faculty! Lord, in your mercy send your blessing upon this loving home, transformed into a refuge of reconciliation. We are gathered here as companions of past struggles to accompany our friend, who is returning to testify to his humility and understanding of your Law!

"O Father! Strengthen him for the long crossing of the river of temporary forgetfulness, enable us to keep his hope alive, and help us now and always to overcome all evil!

"To those who, with the birth of a new child, are now receiving a new ministry of guidance in the home, grant your generous and sanctifying light, which dissipates all darkness! Dear Lord, strengthen their notion of responsibility, open to them your door of sublime trust and keep them in the blessed joy of your dedicated love! Restore their energies so that they may joyfully receive the mission of selflessness to the end, and sanctify their joy so that they may not lose themselves in the abysses of fantasy!

"Lord, this is an act of trust in your infinite goodness, which we wish to honor forever! So, bless our loving work, and above all, Father, we implore your grace for our sister who has reverently given herself to the divine sacrifice of motherhood. Anoint her heart with your paternal magnanimity, intensify her good cheer, and expand her faith in the endless future! May she especially receive our best thoughts, our purest wishes of peace and hope!

"But above all, dear Lord, may your will be done in all corners of the universe, and may we, humble servants of your kingdom, have the incessant joy of revering and obeying you forever!"

Alexandre finished, and I noticed that the room had been filled with new lights. I saw that all of us spirit entities were emitting luminous rays that fell upon Raquel as she wept with sublime emotion. However, the radiant phenomenon was not circumscribed to just this. As soon as Alexandre had become silent, something seemed to reply to his plea. A slight flutter, which faintly resounded in our ears, was felt above our heads. I was truly surprised as I looked up and saw a shining and infinitely beautiful crown coming down from above to rest upon Raquel's head as she knelt in silence. I had the impression that it was composed of etherealized tourmalines that a miraculous goldsmith had turned resplendent. Its brilliance hurt our eyes, and even Alexandre, looking at it, bowed reverently. Held by spirits far superior to us and invisible to me, the sublime crown settled on Raquel's head.

Despite the emotion of the moment, I saw Alexandre motion to the woman holding Segismundo, indicating that she should now deliver the reincarnating spirit into his mother's arms.

Raquel, giving me the impression that she had not seen the luminous crown, raised her tear-filled eyes and received the deposit that heaven had entrusted to her. Alexandre extended his right hand and helped her to her feet, and I saw Adelino approach his wife, embrace her tenderly and kiss her forehead covered in drops of light.

That is when – O divine mystery of God's Infinite Creation! – I saw her pressing Segismundo's infant form to her heart so strongly, so lovingly that she looked like a priestess of the

Power of Supreme Divinity. Segismundo connected to her like a flower to a stem. I then understood that the one who would be flesh of her flesh was from now on soul of her soul.

Alexandre suggested that all the friends present leave the bedroom, except for the Constructors, Herculano and me, and that they take Adelino, comforted and happy, for a little walk outside. Then, very carefully guiding Raquel to her physical body, he said to us:

"Now let us help our friend with his initial contact with denser matter."

Raquel woke up with a feeling of strange happiness in her heart. Instinctively, she hugged her sleeping companion like the fortunate sailor at a port of peace and safety. She had crossed the thick veil of vibrations that separate the physical and spirit realms, and had retained no precise memory of the sublime joy of a few moments ago. However, her feelings of jubilation remained; her hopes overflowed and an intense confidence in the future now warmed her heart. "Will I be a mother for a second time?" she thought happily. This idea, which came into her mind by no mere chance, soothed her soul with delightful joy. She was ready for the divine task of motherhood; she would trust in the Lord as a slave of his infinite goodness.

Adelino's wife could not see that Alexandre and the Constructor Spirits were surrounding her mind with a sublime light, bathing her ideas with the living water of spiritual love.

Noticing that Segismundo's form had connected to her by a divine process of magnetic union, I received my instructor's indication to observe closely his work in aiding Segismundo's final bonding to matter.

Indicating Raquel's reproductive organs and shining his light on them, Alexandre alerted me to the greatness of the event under our observation, reverently pointing out:

"This is the sublime altar of human motherhood. In the presence of this venerable tabernacle, to which we owe the divine light of our lives, we must cooperate in the work of love by keeping our awareness turned toward the Supreme Majesty."

I observed the female structure of our incarnate sister with a reverence I had never felt before.

Assisted by the loving mentor's magnetic help, I began observing the minutiae of the fertilization process.

Through the natural channels, the male germinative elements were running in search of the egg as if they had been prepared beforehand for an elimination race of about three millimeters[16] per minute. Surprised, I saw that there were millions of them, charging forward en masse in an impulsive instinct of sacred competition.

In the sublime silence of those minutes I understood that Alexandre, as the missionary with the highest standing in the operating group, was guiding the critical task of the primordial connection. According to what I could gather, after having carefully studied the future maternal egg, he could see the chromosomal dispositions of all the moving male germ cells as he presided over the preliminary work of determining the sex of the body that would form.

Profoundly absorbed in his work, he followed the forward progress of the minuscule competitors that comprised the fertilizing substance before he identified the one most suitable and fixed his magnetic powers on it, giving me the idea that he was helping it overcome its competitors in order to be the first to penetrate the small maternal sac. The element he was focusing on gained new energy over the others and advanced rapidly toward its target. The female cell, which, compared to

[16] An eighth of an inch. – Tr.

the microscopic spermatic projectile, looked like a small round world of sugar, starch and proteins waiting for the life-giving beam, underwent the laceration of its membrane like a small ship being torpedoed. It then went singularly stiff, closing its tiny pores as if ready to withdraw into its own depths in order to receive the expected visitor face to face while preventing the entry of any of the other competitors that had lost the great race. Still under Alexandre's magnetic luminous influx, the victorious element continued its march after having crossed the egg's periphery, taking a little more than four minutes to reach the nucleus. Both forces, male and female, now formed one whole, turning before my eyes into a very tenuous focus of light. Completely absorbed in his work, the instructor touched the minuscule form with his right hand, maintaining his assistance on the chromatin division – whose specifics are still inaccessible to my comprehension – with the attitude of a surgeon confident in his technical ability. Next, Alexandre adjusted Segismundo's reduced form, which was interpenetrating Raquel's perispiritual organism, over that microscopic globe of light impregnated with life, and I saw that latent life had begun to stir.

Exactly a quarter of an hour had passed from the instant the active element had entered the nucleus of the passive egg.

After a prolonged magnetic application seconded by the efforts of the Constructor Spirits, Alexandre approached me and said:

"The initial connecting operation has ended. May God watch over us."

Sensing the wonder with which I was now following the process of cellular division, in which the germinal vesicle was rapidly forming, the instructor pointed out:

"The mother's body will furnish all the nutrition needed for the formation of the basic physical body, while Segismundo's reduced form, as a living model, will act like a magnet among iron filings, giving consistent form to his future appearance on the world's stage."

I was dumbfounded by what I had been allowed to observe. Guessing that I had found the phenomenon of Segismundo's perispiritual reduction astonishing, Alexandre added kindly:

"Andre, don't forget that reincarnation signifies a new beginning in the processes of evolution or rectification. Remember that the most highly developed organisms of our planetary home proceeded initially from the amoeba. Therefore, to recommence means a 'recapitulation' or a 'return to the beginning'. That is why, in its embryonic development, the future body of a person cannot be any different from the formation of a reptile or bird. What makes the differentiation of the form is its evolutionary state, contained in the perispiritual mold of the being that takes up the fluids of the flesh. Thus, upon returning to the denser sphere, as in Segismundo's case, it is indispensable that the physical body 'recapitulate' all the experiences it has lived during the long history of our evolution, even if only for a few hours or days, quickly repeating the phases it has passed through or the lessons it has learned, and stopping at the point from where it needs to continue the learning process. Soon after the microscopic form of the amoeba in Segismundo's fetal process, the signs of the aquatic era of our evolution will appear, and likewise all the periods of transition or the stages of progress that the creature has already crossed on its incessant journey toward perfection, a journey in which we now find ourselves in the condition of humankind."

It was now very late.

Sensing that Alexandre would not be staying much longer, I once more focused on the fetal formation. The fertilized egg was animated by profound life as it evolved into the germinal vesicle.

The friendly instructor invited me to leave and said:

"My work is finished. However, Andre, considering your need for more experience, I can ask the Constructors to accept your fraternal cooperation in the work of oversight whenever you have the chance to come here."

Delighted, I rejoiced. In fact, I wished for nothing else. The study of embryology under a new paradigm was marvelous and fascinating.

As my inner joy increased, Alexandre made arrangements with the others concerning my concurrent assistance and learning prospects.

A few moments later, as we were exchanging goodbyes, Herculano very kindly and warmly stated that he would be waiting for me whenever I was able to return to Adelino's house to take part in the work of oversight.

14
Watch-Care

The following day, after I had rested from my daily activities and regular tasks, I eagerly returned to Raquel's home.

It was late at night, and I found Segismundo's faithful friend and the Constructor Spirits there, working in the affectionate intimacy that characterizes the meetings of higher spirits.

Apuleio, who was in charge, greeted me politely.

Unlike yesterday, Adelino's wife was not feeling well physically. Although her body was resting, she was overexcited, fidgety:

"Our sister Raquel is beginning to feel the process of adaptation," explained the director. "For now, and for a few more days, she will be indisposed; however, it will be brief."

"She won't be able to sleep?" I asked.

"Later," he replied, "but for now her sleep will be reduced until the blastodermic layers are formed. It is the initial formation effort of the fetus and we cannot dispense with any active cooperation."

Extremely interested, I observed the extraordinary cellular activity in the development of the structure of the new body taking shape, and I noticed the care the spirits were using to ensure that the embryonic disc was sculptured with due precision.

"Organic engineering," said the head of the task good naturedly, "requires perfect foundations. The corporeal body is a delicate and complex building. It is necessary to care for its foundations with serenity and knowledge."

I realized that the cellular segmentation and adjustment of the dividing cells to the mold of the reduced perispiritual body was straightforwardly mechanical, obeying the natural dispositions of the organic field, while the entire microscopic entity of the development of the cellular structure received the magnetic input of the generous spirits, leaving me to conclude that every daughter cell was being appropriately prepared to sustain the task of initiating the future physical apparatus.

Perhaps because he wanted to justify the care being taken, Apuleio kindly explained to me:

"The mission of constructing the fetal mechanism is a great responsibility. We must remove obstacles and assist the unicellular organism of the embryo inside the maternal womb so that the reincarnation, sometimes planned and arranged with such difficulty, does not fail at the start because of a lack of collaboration from our realm, where the commitments have been made."

I listened attentively to his experienced and wise words in order to take advantage of all their educational content.

"That is why," he continued, "miscarriage is only very rarely due to causes from our sphere of action. As a general rule, it originates from the unexpected refusal of the parents to honor their sacred commitments, or from the excesses of frivolousness and criminal thoughtlessness of mothers who are not well prepared for the responsibility and comprehension of this divine ministry. However, even then, when we encounter less noble maternal vessels, we do everything we can to oppose their plans for escaping their duty, when such escape represents a mere whim of irresponsibility without any basis on spiritually constructive plans. Of course, our interference in the matter when struggling with our reincarnated friends who have temporarily forgotten their commitments also has its limits. If the interested parties reneging on their spiritual decisions systematically persevere against us, we are compelled to leave them on their own. That is why there are many human couples without children: they have annulled their generative faculties. If they have not proceeded like this in their present life in their thirst for selfish satisfactions, they did so in the past, causing serious anomalies in their psychic organization. In the latter instance, they experience sorrowful periods of loneliness and thirst for affection until they commendably rebuild the reverence we all owe to God's laws."

The head Constructor's explanations were clearing my mind regarding the serious problems of human struggles.

Interested in learning by taking part, I sought to adopt the position of a worker, looking for a job that I could help out with in the area of magnetic assistance to the cellular organization.

Before leaving, I approached the director in order to gather some information.

I had been impressed by certain details of the work conducted the previous night. Through what process was it possible to situate in Raquel's generative organs the initial connection of Segismundo to his future body? And what about the problem of the most apt male element? Did persons of the status of an Alexandre work on making such choices in every case of fertilization?

Apuleio listened to me with the benevolence that characterizes high order spirits and said:

"Passivity does not mean absence of cooperation. When Raquel accepted the task of motherhood, she did so with determination and constructive obedience. She received Segismundo into her perispiritual organism, and mobilizing the natural powers of her mind, she placed the living mold in the uterine area. She did so with the same spontaneity of other organic processes, supervised by the subconscious mechanical activity, whose automatism translates the multi-millenary experiences acquired by the reincarnated soul. For women the adaptation of creative energies is as easy as the patriarchal and protective attitude is natural for men while the paternal links persist."

Aware of my intent to take advantage of this information in order to use it in my plan to write to incarnate readers, Apuleio stressed:

"It would be very difficult for us to explain to people the phenomenon of the adaptation of creative energies in the maternal womb in the reincarnation process. For the time being, the tendency of most of our incarnate brothers and sisters is directed toward the physical aspect of our explanations. We must wait a little longer to give them certain information that would be incomprehensible for them at this time."

And smiling, he continued:

"Using their perispirit's absorption ability, they are nourished every day with thought forms without using their physical mouths, but they cannot yet feel the extent of these phenomena in their daily experiences. At home, in the street, at work and at play, each person receives the mental nourishment brought by those who surround them, seasoned with each one's individual personal magnetism. In the majority of cases, they depend on this nourishment for their inner states of happiness or sorrow, of pleasure or suffering, particularly the immense percentage of incarnates who have not yet managed to control their emotions. As you can see, humans absorb mental matter at all times of the day, setting it in the innermost areas of their own physiological structure."

The head Constructor looked amused at my expression of surprise at receiving such a simple explanation on such a complex subject, and he added:

"When you were dressed in the corporeal fluids during your last experience down on earth, didn't you ever feel a disturbance in your liver after a verbal disagreement? Didn't you ever experience a momentary imbalance in your heart upon receiving bad news? Why the sometime feelings of organic imbalance when the occasion was of satisfaction and happiness? The answer is that during such moments, humans receive a 'certain quantity of mental energies' in their thought field, just like a wire receives a 'positive electrical charge'. The reception point is in fact in the brain, but if the person is not in step with the law of emotional control – which asks us to select the emissions that reach us – he or she will adapt the disturbing energy within him or herself in the organic cells with great harm to the vulnerable areas."

Apuleio, with great serenity, paused briefly and then considered:

"If it is very hard to explain to incarnates such routine incidents, which happen to them repeatedly – dozens of times a day – how can we inform them with precision and detail about the adaptation of the living mold in the womb for the development of the fetus? We need to wait for the passing of time to bring our experiences together."

Heartened by his explanations, I remarked:

"You're right. Even now, despite the fact that I am discarnate, I am not ready to receive certain news without it affecting my emotional field."

"Very good!" said the director with a tone of satisfaction. "That is because you are on the long road to self-control. Only after you have gained self-control will you know how to select the energies that come your way, adapting to the innermost areas of your soul only those of comforting or constructive content."

Next, giving me the impression that he wanted to continue the subject, Apuleio continued:

"As for your observations relating to Alexandre's collaboration in the choice of the male element of fertilization, I should point out that we cannot rely on this type of assistance in every case – it all depends on merit. However, when the magnetic factor does not come from cooperation from such a high level, we must remember that it will prevail nevertheless, because we know that the passive realm is also impregnated with energies of attraction. If the male element of fertilization is filled with positive energies, the female egg will be full of receptive energies. But if the egg is magnetized by unbalanced energies, it will of course exert a special attraction on the element that is closest to its intrinsic nature. Therefore, my friend, in all cases of fertilization in the physical world, the male cell that reaches the egg first in order to fertilize it is not the most capable in the sense of 'superiority', but rather in the sense of 'magnetic attunement'. This is the law, which surprises geneticists many times when they observe unexpected changes in the structures of various types within the same species. Cells also have their somewhat independent 'individual magnetism' in the field of life-related manifestations."

The director smiled and continued:

"If a woman can exert her decisive influence in choosing a partner, most of the time the female cell can likewise exert its influence in choosing the element that will fertilize it. Of course, we are alluding here to questions of physical science, without referring to spirit-related problems such as necessary tasks, missions or trials."

Noticing my unspoken questioning stance, the director observed:

"Yes, because depending on the duties established for certain reincarnated spirits, the authorities from our realm have sufficient power to intervene in biogenetic laws – within certain limits – adjusting the arrangements for specific objectives."

At this moment our conversation was interrupted.

A small group of spirit friends were requesting Apuleio's presence outside the bedroom.

Very kindly, the head of the task invited me to accompany him.

The group introduced itself quickly. It was composed of two discarnate female friends of Raquel, and a friend of Segismundo, all three wishing to offer them their affection and dedication in the process taking place. They had come from our spirit colony to assist relatives who were still incarnate, and they were hoping to use this opportunity for a loving visit.

The director listened to them attentively and in good spirits, but to my great surprise he said:

"We thank you very much for your attention; however, due to our responsibility for the primordial organization of our brother Segismundo's new body, we cannot authorize a visit at this time. We are taking advantage of the limited time of relative harmony the maternal mind is granting us for delicate work of more urgent cellular magnetization."

And smiling affably, he added:

"However, after the twenty-first day, when the embryo has reached its basic configuration, our friends can be visited at any time, since by then both mother and son will be able to leave their bodies easily. For the time being, our friend Segismundo cannot leave, and our sister Raquel, even in the state of physical sleep, needs to remain close to us."

"But of course!" replied the gentleman from our plane. "We have no wish to disturb the development underway."

"We know that Raquel would be very touched by our personal embrace," commented one of the ladies. "As it is, unexpected happiness can also be a shock."

"And that is what we must avoid," replied Apuleio, satisfied. "Nevertheless, I would like to inform you that Segismundo needs spiritual support from all of us. We have been instructed to notify all his friends about his present reincarnation so that they may come here whenever possible, not only to benefit him with spiritual encouragement, but also to collaborate with their vibrations of sympathy in the harmonious organization of the fetus."

"We will be back as soon as we can," exclaimed the third visitor, who until then had remained silent. "We need to cooperate for Raquel's benefit."

And smiling, she added:

"We have a series of spiritual excursions scheduled for the next few nights. We will do all we can to offer her soul trust and happiness. Several friends are on notice about it."

"Very good!" replied the director kindly.

Soon thereafter, the visitors said goodbye, while I registered yet another precious lesson from the spirit plane.

Alone once again, Apuleio kindly explained to me:

"The moment is delicate and we cannot be distracted."

And thereafter, each night I entered the room where the work of reincarnation was taking place, learning and cooperating for a better understanding of the generosity of the Spirit Benefactors and God's Wisdom manifested in all things.

With the Constructors' magnetic cooperation applied to each cell after the germinal vesicle had taken form, the three blastodermic layers were formed using the mold that Raquel had mentally created for her future child. This mold was then applied over Segismundo's living model in process of reincarnation.

I noticed that the work of the spirit technicians was in every way similar to the work I had witnessed in the session of materialization of discarnate spirits. The technicians were working on behalf of Segismundo; they relied on help from Raquel who, in this case, functioned as the "medium" of life while they mobilized friends, utilized magnetic resources and required direct and positive help from Adelino, Segismundo's future father, just as in a mediumistic session the assistance of the instructor would be required over the passive forces of the medium. The simile was complete, the only difference being that, in the work of materialization of discarnate spirits, a few hours were spent in preparation for an incomplete and transitory resurgence, while in this case nine consecutive months would be needed for a tangible reincarnation of a soul in a more or less long and definitive manner.

As the days went by, Segismundo's new body was formed, cell by cell, in keeping with a simple and intelligent plan.

Continuing my methodical observations, I noticed that, in accordance with the specifications of the living mold, the lower blastodermic layer of cells was rolling itself into the beginnings of the intestinal tube, while the upper layer took on the same rolling impulse to form the epidermal and neural tubes. The middle layer was assuming a very special form to give way to the first outlines of the spinal cord, the muscles and blood vessels.

In certain areas, the intestinal tube began to dilate, giving origin to the stomach and the various kinds of loops, and, immediately afterward, displaying certain movements of external and internal invagination, it gradually organized the inferior and superior layers, consisting of folds, villi and glands.

The cutaneous tube began the complicated task of structuring the skin, while the neural tube gradually folded upon itself, preparing the encephalic area. Meanwhile, the substances of the middle layer changed in a surprising way. Day by day, the lessons I received were more and more beautiful as I observed the marvelous arrangements by which the axial cord is segmented in to vertebrae that embrace the neural tube in its upper part and the intestinal tube in the lower part.

The work of the Constructor Spirits, together with Herculano's dedication, continued to reveal new lessons.

It would be impossible to describe the caring details involved in the construction of Segismundo's new corporeal dwelling. They were working with unsurpassable devotion, developing a large system to guarantee the cellular organizations. Sometimes, during the first stages of the formation of the most important organs, they stopped to pray, pleading for Jesus' blessings for the work at hand, and I noticed that, whenever that happened, sparkling lights came down from above pouring over the bedroom, encouraging their actions.

The work was taking on the characteristics of a truly divine revelation. To focus on its particularities, it would be necessary to forgo the instructional purpose of our simple observations and move into the technical field per se, a descriptive effort that has already been the object of long considerations by experts on the subject, serving researchers with information of a purely material order at the intellectual level.

The first fertilized cell had become a true world of active and wise organization. The embryo had developed noticeably.

The forepart of the intestinal tube had given origin to the esophagus, while the intestine, with its complex arrangements, had become situated in the posterior region; internally, it had been perfectly pleated, indicating that, in the interior area, folds and villi had formed, while projections had begun forming externally, gradually turning into various glands.

The formation of several brain areas, the preparation of the sweat glands and sebaceous glands, autonomous organs, blood vessels, muscles and bones continued swiftly.

On the twentieth day, Apuleio seemed to be very satisfied. He told me that the basic work was ready. Some of the assistants could now leave. To continue the task, only the two who were associated with Herculano's continuous effort would be necessary.

On that day, Segismundo's future physical form, accommodated in the amniotic fluid, gave me the perfect impression of a fish. Not even the gill slits were missing, as they were revealed in the fetus with absolute precision, telling us about the work of recapitulation now in course and of the recollections of ancient times in our passage through marine currents.

On the night of the twenty-first day, the magnetic door to Raquel's bedroom was opened to visitation by loved ones.

Many were the spirit friends who had been waiting for the happy moment.

Detached from her body by the sweet influence of sleep, the future mother was feeling relieved and almost happy.

Apuleio and his companions, as well as Herculano, were greeted with joy and emotion.

Some of Adelino's friends had arrived, also wanting to congratulate him and offer any assistance possible.

I noticed that Segismundo too was relieved. The very delicate threads that link incarnates to their physical bodies when they are temporarily freed were also holding him to the fetal organization. As Raquel moved around, he could too, but it was not possible for him to leave his mother's company. Raquel held him in her loving arms while she smiled with us outside the field of denser matter.

I realized that everyone was taking a break except for Herculano, who did not leave the bedroom as he stood close watch. The Constructors in general were taking a long break from their work, and while Adelino's friends were taking him to other planes in search of certain information that was necessary for him, I accompanied the group that formed, together with Raquel and her child, a gathering of hope and happiness. Several loved ones took them both to a large garden located on the earth itself, and at the moment that the sun distantly announced its reappearance in the hemisphere, we prayed together, praising God's goodness that had filled our evolutionary pathway with blessings.

Immediately afterward, I noticed that many of the discarnate friends present at the gathering were formulating comforting tonics and balms from the emanations of plants and flowers, pouring them over Raquel and her baby son to strengthen them for the trials ahead. It was lovely to witness their fraternal care in those demonstrations of devotion and tenderness. Enthralled, I learned yet another lesson in the spirit realm. Just as migrant birds that know how to search far and wide for soft nest feathers and precious food for their offspring, the souls of devoted and loving mothers know how to cross great distances in search of loving elements for the formation of the nest of flesh into which a beloved child must be reborn.

The fetal organization work continued normally in light of the honorable habits of the couple, who, day by day, seemed more integrated with the assistance from our sphere of action.

The development of Segismundo's future form compelled Raquel to make true organic sacrifices; however, each night, around dawn, their loved ones on our plane continued to take both of them on repeated spirit excursions. Herculano's work merited the assistance of many friends. Rare was the night in which spirits who were thankful to Segismundo did not come to watch over the harmony of his new reincarnation, offering him, his home and his parents various types of help.

With the period of my basic observations ending, I too did not return to Adelino's home with the same frequency. Despite my continued interest in the work in progress, I returned only from time to time, when accompanying Alexandre on other types of service.

However, on the evening before the birth of Segismundo's new physical form, I went there, together with my venerable instructor, who wished to be present and provide assistance to the mother at the culminating moment.

After prolonged efforts, in which I could see once more a mother-spouse's sublime elevation, Segismundo was reborn...

Surprised by the vigorous spiritual assistance that our plane devoted to the matter, I heard Alexandre say movingly:

"The initial work of reincarnation is ready. The full work, with the complete integration of our friend into the physical elements, will only take place in seven years time!"

Surprised and touched in my innermost fibers, I took part in the prayers of thanksgiving that were being offered to the Lord, recognizing the divine treasure that was the blessing of a body of flesh for our experience and learning on the earth.

15
Failure

Considering how much I had learned from Segismundo's case, the always-kind Alexandre told the Constructors' director as he said goodbye:

"Apuleio, thank you for all you have done for Andre over the past several days. Our friend will never forget your kind assistance."

The director smiled, gave me some words of encouragement, and as he was about to leave for good, my instructor remarked:

"Nevertheless, he still needs to consolidate the knowledge he has acquired. Andre has followed a normal case of reincarnation, in which a decent husband yielded from the start to our pleas so that Segismundo could be reborn with the necessary serenity. He saw a sensitive and devoted maternal heart up close, and during his study of the case he was in a conjugal bedroom protected by the sacred power of prayer and comforted by watch-care from the higher realms. So, it would be good for him to observe a different process, the kind that occurs by the hundreds everywhere, and in which we are confronted by all types of obstacles. In that way he would be able to understand the extent and complexity of our efforts to defend the improvident who despise moral responsibility by fleeing their commitments."

And in a gesture of fraternal affection he asked:

"Would you happen to have a case like that presently, where Andre could learn valuable lessons?"

"Yes, we do," Apuleio responded kindly. "The Volpini case."

Since Alexandre was not familiar with the case, he continued:

"Soon after organizing the groundwork for Segismundo, I took on other cases of the same nature. One of them involved our being entrusted with the task of overseeing brother Volpini. You can be sure that we offered him all the assistance we could in order to keep the work from failing; however, judging from my experience, the case is completely unworkable."

"So, you are saying," replied my instructor knowingly, "that the future mother has not lived up to the expectations of our plane..."

"I'm afraid not," continued Apuleio. "When problems arise from the father's side or when they proceed simply from the influence of malevolent spirits, there are resources available to us. However, if the disharmony comes from the mother, it is very difficult to establish effective oversight. The poor woman has already unwittingly caused two miscarriages due to her recklessness, and now it looks like she will be the victim of her own thoughtlessness for a third time. We have offered all the help we can, but to no avail. Seized by the idea of getting only pleasure out of life, the unfortunate sister has fallen in with discarnate spirits of the worst type. In order to strengthen their dark plans, they have separated her from her husband in their eagerness to drag her soul down into the sphere of the lower emotions."

While Alexandre listened silently, Apuleio continued after a long pause:

"Volpini has now reached the seventh month of gestation in his new physical form, but tomorrow night will be decisive for him. I have already received a plea from our coworkers, who have been doing all they can to try and prevent certain extravagances that the future mother has planned for tonight. However, I don't think she will listen to us. The fetus' composition is not in a state to withstand any more instability, and if the poor woman does not wake up to her duty, she will initiate her third failure tonight. We would be very glad if Andre could come with us."

Alexandre seemed to be very circumspect at that moment, and as if he did not wish to make any unconstructive remarks, he considered:

"Our friend will go with you. Sometimes, in order to preserve our health appropriately, we must know about various illnesses; to cultivate the good, we must not ignore the existence of evil."

That evening Apuleio, two of his companions and I arrived at a comfortable and distinguished residence.

The large clock on the wall indicated 7:55 p.m.

We followed the director into a well-furnished room, where three dreadful looking discarnate spirits were present. Due to their low vibratory level, they did not notice us. They were chatting, plotting schemes that we would rather not mention here. At a certain point in the conversation, however, they openly discussed the reincarnation at issue:

"I don't know," said one of those perverse enemies of goodness, "by what infernal art the intruder is so resistant. We must get rid of him as soon as possible."

"When this happens," said another, "it is because there are 'angel hands' working behind the scenes.

"Well, they can go to hell!" exclaimed the other, who looked the crueler. "We shall see who is the strongest. Cesarina is already ninety percent ours. She suits our purposes perfectly. Why should a child mess up our plans? We must fight this to the end."

"But," considered the third, who had been silent until then, "we've been trying in vain to get rid of him for over six months now!"

"Well, we've accomplished a lot," replied the most rebellious. "I don't think he can resist much longer. We might be able to finish this up tonight. A child would rob us of a dependable partner. She would focus all her attention on him and that would be an enormous loss to us. Even if there are 'angel hands' at work, our 'demon hands' are at work as well. We have already won twice; why wouldn't we win again this time?"

"And if the child comes," one of them said, "the husband will come back. We couldn't stave him off any longer if that happened."

"It never shall!" replied the most ferocious adversary in a sinister voice.

How different that scene was in comparison with Raquel's bedroom, where I had made such beautiful observations regarding the reincarnational endeavor! The room was completely devoid of magnetic defenses, and the visits by spirits from the higher spheres that had characterized the formation of Segismundo's new body were noticeably absent.

"See?" asked Apuleio kindly. "Our task is not always carried out in gardens of love. Many times we have to work in true tempests of hatred that disintegrate the elements of our best magnetic cooperation. This is a typical case."

I remembered that Adelino's home had been filled every day by loved ones from the spirit realm, and I asked:

"But doesn't the future mother have relatives in our sphere to help her?"

"Whatever the case may be," he replied, "there are always good friends in zones above the one we are in, but under certain circumstances we willingly distance ourselves from them. Cesarina has many such friendships that she could rely on; however, she herself holds them at bay."

Impressed, I speculated:

"Even so, doesn't she have a father or a mother in our circles who could take on the sacrifice of defending her?"

"She has a father who loves her with all his heart," explained the director, "but he was suffering so undeservedly because of his thoughtless and callous daughter that his superiors in our spirit colony had to submit him to a treatment to temporarily forget his dear daughter until he can remember to approach her without such emotional anguish."

This subject was new to me. So, there were ways for applying forgetfulness in the world of souls?

Apuleio smiled kindly and said:

"Have no doubt about it. In our sphere, hardness and ungratefulness cannot threaten pure love. When reincarnated souls are resistant to appreciation and understanding, we naturally distance ourselves from them – even if they are precious jewels to our hearts – until they integrate themselves into the knowledge of God's laws and are willing to follow them with us. However, even though we may be very loving, we might be weak and feel that we do not have the courage to be apart from them. In that case, if we are deserving of the help of our Superiors, we may be blessed with a magnetic treatment that causes temporary forgetfulness."

Just then, Cesarina entered the room, followed by the Constructor spirits who were caring for Volpini, the reincarnating spirit.

As the woman sat in front of a large mirror, putting on elaborate makeup for a party, Apuleio's coworkers approached and greeted us kindly.

"Unfortunately," said one of them to Apuleio, "the situation is very serious. We cannot continue our efforts of assistance in the hope of success. Our sister is sinking more and more into destructive instability. Having willingly joined up with these unhappy adversaries," and he nodded toward the degrading spirits who surrounded her, "she is now indulging in pleasures and abuses of all types. Her sexual deviances over the last few days have been lamentable, and she has systematically ingested a large quantity of alcoholic beverages, believing them to be harmless. Adding them to the disorderly vibrations of her mental field, we have realized that Volpini's situation is unsustainable despite our best efforts."

Apuleio listened to the serious news in silence and then remarked:

"I already know about her plans for tonight."

"Yes," the other said, "we have appealed to your authority because the fetus will not be able to resist another attack."

The director invited me to examine the pregnant woman. Next to her were the low order spirits referred to earlier. They continued to show they were completely unaware of our presence.

With the excessive care of women extremely vain and impervious to moral responsibility, Cesarina used certain ploys to hide her advanced pregnancy. This led us to believe that she was preparing for a very exciting night out.

With the help of the head Constructor, I focused my attention on the fetus and could not hide my surprise and compassion.

Volpini's case was very different from the reincarnation process that I had witnessed in Raquel's home. The embryo's physical form displayed purple blotches revealing dilacerations. Tiny "monsters" visible only to our eyes were swimming around in the amniotic fluid, invading the umbilical cord and appropriating most of the delicate nutrition reserved for the growing body. The whole placenta had been invaded by them, giving me a terrible feeling.

Due to the intense abnormality of the woman's generative organs, I realized that a miscarriage was not far off.

Apuleio addressed me with an expressive gesture of his head, indicating that he too was very worried.

He suddenly stopped his examination and said to us:

"If this poor woman, obsessed as she is with criminal pleasures, does not restrain herself tonight, the fetus will be expelled by tomorrow."

After thinking for a few moments, he emphasized:

"I will try one last resource."

Apuleio went to another part of the house and returned with an elderly woman.

Nodding toward the woman he said, "This is the owner of the house. She is an old friend of Cesarina and is susceptible to our influence. I will use her help so that in the future our unfortunate sister will not be able to claim that no one had warned her."

In a gesture of kindness that I had already observed in many other high order spirits from our plane, he put his right hand on the new arrival's forehead as she approached Cesarina very lovingly and said:

"My friend, I'm afraid for you ... Please don't go. Beware of unworthy friendships. You are in a delicate condition, Cesarina. Why commit these excesses? A birthday party at a bar can't be good for your present needs. I took you into my home as if you were my daughter and I must look out for you. I'm hopeful that you might get together again with your husband, who I think is only absent due to a simple matter of incompatible personalities; but if you don't defend yourself from evil, how are you going to deal with the situation?"

One of the unfortunate beings of ignorance and darkness, who was persecuting Cesarina due to her carelessness, embraced her as if he wished to transmit his strange and dangerous magnetism to her. I saw that the other low order spirits were carefully observing the older woman and were listening to her sensible words, because they were all making gestures of disgust and displeasure that would be inappropriate to mention.

Allowing herself to be enveloped by the neutralizing influence of evil, Cesarina laughed out loud and added:

"Don't worry, my dear Francisca. You don't need to lecture me about virtue ... I have a commitment tonight and I can't skip it!"

"I don't agree, Cesarina," the woman urgently replied under Apuleio's direct inspiration, "nor am I preaching virtue to your responsible conscience. I want to awaken your inner fibers as a wife and mother. The man whose invitation you intend to accept can't be trusted; he is unworthy of your consideration. Furthermore, your body must be protected. Aren't you worried about damaging your child? Haven't you thought about the future?"

The respectable friend continued to warn her with mother-like sternness, while Volpini's future mother remained in an obviously negative and resistant state.

The conversation went on for two hours, during which Apuleio used high doses of charity, logic and patience; however, at the end of that time, a car honked outside.

Closing the little box of toiletries, Cesarina hugged her disappointed old friend and said:

"Bye; I'll be back later. Got to run."

The car headed off down the paved avenues.

The disturbed spirits accompanied her in the speedy car, but we remained there, waiting for Apuleio to speak.

Somewhat sad, the head of the effort addressed his coworkers:

"Return to our colony and rest. There is nothing else to be done for now. You performed your duties well."

And looking at me meaningfully, he added:

"I myself will go with Andre to get Volpini and take him to an appropriate place."

The feeling was one of consternation. High order spirits may be well-balanced, but they are not insensitive.

I accompanied Apuleio for several silent minutes until we entered a building filled with deafening noise.

The large hall and reserved areas were full of restless men and women, excited by the loud and dizzying music; but the crowd of low order discarnates was much larger, taken by the same delusion of perilous pleasure.

"Keep up your guard," warned the director. "Not many inexperienced discarnates can enter environments such as this one in order to perform protective work."

It is not our intent to describe the sad scenes before our eyes. Let us just say that we had no difficulty in locating Cesarina, who was in the company of an unscrupulous gentleman. They were both holding fine, elegantly disguised glasses of alcoholic beverages.

Apuleio approached and removed Volpini, who had been embracing Cesarina like a semi-conscious child. Next, I saw him very carefully apply magnetic passes to the entire uterine area. I was holding Volpini, whom he had entrusted to me in order to proceed more effectively. He then took him back and he said calmly:

"I have disconnected the reincarnating spirit from the maternal sanctuary; nevertheless, we cannot forget to administer the necessary help to the reckless mother. She must continue the terrestrial struggle as well as possible in order to acquire some benefits from this opportunity."

We left, taking our prematurely disconnected companion to an aid organization; however, after attending to all the duties entrusted to me, as a physician I wanted to see what was going to happen to the poor woman who had failed in her sublime mission.

In the early hours of the morning, I went to the house we had visited the previous night.

I was very surprised to see that Cesarina was not at home. A few minutes later, a neighbor told the woman to whom Apuleio had applied his influence what I wanted to know.

"This morning, Cesarina was taken to the hospital in a very serious condition," explained the concerned woman.

During the short conversation, I got the information I needed regarding the address, and I hurried to visit the unfortunate creature whom we had left at the elegant party last night.

I was deeply shocked to discover that Cesarina had just given birth to a stillborn child and was in a very serious condition indeed.

16
Incorporation[17]

Whenever my usual tasks allowed me as I pursued my studies on the various types of mediumistic phenomena, I would return to the earth plane to learn and work with the group in which Alexandre had the role of guide.

However, due to my duties in our spirit colony, my ability to do so was not assiduous, and therefore I tried to take advantage of every little opportunity to add to my learning experience.

In one of the meetings I attended, one of the coworkers from our sphere approached the compassionate instructor and humbly stated:

---

[17] "Although used for oral mediumistic spirit communications (called Psychophony), the mainstream term lncorporation, if taken literally, would be misleading - two spirits (the medium's own spirit and the communicating spirit) cannot "inhabit" the same body. The communicating entity connects to the medium's mind and transmits its thoughts and commands, which a disciplined medium can either accept or reject. In certain cases of obsession, spirits can control the subject's body, but it is still a mind-to-mind process, as they cannot expel the incarnate spirit from its body to make it their own. See *The Mediums' Book*, Ch. XXIII. - Tr.

"Our incarnate friends have made several requests for the return of our brother Dionisio Fernandes, who, as you know, is presently residing in an assistance organization. They allege that his family is inconsolable, that it would be useful for him to pay them a visit and that it would be interesting to hear an old colleague of their doctrinal endeavors."

Alexandre listened in silence and the friendly coworker continued after a short pause:

"We would like to be duly authorized to take him there ... He could communicate through our sister Otavia's mediumship so that he could in some way be heard by his friends and family."

The mentor thought for a few moments and replied:

"I have no personal objection, my dear Euclides, in light of your argument; but although our group of incarnate coworkers is made up of excellent people, I don't think they have been prepared appropriately to take full advantage of the experience. What they all have in excess in the area of investigation and reasoning, they lack in sentiment and comprehension. They place experimentation far above understanding, and as you know, mediums are not mechanical filters ... Furthermore, Dionisio has not been in our sphere very long and he has not yet been able to leave the care home that is housing him. Add to those factors the family's lack of serenity, little attunement to a living faith, the vibratory differences of the new plane to which our friend is trying presently to adapt, the deep emotion he will feel at such a reunion – which is perhaps premature – and the natural instability of the medium, and we would probably agree that this is not the right time for such an endeavor."

Defending the circle's urgent request, however, Euclides was not discouraged and insisted:

"I realize that your words are as well measured and kind as ever. I agree that we will not succeed at the desired objective;

nevertheless, I would like to reiterate the plea. Even if what happens does not go beyond being a simple experiment ... it's just that these are hard-working brothers and sisters, to whom we owe much here in the work of daily assisting our suffering wards, and we would be happy to be able to show them our recognition and sincere affection."

Alexandre smiled with his characteristic kindness and remarked:

"It is only reasonable that I endorse your request, and since you insist on the arrangement to please our friends, who also feel deserving of your trust and affection, you can tell them that Dionisio will come. I myself will bring him."

Euclides was immensely happy as he thanked him, and Alexandre ended the conversation by adding:

"You can promise them it will be tomorrow night. It is always easier to give joyfully than to receive prudently."

We left.

Because I had asked him about the process of the phenomenon of incorporation, my kind instructor willingly explained:

"Mediumistically speaking, the measures are the same as those used in cases of common psychography, except that we must take special care to protect the language center in the motor zone by making our magnetic assistance reflect over all the speech muscles located in the mouth, throat, larynx, chest area and abdomen."

In reply to my many questions, the instructor offered several explanations of a moral nature on the subject, commenting on the problems involved in spreading the benefits of true consolation among terrestrial hearts that are preoccupied with the unreasonable demands of intellectual research. I was admiring his profound wisdom and sublime understanding of human weaknesses, when we arrived at the aid institution to which Dionisio had been taken. It was located in the lower zones not very far from the planet's surface.

Having spoken to the good spirits who are dedicated to services of Christian love in such zones, he led me to the newly-discarnate, who seemed to be feeling very agitated.

"Dionisio," Alexandre said kindly after the usual greetings, "do you remember our spiritualist study group?"

"Of course! And how I miss it!" sighed Dionisio.

"Our friends in the group are asking for your presence, at least for a few minutes," continued the mentor kindly, "and I have decided to take you there so that you can speak not only to them but also to your family."

"What a blessing!" exclaimed Dionisio, almost in tears of joy.

"But listen, my friend!" replied Alexandre serenely and compellingly. "It's essential that you spend some time thinking about the event. Remember that you will be using a neuro-muscular apparatus that does not belong to you. Our friend Otavia will act as your intermediary. However, in view of the demands of our incarnate brothers and sisters, you must be well aware of the difficulties faced by a medium in order to satisfy the technical particularities involved in the identification of communicating spirits. Do you understand?"

"Yes," replied Dionisio, somewhat disgruntled. "I'm now in the world of the truth and I must honor it. I remember that I was often apprehensive at receiving communications from the invisible plane through Otavia. I often hesitated, believing she was the victim of countless deceits."

Alexandre remarked very calmly:

"Well now, it's your turn to try it out. And if in the past it was so easy for you to doubt others, please excuse the weakness of our incarnate brothers and sisters in case they doubt you in turn. It is possible that we might not be able to achieve our purposes;

even so, our coworkers are insisting on your visit and we should not stand in the way."

Before Dionisio could deliberate further, Alexandre finished:

"Concentrate very carefully on the subject; ask for the divine light in your prayers and wait for me. I will take you to the medium's house a few hours prior to the meeting so you can more easily harmonize with her."

We then said goodbye amid Dionisio's profuse gratitude.

I was very interested in the case and asked Alexandre for permission to follow him closely.

The next day I was authorized to follow the instructor to the institution where Dionisio was being looked after. Alexandre provided him the appropriate help for the planned visit.

With his usual kindness, Alexandre led us to the home of Otavia, the medium. Euclides, the benevolent friend from the previous day, was courteously waiting there for us.

The esteemed mentor bid farewell with great affability, and leaving me in the company of our new colleagues, he added:

"The meeting of our incarnate friends will begin at 8:00 p.m., but I'll be back between 6:00 and 7:00 to go with you to the center."

And looking at me, he kindly concluded:

"Take advantage of your time with Euclides, my dear Andre. A good worker always has profitable lessons to offer."

Smiling and touched, Euclides thanked him and led us into the house, while Alexandre went in the opposite direction.

We stopped inside a modest room.

"Our sister Otavia usually meditates and prays in this part of the house," explained the friendly guide. "That is why the atmosphere here is comforting, light and soothing. Make yourselves comfortable. Since today is one of the days she dedicates to mediumistic work, she will finish preparing the afternoon meal earlier than usual in order to pray and get ready."

I looked at the large clock on the wall. It was precisely 4:00 p.m. and I expressed my wish to see the sister who would act as an intermediary between the two planes that night.

Leaving Dionisio there, Euclides took me to the small kitchen where an elderly woman was carefully preparing some simple dishes. Everything was clean, in order and in domestic harmony. However, I saw that she was a bit pale and sad.

Noticing my subtle observation, my companion told me:

"Otavia is an excellent collaborator in our spiritual work, but due to the trials needed for her redemption, she is married to an ignorant, almost cruel man. While her brutal partner is absent during 'bread-winning' hours, the house is peaceful and happy because our friend does not offer lodging to troubling spirits from the darkness. However, when the unhappy Leonardo enters this little domain, the situation changes because the poor husband is truly a "thorn bush" in the garden of his home. He is accompanied by dangerous elements from the lower zones."

"Wasn't he able to join his wife on her spiritualizing mission?" I asked with interest.

"Not at all," explained Euclides without hesitation. "He is not new to higher understanding but he is stubborn in his errors. He allows his wife to help us because of the insistence of his family members. They are dedicated to our cause, and under our influence, they don't let him stop her. However, the task is not an easy one, because, whereas Otavia obeys the spirits of the good, the husband is obedient to the cultivators of evil. Sometimes it is enough merely to draw up a constructive plan with her help in order for Leonardo to yield to the bringers of darkness and disturb our action, thereby creating serious problems for us."

Noticing that I was aware of the medium's distress, Euclides added:

"Yesterday, I wanted to lift our incarnate friends' spirits, the ones who rely on our sister's mediumistic assistance. But as soon as I joyfully promised them that Dionisio would indeed be coming, the psychic situation of her thoughtless husband got much worse. Leonardo woke up more agitated than usual today, got drunk just before lunchtime, insulted his humble wife and even got physically abusive. The kind woman was so frightened that she suffered a nervous jolt that affected her liver, and at the moment she is undergoing a strong gastrointestinal disturbance. Her nourishment has been deficient throughout the day and she has not been able to maintain the necessary mental harmony to precisely fulfill our aims. I have already brought several resources to help her, including the magnetic help of competent spirit nurses who tried to raise the level of her energies to the necessary level. That is the only reason why the poor woman has not ended up in bed, although she is feeling quite weak despite all the help."

Somewhat downcast, Euclides considered after a short silence:

"As you know, harmony is not something that can be achieved suddenly, and if we discarnates devoted to the good are constantly struggling for our inner enlightenment, mediums, as human creatures, are susceptible to the vicissitudes and imbalances of the physical realm."

"Oh!" I exclaimed, looking at the poor woman. "Isn't there anybody who could replace her? She's about ready to collapse."

"All such work requires preparation and training," Euclides remarked wisely, "and there is no one who could cover for Otavia on the spur of the moment."

"Don't you think she should be in better spirits in order to be more useful?" I asked.

"Who knows?" replied Euclides attentively. "Active missionary mediumship is not incompatible with well-being, and technically speaking, all people who enjoy relative material comfort could seek excellent opportunities of service in their fields of work and edification. However, when favored by the natural tranquility of their physical existence, incarnate souls remain in the area of service that is proper to their individual needs; and since the precise fulfillment of their duty already represents a great effort, they rarely go beyond the boundary of their duties in search of the divine field of self-denial. Nevertheless, intensive struggles increase inner aspirations. When accepted under the light of living faith, suffering is a creative source of spiritual wings."

At this point of his fraternal explanation, my companion smiled and remarked:

"Having said that, I do not mean constructive mediumship must be an appanage of hearts shackled to pain. No. Missions of Higher Spirituality belong to all individuals of goodwill. I have only expressed my conviction that there are souls who are fervent in the ideal of the Good and the Truth, and who make use of obstacles in order to better ascend the mount of divine redemption."

The woman had finished the task of preparing the simple dinner, and before her husband returned home she went to the private room, where, as Euclides had noted, she was used to saying her preparatory prayers.

We entered the room in her company.

Euclides helped settle Dionisio beside her, and while the medium was concentrating in prayer, the dedicated friend applied magnetic passes to her, fortifying the nerves of her viscera and giving her what I perceived to be strong doses of energy, not only to the neural fibers but also to the neuroglia.

Otavia was asking Jesus for enough energy to fulfill her task, and we were moved by her silent, simple and sincere plea. She meditated on the promise that her spirit friends had made the previous evening regarding a communication from Dionisio, who had recently discarnated. By isolating her mind from problems of a material nature, she was trying to put herself in a state to make an effective mediumistic contribution. Little by little under Euclides' influence, a fluidic cord formed, linking the medium to the communicating spirit. Euclides suggested to our discarnate friend that he speak to Otavia with all his mental energies in order to set up a favorable environment for the evening's work.

Dionisio began speaking to her about his needs as a spirit, remarking that he hoped his presence would be felt by his earth family and his old colleagues from his spiritualist studies. I noticed that the medium was registering his presence and language in the form of seemingly imaginary imagery and memory in her field of thought. I observed with interest the width of the vibratory border that separates us from incarnate spirits, because, even though Otavia's mediumistic abilities were well-developed, we still had to begin the work of communication as if we were very far away, slowly overcoming the thick circles of resistance.

The unique dialogue lasted for some time, and at the end of the interesting preliminary conversation between the medium and the communicating spirit, and realizing it had been amply guided by Euclides' fraternal touch in every detail, Otavia seemed to be more in touch with the subject. She was clearly going along with what Dionisio intended to do.

Everything was going well. I was still admiring that unexpected work of mediumistic preparation, when something very serious happened. The man of the house arrived, violently breaking the tranquility of the vibrations in which we were immersed. Shouting from the moment he entered, he forced his wife to get up abruptly. The unfortunate man seemed like a brute in his display of domestic tyranny. A number of thoughtless, wicked spirits made up his entourage.

Otavia served him dinner, performing a miracle of gospel patience.

After the husband and their two older children had enjoyed the simple meal, the noble woman said to her husband privately:

"Leonardo, as you know, I'll be going to my meeting tonight. I'll be leaving just before eight."

"What?" exclaimed her husband, full of wine and stroking his graying moustache. "You won't be going out tonight! There'll be no session! Not tonight!"

Struck by his tempestuous attitude, I asked Euclides, who was following the events very calmly:

"What now?"

"I had already foreseen this," he replied with obvious sadness in his eyes, "and I asked one of our sisters to bring one of boisterous Leonardo's aunts, who will intercede on behalf of our wishes. They shouldn't be long in coming. He'll give in to her without a fight."

Indeed, as Otavia was drying her tears in silence while clearing the dinner table, there was a knock at the door.

Leonardo went to see who it was, and a sweet discarnate spirit entered the house accompanied by an elderly woman with a welcoming and smiling face.

Euclides' coworker approached us and greeted us with a smile. Deeply surprised that there was so much work involved in organizing this small act of consolation, I paid close attention to the conversation that ensued between the incarnates:

"Thank goodness today's struggle is over," said the respectable woman to the medium after the initial greetings. "I've come so you and I can go to the meeting together."

Otavia tried to hide her anguish and made an effort to smile, replying:

"I'm sorry, my good Georgina, I can't go tonight ... Leonardo isn't feeling very well and he wants to go to bed early."

"I know, I know," remarked the visitor with kindness in her words and sternness in her attitude while gazing at the man of the house. "Otavia, you have a commitment you can't skip out on!"

Then she went over and touched the shoulders of her nephew, who was spread out on the sofa, and said to him frankly:

"My son, if you wish to indulge in pleasures and postpone your spiritual advancement through improvidence and ill-will, I cannot stop you. But I must warn you regarding your wife's duties at our Spiritist center of enlightenment, asking that you not put yourself between her and higher determinations. Otavia is an exemplary wife. She has tolerated your insolence her whole life and has made you the father of two grown children, who have been strictly educated in mind and heart. Don't keep her from fulfilling her divine service now. I could go against you and convince her to resist, but I prefer to warn you that your actions against the good will not go unpunished."

I noticed that the venerable woman's words were uttered with strong emissions of magnetic energy, which enveloped Leonardo and forced him to better reasoning. He thought for a few moments, then gave in:

"Otavia can go whenever she wants as long as she goes with you."

The elderly lady thanked him, encouraging him to study the issues of spirituality. When the two women were ready to set out for the study group, Alexandre returned in order to accompany us.

I realized that the instructor had noted at a glance the medium's state of weakness. He perceived the difficulties that would be opposing Dionisio's promised communication, but rather than referring to the warnings of the previous evening, he was the one now showing more optimism, and I noticed that he was stimulating Euclides' enthusiasm for the service of the good.

We reached the large room of the Spiritist center at precisely 7:45 p.m.

As usual, the workers from our plane were numerous, tending to the many tasks of assistance, preparation and vigilance. While a number of eager friends and the communicating spirit's wife and children were waiting for Dionisio to speak, we made an effort to improve Otavia's receptive state.

As on other occasions, Alexandre was taking great care to give an example of sound cooperation. He asked that some of our coworkers work on Otavia's endocrine system, and that they provide her liver with better resources for the immediate normalization of its functions, establishing a certain equilibrium in the stomach and intestines because of the needs of the moment so that the mediumistic apparatus could function with the most harmony possible.

Once the small assembly of incarnate brothers and sisters had gathered, the service began at 8:00 p.m. with a touching prayer from the brother who directed the center.

Making use of the magnetic help that she had been offered, the medium was feeling quite a bit stronger.

Once again, I observed with wonder the luminous phenomenon of the pineal gland as I followed Alexandre's essential work in the mediumistic preparation technique. I noticed that, in this particular case, the tireless instructor was focusing on the cells of the cerebral cortex, the elements of the language center and the parts and muscles of the speech center.

After the prayer, and once the vibratory balance of the environment was achieved with the cooperation of several workers from our plane, Otavia was carefully and partially withdrawn from her physical vehicle. Dionisio approached her and began partially utilizing her faculties. Otavia remained at a short distance, but she could return to her body at any moment at her own impulse. She remained relatively conscious of what was occurring. Dionisio was able to speak by himself, but using faculties that did not belong to him and which he had to use carefully under the direct control of their real owner and the loving supervision of friends and benefactors, who monitored his speech with their gaze in order to keep him in a good state of emotional balance. I realized that the normal incorporation process was more or less the same as that of grafting a fruit tree; that is, the foreign plant displays its own characteristics and offers its own type of fruit, but the grafted tree does not lose its own characteristics and continues operating under its own vitality. In this situation as well, Dionisio was an element that adhered to Otavia's faculties, using them in the production of spiritual characteristics that were unique to him, but naturally subordinated to the medium. Without her mental capabilities, strength and receptivity, the communicating spirit would be unable to reveal his own characteristics to the participants; therefore, it was not logically possible to completely insolate Otavia's watchful influence. Her physical body was her temple, and it was up to her to fend off any destabilizing factors. None of us discarnates had the right to demand that she move further away, since it was her responsibility to guard her physiological powers and preserve them against all evil, both next to us or far from our loving assistance.

Nevertheless, our atmosphere of harmony was not able to calm down the troubling expectations of our fellow incarnates.

Among us, discipline and self-control prevailed; among them, disequilibrium and disquiet. They were demanding Dionisio the man to speak through Otavia's mouth, but our plane was giving them Dionisio the spirit through the medium's transmission. The human family was expecting the emotional father still under the influence of earthly interests and feelings, whereas we were helping our brother keep his soul composed and poised for the benefit of his earthly family members.

The communicating spirit was speaking under a strong emotional state, but Alexandre, who was caring for Dionisio, and Euclides, who was in charge of the medium, were both monitoring his conduct and words so that he would express himself only on the issues aimed at everyone's edification, making him alone responsible for all the negative mental images that his speech might create in the minds and hearts of the listeners.

Consequently, the communicating spirit conducted himself with admirable spiritual dignity during the entire spoken message, performing veritable miracles of inner discipline to avoid certain family situations and to contain the tears that were welling up in his heart.

After speaking for almost forty minutes to his family and colleagues of the human struggle, Dionisio movingly said his goodbyes, repeating a touching prayer of thanksgiving dictated to him by Alexandre.

Our assistance had taken place in complete harmony. The manifesting spirit had offered all possible elements of personal identification, but the small congregation of incarnates did not receive the gift as was hoped. Once their concentration was broken with the closing, they began appraising the experience: four fifths of the audience did not accept the authenticity of the manifestation. Only Dionisio's wife and a few rare friends had actually felt his living and vibrant words. His own children were immersed in doubt and denial.

When questioned by one of the fellow incarnates, the eldest stated:

"Impossible. It couldn't have been my father. If he had been the spirit communicating, he would have commented on our difficult family situation."

Another of Dionisio's children thoughtlessly added:

"I don't believe the manifestation. If it really had been Dad, he would have responded to my inner questions. How could it be possible for parents in the other world not to remember the affection they owe their children?"

Slanderous insinuations began in this group gathered in one of the corners of the room. Only the widow and three other participants remained next to the medium, encouraging her spirit of service through words and thoughts of understanding and joy.

In the group where Dionisio's children were uttering ungrateful words, one of those gathered, influenced by scientism[18], stated solemnly:

"We cannot accept the alleged incorporation of Dionisio. Otavia knows all the details of his past life; she is in almost daily contact with his family, and the communicating spirit did not reveal any particularity by which he could be identified."

After flicking the ash of his cigarette into a small vase nearby, he added sardonically:

"The problem of mediumship is a very serious issue within the Spiritist Doctrine; animism[19] is a widespread stumbling block. Exchange with the invisible plane is full of lamentable deception."

One of the young men present stared in amazement and asked abruptly:

"But do you think Otavia is really capable of deceiving us?"

"Not consciously," replied the follower of scientism with a smile of superiority, "but unconsciously, yes. Most mediums are victims of their own emotional delusions. Usually, communicating personalities are actually the medium's own

---

[18] The application of quasi-scientific techniques to unsuitable subjects or topics. (*American Heritage College Dictionary.*) – Tr.

[19] Phenomena created by mediums without the assistance of spirits. See *The Mediums' Book*, Ch. XIX, nº 223. – Tr.

mental creations. I have patiently studied the subject in order to avoid arriving at implausible conclusions, as happens to so many others. We must avoid the ridiculous, my friends.

Still smiling sarcastically, he stressed triumphantly:

"Immersed in deep hypnosis, the subconscious can confuse the most valorous investigator."

And as if his intricate wording and priceless references represented the final say on the matter, he continued emphatically:

"In order to correct the misuse of the imagination in Spiritism, Metapsychics was created to guide our intellectual research, and we cannot forget that Richet[20] himself died in doubt. Dozens of years of systematic study of the phenomena were not enough for him. Even the materializations themselves did not assure him of the certainty of survival after death. Therefore..."

The small group listened to his words as if listening to an infallible oracle.

In another corner of the room, the same subject was being discussed discretely.

"I don't believe the manifestation was authentic," a relatively young woman said in a low voice to her husband and friends. "After all, the communication was exceptionally banal ... There was nothing new. I think Otavia's words came from herself. I didn't sense any conclusive sign regarding the possible presence of our

---

[20] Charles Richet: Aug. 26, 1850-Dec. 4, 1935. "Pioneer psychical researcher, honored professor of physiology at the Faculty of Medicine in Paris, and winner of the 1913 Nobel Prize in Physiology and Medicine. He was also the honorary president of La Societé Universelle d'études Psychiques, president of the Institut Métapsychique Internationale, and president of the Society for Psychical Research, London (1905)." http://www.spiritwritings.com/charlesrichet.html.

"While he was a student, Richet had a vision, which started his lifelong interest in the paranormal. With Pierre and Marie Curie, he conducted extensive studies on hypnosis and mediums, leading to his Theory of Cryptesthesia, which proposed extra-sensory perception -- 'a faculty of cognition which has no relation to our normal means of knowledge.' He also coined the term 'ectoplasm' to describe the slimy substance produced by the manifestation of spirits, and edited the not- so-scientific journal *Revue Métapsychique* (Metaphysical Review)." http://www.nndb.com/people/207/000125829/ –Tr.

old friend. The realm of discarnates would be very uninteresting if it only provided those who have preceded us with frivolities such as those brought to us by the alleged Dionisio."

"Perhaps there was some sort of disturbance," said her husband. "We aren't free from deceptive spirits of the invisible plane."

The group restrained their laughter.

I had never experienced a disappointment as big as in those instants in which they were examining the process of mediumistic incorporation.

Nobody even thought about the difficulties that Euclides, the good spirit coworker, had had to face in order to bring the comfort of that evening to the gathering. Nobody even thought about the struggle that the event represented to the medium herself, interested as she was in serving the cause of the good with love. Our fellow incarnates seemed to feel that they were owed everything. According to those present, the spirit benefactors would be nothing other than mere servants of their whims, coming back from beyond the grave just to attend to their taste for novelties. With very rare exceptions, nobody had thought about consolation, edification or learning from the experience. Instead of gratitude and constructive observations, distrust and slander were cultivated.

Alexandre noticed that Euclides was following the scene with justifiable disappointment, made worse by the warnings of the evening before; but practicing his dedication to love and kindness, the instructor suggested that he leave, entrusting him with the care of the communicating spirit so that Dioniso could return without delay to where he was recuperating in the spirit world.

The instructor approached me, aware of my great surprise:

"Don't be surprised, Andre. Our incarnate brothers and sisters suffer from complicated limitations."

With a confident and smiling face, he pointed out:

"Furthermore, as you can see, the majority have hypertrophied brains and small hearts. Our friends from the physical realm normally criticize too much and feel too little; they prize being understood; however, they are rarely willing to understand others. But work is a concession from the Lord and we need to trust in the Father's providence, always working for the best."

He gave a few recommendations to some friends who would remain in that place of spiritual fulfillment and said:

"Let's go."

As we left, a gentleman next to the door was saying to the director of the service:

"We all have the right to doubt."

I did not hear the incarnate director's reply, but with the expression of an optimistic and kind father, Alexandre offered:

"Almost all incarnates who take advantage of our cooperation feel they have the right to doubt. Only rarely do we see a fellow incarnate come forward feeling the duty to help."

17
Spirit Counseling[21]

The work of one of the regular gospel study meetings was just finishing up, when a very likeable spirit approached us and greeted my instructor, who responded with spontaneous joy.

It was a loving mother, who openly explained the painful troubles that had invaded her soul. Right after they had begun conversing, she requested Alexandre's help:

"Oh! My friend, even today I'm continuing to struggle with my unfortunate Marinho. Despite my most ardent efforts, the poor thing is still a prisoner of dark powers. Nevertheless, I'm hopeful that his renewal is possible and I'm asking for your cooperation in helping his unhappy soul!"

"Another counseling session?" asked the mentor solicitously.

"Yes," said the distraught mother, wiping her eyes. "I've already resorted to several other friends who work at the spirit support post. I know of your work there as an instructor, and they have all promised to give me fraternal assistance."

---

[21] Dialogue with spirits in need at mediumistic meetings. – Tr.

"Have you noticed any evidence of inner transformation in Marinho?" asked Alexandre.

She nodded and continued:

"For over ten years now, I've been trying to dissuade him from the path of evil by influencing him indirectly. More than once I led him to situations of clarification and enlightenment, but without results, as you know. However, I've noticed that his inclinations have changed a bit. He doesn't feel the same enthusiasm when he receives the malevolent suggestions of his unfortunate companions in revolt and despair. He feels an indefinable boredom in this unbalanced position, and several times I've had the satisfaction of leading him to pray by himself, although I have not been able to steer him clear of the depths of rebelliousness."

The venerable spirit paused briefly and then continued in a pleading tone:

"Who knows but that maybe now the divine moment of inner light has arrived for him? I've been suffering so much for this poor son, who has strayed from the path of the good, and it's possible that the Lord is now granting me the grace of restoring him to it ... To that end I am gathering my purest affections."

Then, looking at my mentor with a strange light in her eyes, she implored:

"Oh, Alexandre! I'm counting on your decisive support! I need to work for Marinho, as I deem myself partially to blame for his misfortune; and I must confess to you, my friend, that I feel tired, in a state of deep spiritual exhaustion!"

"I know what you mean," exclaimed Alexandre, moved. "The constant struggle to free a beloved soul imprisoned in darkness is enough to exhaust anyone of us. But be patient. If Marinho is now tiring of his companions in criminal deviation, then it will be easy to help his spirit and set him back on the path of true spiritual growth. If that were not the case, I would not venture to help him. Trust in our assistance and let's do everything possible for him within our abilities. Are all the preparations ready?"

"Yes," replied the respectable discarnate woman, "I have some friends who will help me bring him, while others will be in charge of helping Otavia bring up the issue at the right time in the group."

"Very well then," concluded Alexandre attentively. "I'll be there on the appointed evening and will help as much as I can on his behalf."

After she bade us an emotional farewell, we were alone once again.

"Why the counseling in the environment of incarnates?" I asked. "Is such a measure necessary for this level of work?"

"No," explained the instructor, "it's not a crucial measure. There are several groups of workers on our plane who are exclusively dedicated to this type of assistance. The regeneration activities in our colony are full of institutions dedicated to fraternal charity in the area of enlightenment for those have gone astray. The rescue outposts and the emergency organizations in the various departments of our sphere of action can count on advanced service centers of the same type. In certain cases, however, the help of human magnetism can influence more intensely the needy who find themselves prisoners of the sensorial fields of the physical realm. But even there, the collaboration of our earthly friends, although considerable, does not constitute an absolute and indispensable factor. Even so, whenever possible and useful we employ the help of human mediums and instructors not only to facilitate the desired solution but also to offer live instruction to our fellow incarnates, thereby awakening their hearts to spiritual matters."

The mentor smiled and continued:

"By helping unbalanced spirits, they will be helping themselves; by counseling them, they too will end up being counseled."

Satisfied with these explanations, I began to consider the personal case of the sweet spirit who had visited us. Why would an enlightened spirit work so long for someone who enjoyed the darkness? Would it be fair to tie maternal hearts to unrepentant children?

The supervisor answered my questions by explaining:

"The dedicated friend who visited us is a poor mother who has been struggling ever since her physical death."

"Who was she referring to in her intercession?" I asked.

"A son who used to be a priest."

"A priest?" I asked, deeply surprised.

"Yes," said Alexandre. "The deviations of souls who received tasks of a religious nature are always more serious. There are priests who, contrary to all hopes on our plane, yield completely to the literal meaning of the teachings of the faith. They receive the titles of the priesthood like doctors who have no love for the work of healing, or like lawyers who have no devotion to the law. They see to their immediate interests, seeking human accolades, and at the end of their transitory existence they find that they have sadly failed their conscience. However, accustomed to the incense of the altar and the submission of incarnate souls, they usually do not acknowledge their own failings, and they prefer to withdraw into a lamentable state of revolt, which turns them into spirits of the darkness. In such cases," emphasized the instructor, changing his tone of voice, "we must realize that such a condition on this side of life is that of all men and women of notable intelligence, who were blessed with the excellence of earthly education but went astray of the true path of moral ascension. It is common for the more sensitive and educated people to create a world peculiar to them, and they hope to escape the law of giving testimony in the sphere of edifying virtues. Accustomed to the easy acquisition of conventional advantages while on the earth, they try to resolve their spiritual problems by the same means after having lost their physical bodies. But when they encounter only the law that requires that each one be rewarded according to his or her deeds, they quite often make their situation worse by entering the dark region of despair, where they join up with countless fellow spirits of the same type. Amongst these types of individuals there is a very high percentage of ministers of the various religions. Referring only to those of the Christian denominations, we can see that the majority do not follow the example of the Divine Master. They close their eyes and ears to the sacrifices of their office. Simon Peter, John the Evangelist and Paul of Tarsus represent figures who are too far removed from them. They cling to the merely conventional decisions of the Councils; they study only books on theology and they resolve all the transcendent questions of the soul through absurd programs under the domination of outward worship. They build elaborate basilicas, forgetting the living temple of the spirit within. They pay homage to the Lord in the same way that the proud Romans revered the statue of Jupiter by trying to bribe the heavenly power with large material offerings. But woe to them! They forget the human heart; they belittle the spirit of humanity, and they ignore the afflictions of the people to whom they were sent to serve. And blind to their own folly, they still anticipate a fabulous heaven that enthrones their criminal vanity and their insensible idleness."

As if called to deeper reflections, Alexandre became silent for a few moments, and then continued:

"For them, Andre, the death of the body is an awful event. Some bravely face the necessary and beneficial disillusionment.

Most, however, run from the dolorous process of readapting to reality and descend into the lower realms of conceited nonconformance, organizing perilous groups of rebellious souls, with whom we, in turn, have to struggle ... Almost all religious sects speak of a hell of anguishing and horrible punishment, where the condemned experience everlasting torment. But very few teach the truth of the fallen conscience within us or explain that the realm of hell and its diabolical expressions finds its beginnings in the inner sphere of our own souls."

The friendly supervisor paused again, and after thinking for a few instants, he considered:

"You can understand ... Those who fall due to ignorance accept correction joyfully as long as they maintain a level of sincere goodwill. Those who heed the suggestions of pride and thus tumble into disequilibrium, however, experience great difficulty accepting any inward corrections. They have to build up a larger store of humility before they can initiate the renewal they need so much."

Noticing that the mentor had once again become silent, I asked:

"But if the willful error belongs to the priest in the case in question, how can we explain the mother's torment?"

Alexandre did not hesitate.

"There are sublime cases of selflessness on our plane," he exclaimed movingly, "in which individuals are willing to sacrifice themselves for others for many, many years. But in this particular case, our friend herself is partly to blame. As a mother, she wanted to force her young son's inclinations. In reality, he had been reborn for an elevated task in the area of spiritualist philosophy, but he was in no way prepared for the job of leading souls. Nevertheless, his mother forced him to enter seminary, thereby violating his ideals and indirectly contributing to the build-up of his pride.

Interpreting his inclinations toward edifying philosophy as a call to the priesthood, she imposed the cassock of the Jesuits on him, which he tainted with his excessive vanity. Of course, our sister was motivated by the holiest of intentions; however, she now feels the duty to share in her son's suffering – a suffering that he himself has not yet experienced to the fullest due to the crust of insensitivity with which rebelliousness has clothed his wayward soul."

As Alexandre was taking a longer pause, I asked:

"But if the son was driven into a difficult situation, one for which he was not duly prepared, is he really so blameworthy?"

The instructor smiled in light of my continuous questioning and explained:

"The mother erred through improvidence, whereas he failed through criminal abuse of an opportunity for sacred service. Out of excessive love, someone might open the door of a castle to us, but just because it is made easy for us, that doesn't mean that we are guilt free if we disparage the gift and destroy the treasures set before us. That is why this dear mother is involved in the loving correction of a mistake, whereas the unfortunate son will have to expiate serious wrongs."

This explanation ended our discussion on the subject.

On the previously arranged evening, I accompanied the small group that was searching for Marinho to offer him spiritual help.

Our small expedition was made up of only four: Alexandre, the discarnate mother, another fellow worker and myself. I was very surprised to discover that the other fellow, Necesio, was going to act as an interpreter for the unfortunate priest. Necesio too had been a rebellious priest, and had kept himself on a vibratory level accessible to the perception of lower order spirits. Alexandre told me that Marinho would not be able see us, but that he would be able to see this ex-colleague, who would speak to him so that he could receive our suggestions.

Admiring the wisdom governing such activities of fraternal cooperation, I attentively followed the group as it headed for an old church.

If I had still been in the flesh, perhaps the scene I witnessed would have caused dreadful terror, but now, the state of being discarnate imposed an emotional discipline on me. The church was filled with criminal figures. Countless spirits from the lower planes were congregated there, cultivating beyond death the same ideas of minimal effort in the area of religious edification. A few priests in black vestments were standing at the altar, while another, who seemed to be leading the group, was commenting from a pulpit on the power of the exclusivist church to which they belonged, craftily expounding new theories about heaven and blessedness.

Astonished, I heard Alexandre kindly explain:

"Don't be so surprised. The desperate and the lazy also get together after the transition of physical death according to their personal tendencies. As is the case with the gatherings of rebellious individuals in the physical realm, the more intelligent and shrewd assume control. Many evils are practiced unconsciously by these unfortunate brothers."

"Oh!" I exclaimed, surprised, "How can they enthrone ignorance to such a degree? Who could believe what we are looking at? If they are aware of what the truth is, why do they still indulge in the practice of evil?"

"It's a question of unconscious malefic action," Alexandre kindly explained.

"But," I replied, confounded, "by what nonsense would souls who are aware of the distance that separates them from the flesh not yield to the law of the good?"

The instructor smiled and replied:

"Well, you can find the same phenomenon in incarnate humanity itself. Humans have known of Christ's teachings for more than a thousand years. They have known fully well about the sufferings of the Master and his followers, and have been aware of the lessons of the manger and the cross. They have been invested with the power of the evangelical treasures. Nevertheless, they have engaged in so-called holy wars, exterminating each other in the name of Jesus. For instance, they set up the courts of the Inquisition, where people of all social conditions were tortured by the thousands in the name of the charity of our Lord. As you can see, ignorance is ancient and the simple change of attire imposed by physical death does not modify the inner soul. There are no 'automatic heavens'; there are only realities."

Without hiding my astonishment, I asked:

"But how do these unfortunate creatures live? Do they obey their own organizations? Do they have special systems?"

"The majority," explained the instructor, "is composed of discarnate spirits in a parasitic state. They naturally influence the psychic energies of the persons to whom they attach themselves and the atmosphere of the homes that welcome them. However, don't think that there are no organizations in the lower zones. They do exist, and in large numbers, despite the elements of pride and rebellion that inspire their foundations. In these types of groups, the spirits of deliberate perversity dominate. What we are looking at here is merely a gathering of suffering and lost souls. You still have not experienced a true den of evil."

And with an expressive gesture, he stressed:

"We do not live in peace with these centers of organized evil. We must fight against them until there is a total victory of the good."

Once more I felt the extent and magnitude of the work that awaits Jesus' faithful servants after the death of the physical body.

I was listening with interest to the ingenuous preaching of the discarnate leader, when our new coworker gave us a light signal at some distance from us in an effort to avoid contact with the crowd because of his condition of visibility to those present. Alexandre answered immediately, followed by the afflicted mother and myself.

Our companion had located Marinho and was calling us to work.

The poor soul was meditating in a dark corner of one of the old areas of the church. His caring mother approached him and stroked his brow, but as happens with most terrestrial persons when being influenced by higher souls, the poor son only felt a vague joy in his heart. However, he could see our new friend, with whom he struck up an interesting dialogue.

Soon after receiving his affectionate greeting, Marinho asked him in surprise:

"You too used to be a priest?"

"Yes," replied Necesio sympathetically.

"Do you belong to the submissives or the fighters?" asked Marinho, somewhat ironically, giving the impression that he considered submissives to be all those colleagues who cultivated evangelical humility, and fighters to be all those who, not having found spiritual reality to be in accordance with the false promises of outward worship, had yielded to the ungrateful drudgery of rebellion and despair.

"I belong to the group of goodwill," replied Necesio intelligently.

Incapable of perceiving our presence next to him, Marinho looked at our companion sarcastically and sadly at the same time, and asked:

"What do you want?"

"I know that you, my friend," explained Necesio movingly, "are experiencing certain inner difficulties, which I too have been suffering. The problem in getting to know the good and the weariness of remaining in evil, the need for affection and the boredom of inferior company have meant great suffering for me."

As the sad priest changed his facial demeanor, Necesio continued:

"It is very bitter to realize the impossibility of living without hope, while at the same time preserving in the disillusionment of living."

"Oh! Yes, that's so true!" exclaimed Marinho, touched by the remark.

"So why don't we work against it?"

"But how?" asked Marinho, in a pain-filled tone of voice. "On earth they promised us a heaven that would open to us because of our titles, but death has revealed a situation that is patently just the opposite. Didn't we administer the sacraments? Weren't we clothed with power? They entrusted us with domination but here they have imposed painful humiliations on us ... To whom can we appeal? Insubordination is now a duty."

I noticed that our colleague was about to reply with a solid Gospel-based argument, talking to him about earthly vanities and arbitrary human interpretations in the field of divine law; but before Necesio could impress any sign of contention on the conversation, Alexandre kindly warned him:

"Don't argue."

Necesio changed his disposition and offered politely:

"Yes, my friend, each conscience has its own struggles and problems. I haven't come to argue for your compulsory renewal. I've been asked by some friends on a higher plane to invite you to a meeting. They are interested in your happiness."

"Are they going to try and change my ways again?" asked Marinho, curious.

"Of course, they have been informed of your new inner state," added Necesio decisively, "and perhaps they are planning to offer you some new advantages. Who knows?"

Marinho thought for a few minutes and then asked some questions about his potential benefactors. However, our companion serenely informed him:

"We don't have time for too many explanations. My friend, I think you will profit much from it, just as I did. So, if you would like to resolve your situation, we don't have a minute to lose."

One could see that Marinho was entering the dark realm of indecision; however, his discarnate mother embraced him with even more affection, mentally asking him to go with the messenger without hesitation. Unable to offer any resistance to that vigorous magnetic imposition of maternal love, he resolutely exclaimed:

"Let's go!"

Necesio offered his arm like a brother, and we left in a hurry out one of the small side doors.

In just a few minutes, we entered the well-known room of prayer and spiritual work.

I noticed that many workers from our plane were holding hands, forming a protective current around the table consecrated to the evening's work. This scene was new to me.

Alexandre explained discreetly:

"This magnetic chain is necessary for the efficacy of our counseling task. This web of positive energies provides indispensable protection. Without it we would not have the elements to contain perverse and obstinate spirits."

The instructor made it clear that this was not the right time for conversation, and he helped Necesio place Marinho within the magnetic circle, where I was surprised to notice the presence of several suffering discarnates who had been brought by other small groups of spirit friends, and who in their turn were also awaiting the opportunity for counseling.

Having sensed the environment where he now found himself, Marinho wanted to retreat, but was unable to. The vibratory border established by our coworkers a short distance from that table of fraternity prevented him from escaping.

"This is a scam!" he shouted angrily.

"Compose yourself!" replied Necesio, maintaining his serenity. "You will experience great relief. Wait! You will be able to talk about your anguish and listen to compassionate words from a still-incarnate Christian instructor. And then, who knows? Maybe you will be able to see a loved one who is an inhabitant of the higher spheres, waiting for your improvement and enlightenment."

"I don't want to! I don't want to!" yelled the unfortunate man.

"Do you want to know the truth, my friend?" asked our companion kindly. "Can you guess where today's assistance is coming from? Can you remember the person who sent me to find you?"

The discarnate priest gazed at him with a dreadful look in his eyes, but Necesio, without losing his serenity, spoke after a longer pause:

"Your mother!"

Marinho hid his face in his hands and broke into bitter weeping.

At that moment, seconded by several assistants, Alexandre began extending abundant doses of magnetic energy to Otavia's organism. I then understood that if there was a need for assistance from our plane for the mediumistic endeavor in the case of exchange with enlightened discarnates, in this case the cooperation had to be much greater because of the dolorous and lamentable condition of the participants. In fact, Otavia, the medium, was receiving huge amounts of magnetic resources for the execution of her task.

A few minutes later, Marinho's incorporation was arranged and he took over the intermediary in a state of great agitation. Otavia, now temporarily disconnected from her physical vehicle, had become a bit confused due to her exposure to unbalanced fluids, and she lacked the same lucidity that we had observed in her previously. However, the assistance she was receiving from our plane was much greater too.

An instructor of an elevated hierarchical status replaced Alexandre next to the medium, while my guide began to directly inspire the incarnate coworker who was heading the meeting.

While this was taking place, several helpers were collecting the mental energies emitted by the brothers and sisters present, including those that were flowing abundantly from the medium's body. Although it was nothing new to me, I was surprised because of the different characteristics with which the work was being carried out.

I could not contain myself and I inquired of a friend who was acting in this capacity.

"That matter," he kindly explained, "represents vigorous pliable energies that will enable the benefactors on our plane to make themselves visible to the disturbed and afflicted brothers and sisters, or will enable them to temporarily materialize certain images or scenes that are indispensable for rekindling the emotions and trust of the unfortunate souls. With the many different types of rays and energies emitted by incarnate humans, we can carry out certain important services for all those who are still bound to the vibratory pattern of ordinary humans, in spite of being far from their physical bodies."

I understood the explanation and realized that if it is possible to carry out a materialization session for incarnates, in another sense the same task could be carried out for our discarnate brothers and sisters in lower conditions.

Admiring the excellence and breadth of the activities of our supervisors, I focused my attention on the conversation that had been established between Marinho, through Otavia's mediumship, and the human instructor, intuitively guided by Alexandre.

At first, the priest displayed intense despair and uttered strong words that exposed his rebelliousness. However, the human instructor spoke to him with Christian serenity, revealing to him the superiority of the living Gospel over the interpreted Gospel.

At a certain point in the counseling, I noticed that Alexandre called to one of the many coworkers who were manipulating the fluids and energies collected in the room, recommending that he help Marinho's mother become visible to him. With the help of other workers, the discarnate woman complied immediately, while Alexandre momentarily left his position next to the instructor in order to apply magnetic passes over Marinho's visual area. I then understood that interesting principles of cooperation were in play. The loving mother acquiesced to being enveloped in denser vibrations for a few minutes, while her son raised his visual perception to the highest level available to him so that they could initiate a temporary reunion of beneficial consequences for him.

Alexandre returned to the human instructor's side, and I was surprised to hear our incarnate friend challenging the exasperated Marinho, acting openly by intuition with his voice warm with sincerity in the ministry of fraternal love:

"Look around you, my brother!" exclaimed the instructor movingly. "Do you recognize the one who is at your side?"

The priest let out a terrible cry:

"My mother!" he said, alarmed with pain and shame. "My mother!"

"Why not surrender to the love of our heavenly Father, my son?" asked the mother, embracing him with great emotion. "Let's stop these useless arguments and intellectual debates! Marinho, the door to our earthly illusions closed with our physical eyes! ... Don't bring our mistakes of the past to this side! Listen to me! Don't rebel anymore! Humble yourself before the truth! Don't make me suffer any longer!"

The incarnates present could see only Otavia's body controlled by the priest, who remained invisible to them. He was nearly bursting with tears. But we saw beyond this. The poised discarnate woman stood next to her son and began kissing him in tears of recognition and love. They were one in their copious weeping.

Gaining new strength, the mother continued:

"Forgive me, my dear son, if in days past I led your heart into ecclesiastical responsibilities, changing the direction of your tendencies. Your current struggles pierce my afflicted soul. Be strong, Marinho, and help me! Rid yourself of your evil companions! It isn't worth it to rebel. We will never escape the law of the Eternal One! Wherever you are, the divine voice will make itself heard in the core of your conscience."

At that moment I noticed that the priest instinctively remembered his friends and was hit with profound fear. Now that he had been reunited with his caring mother, who was devoted to God, and now that he felt the comforting vibration of an environment of fraternity and faith, he was afraid to go back to his colleagues hardened in evil.

He squeezed his mother's hand trustingly and asked:

"Oh, dear mother! Can't I stay with you forever?"

The loving spirit contemplated him with redoubled love, and through the veil of tears she replied:

"Not yet, my son! You can at this moment distance yourself from disequilibrium and sever all the ties that bind you to the lower zones, abandoning them forever; however, you must transform your vibratory condition through inner renewal toward the good, through which our reunion will soon be possible in the Divine Home. But don't be afraid. We will arrange for all the necessary resources for your new life as long as you sincerely change your spiritual aims. Show us your faithful goodwill and Jesus will help us with the rest! ... We have a caring friend here who will give us his valuable assistance. I'm referring to Necesio, the good brother who brought you to meet me. He will put at your disposal precious resources for a change in behavior. At first, Marinho, you will experience difficulties and sorrows, and you will be persecuted by your old companions, who will become your adversaries; however, without the struggle that enables us to acquire real values, we won't find our true place in God's work."

The unfortunate son promised to change.

After encouraging him with measured tenderness, the devoted woman left him in the care of Necesio, who was pleased at having received the mission of guiding him in the sphere of new duties.

After saying goodbye to his selfless mother, who returned to our company, the priest continued to speak for a few more moments with the incarnate director of the meeting, surprising him with his sudden change.

In fact, a gift had been granted from the Lord. Maternal dedication had produced healthy effects in that exasperated and disillusioned heart.

Marinho could not be wrested from the darkness and brought to the light solely in virtue of the loving cooperation from our plane, but he had received our fraternal help and would use these new elements to put himself on the path to the Higher Life. Wondering at our Father's justice, I realized that his dedicated mother could not hand him her own harvest of light, but she could furnish him valuable seed so that he could cultivate them as a good laborer.

Other groups coming from other regions were bringing their wards for instruction, following the plan pre-established for them.

Four spirits received this type of benefit directly through Otavia and another medium.

In all cases, magnetism was used to a large extent by our instructors. One case in particular stood out. It involved a poor businessman who was not yet aware of the fact that he had died. Displaying a certain amount of stubbornness when faced with the truth, one of the spirit supervisors of Alexandre's hierarchical standing imposed his strong will on him and made him see his decomposing remains at a distance. Upon examining the scene, the unfortunate man screamed in grief and finally gave in to the evidence.

In all the tasks, the pliable matter collected from the emanations of the incarnate coworkers was used effectively. It was not only utilized by our friends of a more noble condition, who needed to make themselves visible to the communicating spirits, but was also used for the momentary production of temporary scenes and thought-forms, which had a beneficial effect on the minds of the unfortunates who were struggling with themselves. One of the needy spirits who had taken over the medium under great excitement wanted to attack the participants at the table as they carried out their fraternal assistance. But before he could put his sinister plan in motion, I saw that the technicians on our plane were working hard to compose a form which did not have a life of its own, and which they brought immediately, putting it next to the potential aggressor. It was a terrible looking skeleton, which he stared at from top to bottom, making him tremble in humiliation and forget about his sad plan to harm the benefactors.

After complex work in our sphere, the session ended with great benefit for all.

New worlds of thought germinated inside me.

In each individual case, the work was like a different lesson for my soul. And bewildered by the diffusion of light that was becoming ever more intense and alive in my mental realm, I realized that celestial spirits could bring the most beautiful and effective help to the spirits of darkness; that, moved by mercy and love, they could establish abundant repositories of blessings next to suffering spirits; but that, in accordance with the Eternal Law, the needy could only receive the divine benefits if they were willing to adhere, on their own, to the work of the good.

18
Obsession[22]

On the advice of experienced supervisors, the group to which Alexandre lent his valuable help would meet on previously arranged evenings to deal with cases of obsession. It was necessary to reduce as much as possible the vibratory heterogeneity of the environment, which compelled the director of the Spiritist center to limit the number of incarnates involved in the services of spiritual assistance.

This area of our activities always had quite an impression on me, and for this reason, after obtaining Alexandre's permission to accompany him, I asked him with my usual curiosity:

---

[22] "Of all the difficulties presented in the practice of Spiritism, among the worst we place obsession, which is the domination that certain spirits may acquire over certain individuals. This domination is always the work of little-evolved spirits, for good ones never exert any kind of coercion whatsoever; instead, they provide counsel and fight against the influence of evil spirits, and whenever they are not listened to, they prefer simply to withdraw. Evil ones, on the other hand, latch onto whomever they can control. If they manage to dominate someone, they identify with the victim's spirit, leading the person as if he or she were a child." (Allan Kardec, *The Mediums' Book*, Ch. XXIII, Question 237.) – Tr.

"Is every obsessed person a medium in the real sense of the word?"

The instructor smiled and considered:

"My friend, we are all mediums, including us discarnates, because we are the intermediaries of the good that comes from the higher realms when we elevate ourselves or we are the carriers of the evil picked up in the lower zones when we lose our equilibrium. The obsessed, however, more than being mediums with disturbed energies, are almost always unwell persons and represent a legion of sick spirits who are invisible to human eyes. That is why in all circumstances obsession is a special case requiring much attention, prudence and care."

Recalling the conversations I had heard amongst our incarnate fellow spirits and Alexandre's and other instructors' assiduous coworkers, I added:

"According to what you are saying, I can understand the difficulties relating to healing; nevertheless, I recall the optimism with which our friends have commented on the condition of the obsessed who are brought in for treatment."

My generous mentor gave me a fatherly smile and remarked:

"For the time being, they cannot see anything other than the present act in the centuries-long drama of each individual. They do not consider the fact that both the obsessed and the obsessor are two souls who have come very far, and who are strongly bound together in the disturbances particular to them. Our brothers and sisters in the flesh proceed correctly by joyfully getting involved in this sort of work, because from every worthy effort something good results that will be indestructible in the spirit realm. Nevertheless, they should be more moderate in their promises of immediate improvement in the physical realm, and in no way should they form any premature judgment in each case, since, with the restricted sight of the earthly body, it is very difficult to identify who the true victim is."

After a short pause, he continued:

"I too have observed the exaggerated optimism of our incarnate friends; some of the more inconsequential ones have gone so far as to make formal promises of healing to the patients' families. Of course, the benefits to be reaped by the patients will be enormous; nonetheless, although we should be optimistic, we must disapprove of unbalanced and aimless enthusiasm."

"Are you already familiar with all the cases?" I asked.

"Yes," replied Alexandre, without hesitation. "Of the five that will be the object of the next meeting, only one young woman has displayed any potential for more or less quick improvement. The others will come only for help in order to avoid worsening their necessary trials."

I thought the particular case he had mentioned was very interesting and asked:

"Does this young woman enjoy a different type of protection?"

The instructor smiled and explained:

"It's not a matter of protection, but of personal effort. Not only are the obsessed ill and representatives of other sick spirits, but they are almost always individuals with a load of tormenting spiritual problems. If they lack a strong will for self-education and self-discipline, they will almost certainly prolong the duration of their painful condition beyond death. For example, what happens to a man who is indifferent regarding the management of his own home? Of course, he is assaulted by a thousand and one issues every day and will end up defeated and will become a plaything of circumstances. Now imagine that this indifferent man is surrounded by enemies of his own making – adversaries who keep an eye on his smallest gestures and who are usually motivated by sinister purposes ... If he does not wake up to the realities of the situation and take up the means to resist and use the outside help offered by his friends, it is reasonable to suppose that he will remain crushed. This is how the largest percentage of the spiritual cases we are treating can be defined. But this is not an exclusive characteristic of obsessions in general. There are also the painstaking liberating processes, in which, after the elements of disturbance and darkness are removed, the expiatory situations continue. In all instances of this type, however, one cannot do without the support of those directly interested in the healing. If obsessed persons are satisfied with their state of disequilibrium, it is necessary to wait for the end of their blindness, the lessening of their rebelliousness or the removal of the ignorance that prevents them from understanding the truth. Although we are fervently called by those who love these ill individuals in particular, when we are faced with obstacles of such nature, we can do nothing except sow the good for a future harvest but without any hopes for immediate benefit."

Alexandre paused for a few moments, and because he saw that I needed further explanation, he continued:

"The young woman to whom I referred has been trying to restore her psychic forces by herself. She has been constantly fighting against the attack of evil spirits by using all her resources in the areas of prayer, self-control and meditation. She is not expecting the miracle of a healing without effort, and despite being terribly persecuted by less evolved beings, she has been taking advantage of all types of assistance that helpers on our plane project into her personal circle. So the difference between her and the others is that by using her own energies, albeit slowly, she will enter into contact with our current of assistance, whereas the others will continue – as everything seems to indicate – in the impassive state of those who willfully abandon the constructive struggle."

I understood the explanation and waited for the evening of assistance to the obsessed, as Alexandre called this type of service.

A few days later, I was filled with interest as I entered the well-known room in the company of the instructor.

There were not many there this time. Around the table there were only two mediums, six brothers and sisters who were experienced in the knowledge and practice of spiritual problems, and the obsessed individuals being treated.

The five patients displayed special characteristics. Two of them, a relatively young woman and a mature gentleman were highly agitated; two others, young brothers, seemed to be completely incapacitated mentally; and lastly, the fifth, the young woman to whom Alexandre had referred, was making a supreme effort to control herself in light of the attacks directed at her.

There were several little-evolved spirits surrounding the patients. None of them detected our presence due to their low vibratory level, but they felt comfortable with their contact with the incarnates. They talked to each other with great interest, and as they did so they exposed their terrible plans of attack and vengeance.

I was closely watching what they were doing when I was surprised by the arrival of two workers from our plane. The obsessing spirits looked at them with some fear.

"These are our interpreters for the persecuting spirits," explained Alexandre. "Because of their condition, they can be seen by the obsessors while maintaining a close connection with us at the same time."

Observing the serenity with which they were smiling at us, without implying a direct contact with the instructors from our sphere, my guide explained:

"They have already received precise instructions for tonight's work."

The obsessor spirits, congregated there in suffering perturbation, changed their manner of speaking somewhat at seeing the two missionaries. Judging by this change, I realized that both were already known to them.

One of the obviously cruel obsessors discretely said to one of his companions:

"The preachers have arrived. Hopefully, they haven't brought any more demands."

"I don't know what these emissaries want," answered the other slightly ironically. "After all, advice and water are given to those who ask for it."

"It seems like they have invited those sitting at the table to tire us out until we forget our aims of serving justice with our own hands."

"Words go with the wind," added the other.

At this point, the newly arrived missionaries started addressing the spirits of darkness. One of them spoke kindly to an unhappy discarnate woman, who was connected to one of the mentally impaired patients:

"So, my sister, it seems that you are feeling a bit better, a bit stronger! That's great!"

She burst into a fit of weeping. However, the missionary continued patiently:

"Now settle down! Vengeance only makes the crime worse. In order to re-establish lost happiness, my friend, we must forget all evil. As long as you harbor thoughts of hatred, you will not be able to obtain the improvement you desire. Continued anger maintains a permanent state of destruction. You will not be able to experience any inner peace until you can forgive with all your heart."

"That would be almost impossible," replied the woman. "This man dishonored my female ideals; he led me into corruption, scoffed my fate and transformed my destiny into a stream of evils. Isn't it fair that he pay now? Don't you proclaim that the Father is just? Well, I can't see the Father so I must render justice using my own strength."

And because the discarnate counselor was looking at her compassionately, she asked:

"What if you were the woman? Put yourself in my shoes and think about what you would do. Would you be willing to forgive the wicked person who cast your heart into the mire? Would you close the doors of your memory, dulling the most beautiful sentiments of your character? I don't think so. You too would act as I have. There are conditions for forgiveness. And as the victim, the condition I impose is that my persecutor must also experience the disdain of fate. He disgraced me and returned to the world, where he prepared himself for a life of social benefits. He earned his degrees to win the esteem of others. Well, what about what he owes me? In days gone by, wasn't I also worthy of everyone's respect? Hadn't I prepared for a hard-working and honest life with the firm purpose of serving God?"

I followed the discussion with great interest, admiring the individuality that characterizes each person, even beyond the death of the body.

The interpreter from our sphere contemplated her without any anger, and remarked:

"My friend, all your points are apparently very respectable. However, we must calmly examine what the percentage of our own share is in all the disasters that happen to us. Only in very rare situations could we really claim to be victims. In most instances of this nature, we must share the blame. We cannot keep a bird of prey from flying across the sky above us, but we can keep it from making a nest on our head."

At this point the woman looked quite chagrined and exclaimed harshly:

"Your words are the offspring of religious preaching, but I am in search of justice."

And with an ironic laugh she finished:

"In fact, the very justice that Jesus himself proclaimed."

The missionary did not react to the sarcasm of the gesture that accompanied the ungracious comment and said to her kindly:

"Justice! How many crimes are committed in the world in its name! How many men and women only encourage the tyranny of the self while searching for justice for themselves? You mentioned the Divine Master. What type of justice did the Lord ask for himself when he was hanging on the cross? Regarding justice, my friend, Christ left us with rules we should not forget. The Master was watchful in all actions regarding justice for others. He defended the spiritual interests of the community all the way to his supreme act of selflessness. But when the time for his trial came, he was silent and resigned until the very end. Obviously, the Master did not intend for this attitude to disregard the sacred service of upright judges in the physical world, but he preferred to adopt it for himself and to establish the standard of judiciousness for all disciples of his Gospel for a variety of different situations. When dealing with the interests of others, my sister, we must be speedy regarding true justice; however, when difficult and dolorous matters involve the *self*, it is worthwhile to moderate our impulses for vindication. Our incomplete vision does not always allow us to perceive the full amount of the debt we carry. And when in doubt, it is better to abstain. Do you think that Jesus had some sort of debt to warrant his condemnation? He knew what crime was being committed; he had solid reasons to ask for help from the Law; however, he preferred to remain silent and go through with it, waiting for our true understanding. This is because the Master taught us to 'love one another' above the 'eye for an eye' of the ancient provisions of the Law, and he practiced this unwaveringly. He confirmed the legitimacy of justice, but proclaimed the divinity of love. He showed that it is always a heroic act to defend those who deserve it, but he abstained from carrying out justice for himself so that disciples of his doctrine would learn to appreciate human discretion and divine fidelity in dealing with the serious problems of the personality, escaping from the madness that the passions of the self can unleash upon the pathways of the world."

In light of this forceful and beautiful argumentation, the woman became silent and was strongly impressed.

Alexandre, who was truly moved as he followed the interpreter's explanations, remarked to me:

"The work of spiritual enlightenment for persons after death requires much attention and tenderness on our part. We must know how to sow in the 'God-forsaken land' of disillusioned hearts that have left the physical realm behind under the storms of hatred and unknown anguish. The Sacred Book says that in the beginning was the Word... Here too, in view of the desolate chaos of unfortunate spirits, we need to use the word in the principle of true enlightenment. We cannot create without love, and only when we are duly prepared will we be able to successfully edify ourselves for life eternal.

Once the spirit who had been so carefully warned became silent, I noticed the first young woman showing signs of strong irritation, which concerned the incarnates who were present. Several obsessors – invisible to terrestrial eyes – stood beside her, imposing terrible disturbances on her. But amongst them, one unfortunate obsessor stood out due to his cruel demeanor. He had stuck himself to her whole body, dominating all the centers of organic energy. I noticed the victim's almost useless struggle in trying to resist.

My kind instructor perceived my surprise:

"Andre, this is a case of complete possession."

Addressing the interpreter who had been presenting his arguments a few moments earlier, he recommended that he establish a light dialogue with the fearsome persecutor so that I might be informed on the subject.

Feeling the touch of the loving hand of our fellow missionary, the wretch cried out:

"No! No! Don't try to teach me the way of heaven! I know my situation and nobody can sway my avenging hand!"

"We do not wish to coerce you, my brother," our friend emphasized with Gospel serenity. "Compose yourself! As long as you continue to nourish your vengeful purposes, you will be punishing only yourself. Nothing but your own conscience is bothering you. The shackles that chain you to anguish and pain were produced by your own hands!"

"Not so!" yelled the wretch. "Not so! What about her?"

His question was accompanied by a dreadful look and he continued:

"You who preach virtue, do you justify the slavery of free men? Do you believe in the right to build slave's quarters to humiliate the sons of one and the same God? This woman was cruel to all of us. Besides my own vengeance, other hearts beat with a hatred that will not let her rest. We shall persecute her wherever she goes."

With a sinister gesture he continued:

"She sold my wife and children on a whim! Isn't it just that she suffer until she restores them to me? Could Jesus, the ultimate Savior, applaud slavery?"

Our interpreter replied very calmly and respectfully:

"Our Master would not approve of slavery; however, my friend, he stated that we must forgive one another; otherwise, we will never free ourselves from the tangle of our wrongs. Who amongst us former inhabitants of the flesh can display a past free of crime? At this moment your eyes behold the guilt of an unfortunate sister. However, your soul, dear brother, remains bewildered by a whirlwind of rebellion. Therefore, your memory is imbalanced and cannot yet bring forth the recollections that are pertinent to you. Since you are not able to remember the past precisely, wouldn't it be more reasonable in your case to wait for the Righteous Judge? How can you judge and execute somebody with your own hands if you are still not able to evaluate the extent of your own debts?"

The obsessor seemed to be struck by such arguments, but far from giving up his position of persecutor, he replied harshly:

"Your observations might be valuable for the weak, but not for me; I am well aware of the subtleties used by preachers from your sphere. I shall not abandon my purposes. My situation will not be resolved by mere words."

Understanding the antagonist's hardheartedness and lamenting his ignorance, the missionary continued fraternally:

"It is not a matter of subtlety but rather of common sense. Moreover, I do not wish to take away your individualistic reasons, especially since strong ties bind your influence to the victim's mind. However, I am appealing to the noble sentiments that still vibrate in your heart, enabling you to realize that, without mutual forgiveness, we will never liquidate our debts. The demanding creditor is usually blind to his own commitments. In essence your complaint might be legitimate; nevertheless, strange is your method of collection, in which I cannot see any advantage, since your activities as an avenger not only deepen your inner wounds but also make you appear unsympathetic in the eyes of all the others."

Wounded perhaps more deeply in his vanity, the obsessor became silent, while the interpreter turned to us, asking my instructor if magnetism would be appropriate to induce the unfortunate spirit to tap into a few reminiscences of scenes from the distant past.

But Alexandre reasoned:

"It would not be appropriate to expand his memories. He wouldn't comprehend them. Before expanding his comprehension, his suffering must continue for a while."

Taking advantage of a long pause, I observed the poor obsessed woman in greater detail. Surrounded by aggressive spirits, her body had become like a dwelling for this cruelest of persecutors. He occupied her body from head to toe, imposing great reactions on all her centers of cellular energy. Tenuous but vigorous filaments united both of them, and while the obsessor displayed a psychological picture of satanic lucidity, the unfortunate woman showed the incarnate coworkers an opposite image, revealing distress and unawareness.

"Save me from the Devil! Save me from the Devil!" she screamed without ceasing, moving the incarnates seated around the simple table. "Oh my God! When will my torment end?"

With her eyes bugging out as if gazing at enemies invisible to ordinary sight, she would shout out after brief moments of silence:

"They've all come from hell! They're here! They're here! Oh no! Oh no!"

Her cries were like long agonizing hisses.

Answering my expectant look, Alexandre explained:

"This young woman is displaying a dire case of possession. She has been hounded by tenacious adversaries from her past since childhood. However, as long as she remained single and within her parents' protective environment, she somehow managed to escape the full influence of her persistent enemies, although she sensed their actions in a less perceptible way. But when she took on the responsibilities of marriage, in which, more often than not, the wife receives the greater share of the sacrifices, she could no longer resist. Soon after the birth of her first child, she fell into an intense prostration, thereby offering the dreaded persecutors their opportunity; ever since then she has experienced pain-filled trials."

I was about to voice new questions about the case, but my friendly instructor indicated that the incarnates' part of the assistance meeting was about to begin.

We needed to maintain watchful, fraternal cooperation.

Pleasantly surprised, I observed the magnetic emissions of those meeting there for the activities of assistance, as they were motivated by the most saintly impulse of redemptive charity. Our advanced technicians took advantage of the abundant flow of beneficial energies, improvising admirable resources for the assistance not only of the obsessed but also the unfortunate persecutors.

Of the five psychically infirm individuals, only the resolute, second young woman referred to earlier was able to benefit one hundred percent from our help. I witnessed her brave efforts at reacting against the attack of the dangerous spirits surrounding her. Enveloped in the current of our fraternal vibrations, she had recovered absolute organic normality, albeit temporarily. She felt calm, almost happy.

Although he was actively at work, Alexandre called my attention to this fact.

"This sister," he said, "is actually on her way to being healed. She realized in time that medication, whatever it may be, is not all that is needed for the restoration of physical balance. She knows that help on our part should be used by patients desirous of recovery. For this reason she is developing her full capacity of resistance, cooperating with us for her own good. Observe."

In fact, feeling herself assisted by our extensive web of protective vibrations, the young woman emitted a vigorous flow of mental energies, expelling all the malevolent ideas that the misfortunate obsessors had deposited in her mind. Immediately, she began to absorb the regenerating and constructive thoughts that our influence offered her. Approving my detailed examination with a meaningful gesture, Alexandre continued:

"Only patients who have willingly made themselves their own physician achieve a positive healing; the principle is the same in the dolorous field of obsession. If victims capitulate unconditionally to their adversaries, they will surrender completely and become possessed after becoming an automaton at the mercy of the persecutor. If they have a weak and indecisive will, they will become accustomed to the persistent actions of their persecutor and will become accustomed to the circle of irregularities, a situation very difficult to correct, because, little by little, it will become a pole of strong mental attraction to the persecutors themselves. In such cases our activities are nearly limited to simple tasks of assistance aimed at results far into the future. However, when we find patients who are interested in their healing, taking advantage of our resources in order to apply them to their spiritual evolution, then we can foresee immediate gains."

As Alexandre became silent, I continued to observe the work being carried out in the room.

Filled with beautiful sincerity, the incarnate counselor was the center of a remarkable scene. His chest area had become a radiating focal point, and each word that came from his lips seemed like a spray of light reaching its target directly, whether the disturbed ears of the patient, or the hearts of the cruel persecutors. In fact, his words were of an enchanting simplicity, but the emotional substance in each one was surprising in its sublimity, loftiness and beauty.

Noticing my astonishment, Alexandre came to my aid and explained:

"This is a spiritual school. The human instructor is in charge of transmitting the lessons. However, you can notice that, in order to teach successfully, it is not enough to know the disciplines of the course and teach them. Before anything else, it is necessary to feel them and live their essence in the heart. People who preach the good should practice it if they do not want their words to be carried away by the wind as the mere echo of an empty drum. Persons who teach virtue while living its greatness within themselves have words charged with positive magnetism, working spiritual edification in the souls who listen to them. Without that characteristic, counseling is almost always useless."

Having witnessed the impressive scene analyzed by my instructor's explanation, I understood that contagion by example is not a purely ideological phenomenon, but rather a scientific fact in magnetic-mental manifestations.

Except for the poor sister who was possessed, the other obsessed individuals were free of the direct influence of their persecutors for the time being; however, with the exception of the young woman who bravely resisted, the others displayed a peculiar uneasiness, anxious to be reunited once again to the field of their persecutors' attraction. Our assistants had already removed the persecutors by expelling them from those infirm and tormented bodies; nonetheless, those who were seeking physio-psychic improvement characterized themselves by their inner absence, remaining very distant spiritually from the teachings the incarnate instructor ministered with admirable sentiment under the influence of the mentors from the Most High. Their attitude was one of dissatisfaction and anxiety. One could say that they could not stand being separated from their invisible obsessors. Used to patients who at least demonstrated the apparent desire to be healed, I was surprised by the mental attitude of this small group, so lamentably uninterested in the remedy that Spirituality offered them out of love.

Alexandre noticed my surprise and pointed out:

"Usually, ninety percent of the cases of obsession that we observe are made of painful and intricate problems. Almost always, obsessed persons suffer from a regrettable blindness regarding their own infirmity. Even though they do not answer the call of truth due to their crystallized individualism, they are responsible nonetheless, and they become easy and unwary prey of dangerous enemies from the regions of debased activities. Normally, these types of cases have happened because of the strong and deep ties of misdirected affection or by the horrible bonds of hatred, which, in all circumstances, represents imbalanced trust turned into a monster."

My supervisor took a long pause to check on the work in progress, but as someone who wished to help me with unforgettable lessons in practical struggle, he continued, despite his consuming responsibilities at the time:

"That is why, Andre, even for psychiatrists enlightened by the insights of Christian Spiritism, the majority of these types of cases are frankly disconcerting. In light of the sentimental influences, each of these problems requires a different solution. Furthermore, it is important to note that our fellow incarnates see only one side of the question, whereas each of these processes is characterized by infinite particularities entailing the past of the incarnate and discarnate protagonists. Looking at the obsessed, they focus only on the immediate imperative – to remove the obsessor. But how is it possible, from one instant to the next, to break secular shackles forged in reciprocal commitments of a life in common? How to separate beings who anxiously cling to each other because they understand that in the torment of such a union rests the price of their redemption? As a matter of fact, although it is rare, there is no lack of cases involving almost instantaneous deliverance. However, what we see in them is the end result of a laborious redemptive process, or we find a patient, who, in fact, commits violence against him or herself in order to shorten the healing."

Examining the extent of the obstacles to the complete recovery of the psychically ill, I considered:

"So, may we gather that..."

Alexandre did not let me finish. Interrupting my untimely statement, he replied:

"I know what you are going to say. In light of the difficulties regarding your natural learning experience, you are wondering if our work might not be useless and if it might not be better to leave the obsessed to their own fate. That is a nonsensical observation. If you were on the earth and still in the flesh, and you saw a beloved son who was about to die, deemed incurable by human medicine, would you have the courage to abandon him to the whims of the circumstances? Wouldn't you trust in an unexpected recourse from Divine Providence? Wouldn't you anxiously await the favorable manifestation from nature? Who can claim to be so firmly set in the core of their heart to say with mathematical precision if he or she will react against evil or not, if he or she is inclined to idleness or active work? Truth is, we cannot use any intellectual argument to escape our duty to extend fraternal assistance to the ignorant and suffering. It is imperative that we fulfill our part of immediate responsibility, understanding that the building of love is also the work of time. No word, no gesture or thought in the service of the good is lost."

I understood the worthiness of his remark and was silent. Because my instructor had returned to actively take part in the work in progress, I proceeded to examine the psychically ill while the incarnate counselor continued with his enlightening undertaking of evangelization.

The young woman who was fighting against the dangerous influence of the inhabitants of darkness showed normality in her physiological apparatus. She seemed like someone who had mobilized all her defensive abilities in order to keep the balance of her own dwelling intact; the others, however, displayed deplorable organic conditions. The unfortunate possessed woman displayed serious disturbances from her brain down to the lumbar and sacral nerves, demonstrating a complete disorganization of the center of sensitivity as well as a dreadful relaxation of her motor fibers. These imbalances appeared not only in the nervous system but also in the glands in general and in a number of organs. Amongst the other obsessed individuals, the physical degradation was no less. Two of them displayed strange liver and kidney intoxications. Another showed a peculiar imbalance in the heart and lungs, tending toward cardiac failure on top of an advanced pre-tuberculosis.

While I carefully examined these disturbing clinical conditions, the group's incarnate supervisor had become an interpreter of great benefactors from our plane of action and was spreading a large amount of Christian love and evangelical knowledge, carrying out with extreme fidelity to Christ the sowing of charity, light and forgiveness.

Desiring my spiritual growth in these constructive activities, Alexandre remarked:

"Observe the work of authentic fraternity. There are no miracles of sudden transformation, nor is there an immediate promotion to higher planes for those who linger in the lower realms. The task is one of sowing, of care, persistence and watchfulness. The fetters of many centuries cannot be broken in an instant, nor can a city be built in a day. It is essential to wear down the shackles of evil with perseverance and to practice the good with evangelical joyfulness."

The work was coming to an end.

Perceiving that my instructor had eased back into our conversation, I exposed my observations by asking:

"In view of the physiological disturbances that I was able to identify in the psychically ill, should I consider them as infirm in body also?"

"Indeed," stated Alexandre. "The imbalance of the mind can determine the general perturbation of the organic cells. That is why obsessions almost always are accompanied by highly dolorous symptoms. The poisons of the soul determine the illnesses of the body."

Before I could ask another question, I noticed that the meeting was being closed by our incarnate friends. The defensive magnetic chain had been broken. Surprised, I saw that the young woman resolute and firm in her faith had achieved considerable improvement, while the possessed woman was about to leave with her situation unchanged. I looked at the other three patients. As soon as the current of the established beneficial vibrations was broken, they started to attract their invisible persecutors, to whose influence they had become accustomed, showing little improvement from the session.

Taking advantage of the time, I approached Alexandre in order not to miss his lessons on the subject, and asked:

"How can we reach the conclusion in the treatment of the obsessed?"

He smiled and answered:

"In all our activities of assistance, there is always immense profit, even when its extent is not perceptible to ordinary eyes. And any such patients willing to cooperate with us for their own benefit by decisively taking part in the restoration of their mental activities and regenerating themselves in the light of a life renewed in Christ can expect the reestablishment of health regarding the earthly body. However, when they call for Jesus' help with their lips but without opening their heart to the divine influence, then they should not expect miracles from our assistance. We can help, aid, contribute and enlighten, but it is not possible to improvise resources whose organization is the exclusive work of the interested parties."

"Nevertheless, I am impressed by the clinical situation of the obsessed," I considered. "How grievous their physical condition is!"

"Yes, yes!" replied the instructor. "The problem of responsibility is not restricted to words. It is a vital issue on the pathway of life. In order to preserve his children against the dangers of downfall, God created the means of religious enlightenment, awakening souls to immortal glorification. Nevertheless, few are those who are willing to respect the objectives of religion, willfully forgetting that the smallest failures and the least addictions remain imprinted in the soul, demanding rectification. You have observed a few unfortunate, obsessed persons who are in a positive treatment process, but you are forgetting the countless individuals still in the flesh, who, although having been informed by religion on the needs of the spirit, have allowed themselves to be carried away by addictive attachment to sensations of all sorts, contracting debts, taking on heavy commitments and dragging others into their degrading adventures, forging strong bonds for the painful dramas of future obsessions."

And after smiling paternally, he added:

"What do you expect? It is obvious that we must work as hard as we can for the good of others, but we cannot exonerate our brothers and sisters from the obligations they have contracted. The faithful servant is not the one who weeps at contemplating the misfortune of others, nor the one who observes them impassively under the pretext of not wanting to interfere in the work of justice. Sick sentimentality and measured coldness do not build up the good. Good workers are those who help while maintaining the necessary balance, doing all the beneficial work that is available to them, conscious that their effort represents the Divine Will."

Alexandre could not have been clearer. I understood his instructive explanation, but noticing the exit of the patients under the vigilant assistance of their relatives waiting for them at the door, I asked again:

"My friend, what if we were to succeed in removing the implacable persecutors for good? As a former doctor in the world, I realize that these psychically ill individuals do not have the diseases they display, which are circumscribed to their minds. With the exception of the young woman who is fighting bravely, the rest are displaying strange imbalances in their nervous systems, with disturbances of the heart, liver, kidneys and lungs. Let us suppose that the conversion of the persecutors that torment them could be achieved. Would they return to organic normality? Would they attain complete health?"

Alexandre thought for a few moments before replying, and then stated:

"Andre, the body of flesh is like a violin that has been handed to an artist, in this case the reincarnate spirit. It is indispensable to preserve the instrument from destructive agents and to defend it from thieves. Did you notice the young woman who is doing everything to protect herself from evil? She has been stumbling under blows of persecutors who mercilessly attack her heart. However, as someone who, trusting in God, crosses a long and dangerous bridge over an abyss, she has incessantly resorted to prayer, watching herself and mobilizing resources at her disposal so as not to disturb her inner equilibrium. In the temptation of which she is a victim, this sister has found the trial that redeems her. However, in the silent heroism of her effort, she has been enlightening her very persecutors, encouraging them to meditation and discipline. As you can see, this fighter knows how to preserve the body that was entrusted to her, and having become the counselor of her persecutors by her example of resistance to evil, she is transforming them, thereby enlightening herself. With this type of collaboration, the matter of healing is greatly facilitated. However, the same will not happen with those who are not careful about defending their corporeal instrument. Handed over to evildoers, our symbolic violin can be half destroyed. And even if it is restored to its legitimate owner, it cannot be as precisely harmonious as before. A Stradivarius may be authentic, but it will not be heard if the strings are broken. As we can see, cases of obsession present natural complexities, and we cannot solve them without the direct collaboration of the interested parties."

"I understand!" I exclaimed.

And because of the mentor's pause, I argued:

"However, let's say that the persecutors convert, that they forsake forever the pathway of evil after having battered the body of their victims for so long ... In that case, wouldn't the latter have an immediate recovery? Wouldn't they recover their whole physiological balance?"

With his habitual kindness, Alexandre replied:

"I have already seen such situations, and when they do occur, former tormentors become friends, anxious to repair the evil they had practiced. Sometimes, by receiving help from the higher planes, they manage to restore the organic harmony of those who have suffered their inhuman influence. However, in the majority of cases, the victims cannot reestablish the equilibrium of the body."

"Do they remain in deficient health all the way to the grave?" I asked, strongly impressed.

"Yes," explained Alexandre calmly.

At noticing my surprise, the instructor added:

"Your astonishment is still linked to a deficient human analysis. The persecutor, recognized as such amongst our fellow incarnates, can display modifications, but perhaps the alleged victim has not been converted. In obsession, the difficulties are not unilateral. The eventual removal of the persecutor does not always mean the end of the debt. In any part of the universe, Andre, we shall always receive according to our deeds."

The matter was suggestive of great and beautiful questions, but other demands were calling us elsewhere.

Alexandre was ready to leave and he affectionately said goodbye to the coworkers. I followed him in silence, thinking about the greatness of even the smallest provisions of Divine Justice.

19
Passes

In all the group meetings in which Alexandre participated as an instructor, there are many different types of services developed under the responsibility of our discarnate coworkers. It had always been possible for me to study them separately; however, I could not hide my strong desire for the respectable instructor to explain a few of them. One of these activities was the service of magnetic passes ministered to people who frequently attended the center.

This work was attended to by six spirits dressed in very white tunics, who acted as watchful nurses. They rarely spoke and they worked intensely. All the persons who entered the room received their wholesome touch, and after attending to the incarnates, they ministered effective help to unfortunate spirits from our plane, especially those who composed the family entourage of our incarnate friends.

I asked Alexandre about this spiritual activity, and nodding toward these workers as they went about their silent efforts, the mentor explained with his usual kindness:

"These particular individuals are magnetic assistance technicians who come here to dispense healing passes. It is a delicate department of what we do and it requires much discretion and responsibility."

"Do such workers need any special qualifications?" I asked.

"Yes," explained the friendly mentor. "As they do their work, goodwill alone is not enough, as is also the case in other areas of our work. They need to display certain qualities of a superior order and certain specialized knowledge. Even when discarnate, servants of the good cannot act satisfactorily in this type of service if they cannot yet maintain a higher standard of continuous mental elevation, an indispensable condition for the exteriorization of radiant[23] faculties. Missionaries involved in magnetic assistance, either on the physical plane or here in our sphere, must have great self-control, naturally balanced sentiments, a purified love for their fellow beings, a higher understanding of life, strong faith and a deep trust in the Divine Power. However, I must point out that, on our plane, these requirements are demands that one cannot be exempted from, whereas on the physical plane, sincere goodwill can overcome this or that deficiency in many cases. This is justifiable because of the assistance given by the benefactors from our realm of action to human workers who are still incomplete in terms of desirable qualities."

As I listened to my supervisor's thoughts on the matter, I recalled that every now and then, in the usual meetings of the group, one could, in fact, see mediums dispensing passes while accompanied closely by such spirits. I thus used this opportunity to increase my learning on the subject.

---

[23] Radiant energy: Energy transferred by radiation, esp. by an electromagnetic wave. (*The American Heritage College Dictionary.*) – Tr.

"Generally speaking, could incarnates help out in these activities of magnetic assistance?" I asked.

"In different degrees of intensity, all of them would be able to extend their fraternal help in this sense," replied the instructor, "because once an authentic desire to cooperate for the benefit of others is displayed by this or that worker, the authorities from our realm appoint wise and benevolent spirits who indirectly guide the newcomer by using his or her goodwill and by enriching his or her personal qualities. However, very few demonstrate a vocation to serve willingly. Notwithstanding their good and authentic convictions, many await healing mediumship as if it were a miraculous event in their lives and not a service for the good that asks the candidate for a painstaking effort from the start. Of course, when we refer to our incarnate brothers and sisters, we cannot demand anybody's cooperation in our usual field of work; however, if any of them come looking for us, requesting admission to the tasks of assistance, they will of course receive our best guidance in the area of spirituality."

"So, even if human helpers display few qualities, can they still be utilized?" I asked curiously.

"Of course," Alexandre added attentively. "As long as they remain interested in the sacred acquisitions of the good above any transitory concerns, they can expect the continuous progress of their faculties of radiance[24] not only from their own efforts but also from well-deserved help from On High."

Not far from us, the spirit magnetic technicians were performing their methodical procedures. I could see a whole new world of lessons in their silent work, inviting me to useful experiences. Nonetheless, having made note of Alexandre's

[24] Radiance: The radiant energy emitted per unit time in a specified direction by a unit area of an emitting surface. (*The American Heritage College Dictionary.*) – Tr.

explanations and wondering about the possibility of contributing an explanation on the subject to incarnates, I asked:

"While we are still enveloped by the denser fluids of the physical realm, how can we develop our radiant faculties after fostering our true goodwill to serve our neighbor?"

Alexandre understood my intention and immediately explained:

"Once the basic qualities are obtained, candidates must consider the need for immediate elevation so that their work can be raised at the same pace. We are only talking about the most immediate and simplest gains that they need to accomplish within themselves. Before anything else, they must balance their emotions. It isn't possible to offer constructive energies to somebody else, even if acting as a useful instrument, if one systematically wastes one's own vital radiations. A worn out and oppressed nervous system is a channel that does not respond to the interruptions that take place. Excessive bitterness, unbridled passion and obsessive anxiety are barriers that impede the passage of auxiliary energies. On the other hand, it is also necessary to examine physiological requirements as well as requisites of a psychic order. The monitoring of elements destined for the cellular reservoirs is indispensable for anyone interested in attending to tasks of the good. Excessive eating produces fetid odors that emanate through the pores as well as through the outlets from the lungs and the stomach, harming the radiating faculties because it causes abnormal ejections and great disharmony in the gastrointestinal system, which in turn affects the inside of the cells. Alcohol and other toxic substances create disturbances in the nervous centers, altering certain psychic functions and annulling the best efforts for the transmission of regenerative and salutary elements."

The mentor paused for a bit longer, and looking to see what effect his words were having on me, he concluded:

"When the building of sincere goodwill begins, loyal workers understand the need to develop the qualities we have mentioned because, being in constant contact with the discarnate benefactors who make use of them in their mission of helping others, they indirectly receive suggestions for improvement that lift them to higher states."

Alexandre's observations could not have been clearer; however, I ventured to consider further:

"But let's assume that there was an immediate need to help somebody in the circle of incarnates, and let's consider the hypothesis that a human instrument is absolutely essential. Let's imagine that, at the time, a complete and adequate vehicle for the influence from higher powers is not immediately available in the vicinity of our task. However, there is an individual nearby in a normal state, who, immersed in ignorance, still does not perceive the dangers to which his body will be exposed, but who, nonetheless, allows himself to be utilized by our spiritual endeavor on behalf of someone else. Couldn't he be utilized?"

The instructor smiled benevolently and considered:

"That would be too strict. Wherever there is merit in those who suffer and goodwill in those who help them, we can administer spiritual benefits with relative efficiency. All infirm persons can seek health; all misguided ones can return to equilibrium when they so wish. If the practice of the good were restricted solely to good spirits, human redemption would be impossible. Any degree of goodwill and spirit of service receives the greatest attention on our part."

Alexandre paused briefly, thinking for a moment, and explained:

"When we refer to the necessary qualities for workers in this area of assistance, we do not wish to discourage anybody, but rather to guide the worker's aspirations so that his or her work may grow in positive and eternal worth."

Just then, one of our coworkers approached asking for Alexandre's help.

He kindly agreed. Before leaving, he led me to a small group of spirits who were in charge of the passes, and introducing me to the one directing the work, he kindly explained:

"Anacleto, our brother Andre Luiz practiced as a physician during his last earthly experience and he would like to receive some clarification regarding your specialty. I thank you in advance for anything you can do for him."

The director of that department of assistance greeted me fraternally, and either because he was busy or because he was a man of few words, he did not waste any time inviting me to directly observe the activities under his command.

He carefully placed me next to a respectable woman seated at the table not far from the center's supervisor.

"Let's take a look at this sister," exclaimed Anacleto, getting ready for his affable assistance. "Observe her heart, especially the mitral valve."

I made a detailed examination of the area, and I did in fact notice a thin black cloud covering a large part of it, affecting even the aortic valve and casting almost imperceptible filaments over the sino-auricular node. I told my new friend about my findings and he answered:

"Just as the physical body can ingest poisonous foods that intoxicate its tissues, the perispiritual body can also absorb degenerative elements that corrode its energy centers with repercussions on the material cells. If an incarnate person's mind has not yet managed to discipline the emotions, if it nourishes passions that disharmonize it with reality, it can at any moment become poisoned with the mental emissions of those with whom it lives, and who are also in the same state of imbalance. Sometimes, these absorptions are simple phenomena of no major importance; however, in many cases they are susceptible of causing dangerous organic disasters. This happens particularly when the interested parties do not have a prayer life, the beneficial influence of which can annul many ills.

He pointed to the woman's heart and continued:

"This morning she had a bad argument with her husband and entered a serious state of inner disharmony. The small cloud surrounding her vital organ represents fulminating mental matter. The permanence of such residues in her heart could cause a dangerous illness. Let's help her."

As I watched, Anacleto assumed a new attitude, indicating that he was about to use his radiating faculty, and then he immediately began the passes. He put his right hand over the patient's epigastric area below the sternum, and I was surprised to see that, placed in this way, his hand emitted sublime rays of light that were being directed at the infirm woman's heart. I could clearly see that the rays of luminous vitality were being driven by the intelligent and conscious power of the transmitter. Besieged by these magnetic principles, the small amount of black matter enveloping the mitral valve slowly moved away, and as if attracted by Anacleto's strong will, it reached the upper tissues, scattering under the radiating hand along the epidermis. Then the spirit magnetizer began the more active phase of the passes, discarding the evil influence. He made a double pass over the epigastric area by lifting both hands and immediately bringing them down very slowly past the hips down to the knees, repeating the same pass and operation over the area several times. In just a few moments, the infirm woman's body returned to normal.

I was astonished. And since the subject involved highly significant spiritual aspects, as soon as the instructor finished his work, I asked:

"Forgive me for asking, but in case this sister had not received assistance at a Spiritist center, how would she have dealt with the hidden illness? Would she be helpless?"

"Not in the least," replied Anacleto, smiling. "There are veritable legions of workers in our specialty assisting individuals who, through higher aspirations, search the right pathway in religious institutions of all hues. The manifestation of faith is not restricted to a simple, mechanical affirmation of trust. Persons who are mentally and viscerally living the religion that is teaching them the path of the good are involved in an intense and renewing activity, and for that reason they are receiving the strongest contributions of spiritual assistance, because they are opening the living door of their soul to help from the Most High through prayer and an active attitude of trust in the Divine Power.

My new companion nodded toward the sister who had just been freed from the dangerous influence, and after a short pause, he explained:

"Our friend is searching for the truth, filled with sincere trust in Jesus. A lamb battered by the storms of the world and inexperienced in the realm of enlightenment, she has turned to the Divine Shepherd like a fragile child, longing for motherly affection. Whether she was praying in a Roman Catholic church or in a Buddhist temple, she would receive help from our sphere by means of this or that group of Christ's workers. Of course, here in an organization that is free of the shadows of prejudice and dogma, our fraternal help can be more effective and purer, and the possibilities for her profiting are much greater. However, I need to point out that magnetic helpers go wherever there are requests of sincere faith, distributing the Divine Master's assistance with their best efforts. Wherever sincere and uplifting sentiments vibrate, a pathway to God's watch-care is opened."

I was very pleased at hearing this explanation revealing impartiality in the distribution of benefits from our plane. However, another question immediately occurred to me:

"But my friend," I considered, "let's suppose that this sister was foreign to any sort of activity of a spiritual nature. Let's imagine that she had no faith at all, no affiliation with any religion and no certificate of merit in the practice of virtue. In that case, would she still receive the benefit of liberating passes?"

With the same patient kindness that I had come to know in Alexandre, Anacleto remarked:

"If she were a person with upright sentiments, although hostile toward religion, in her natural meditations she would receive help, albeit reduced due to her inability to more intensely receive our radiating energies. But if she were completely immersed in the darkness of ignorance or evil, she would be without help of a higher order and her physical energies would suffer violent and inevitable wear and tear due to continuous mental intoxication. Those who close themselves off to regenerative ideas and flee from the laws of cooperation will suffer the appropriate consequences."

Satisfied with these explanations, I realized that I should not be interrupting the work's progress just to satisfy my personal curiosity.

My new friend moved on to a different area.

We were now standing next to an elderly gentleman and Anacleto asked me to observe his body.

I analyzed it carefully. I was surprised to notice that his liver was profoundly altered. Another cloud, also very dark, covered a large part of the organ, compelling it to strange imbalances. The whole gallbladder was affected, and I clearly saw that the black manifestations of that small portion of toxic matter were reaching the duodenum and the pancreas, affecting the digestive process. A few minutes of silent observation enabled me to realize the extreme perturbation affecting the gallbladder. The hepatic cells seemed to be prisoners of dangerous vibrations.

I looked at my spirit friend with astonishment.

"You noticed?" he asked kindly. "Every mental disturbance opens the way to serious pathological processes. To afflict the mind is to alter the functions of the body. That is why any inner disquiet is called disharmony and organic disturbances are called illnesses."

He put his right hand over the gentleman's head and added:

"Although this brother has a very strong temperament, he also has many positive values of human character. He has been through numerous experiences in past struggles and has learned how to control things and situations with enviable strength. Now, however, he is learning to control himself, to overcome himself for inner enlightenment. Nevertheless, he is experiencing large jolts because his dominating personality is being compelled to abandon a number of concepts that used to be precious and sacred to him. In this struggle he uses the teachings of Christ himself as his model for renewal, and in certain circumstances they strike him inside like hammers. Even so, he is sincere and does in fact wish to reform, but he suffers intensely because he must move away from his narrow-mindedness onto the pathway of the vast territory of general understanding. Within the circle of conflicts of this nature, since yesterday he has been struggling within himself to adapt to certain impositions of human nature that are required for his spiritual learning, and in this gigantic mental effort he has produced dreadful and destructive thoughts that secreted poisonous matter, which was immediately attracted to his weakest organic point, the liver. He has kept himself in a state of regenerative prayer, and that will make our work of assistance through the emission of beneficial energies easier. If it were not for prayer, which renews his reparative energies, and if it were not for the immediate help from our sphere, he could become the victim of terminal illness. The continued permanence of toxic matter within this vitally important organ would act destructively on the red blood cells, would complicate the combined actions of digestion, and would fatally disturb the metabolism of proteins."

Anacleto paused at length, smiled cordially and pointed out:

"But that will not happen. In his titanic inner struggle, his strong will to succeed is his saving grace."

I was so surprised by the lesson that I did not dare ask any more questions.

Anacleto continued standing and applied a longitudinal pass over the man's head, starting with a simple contact and bringing his hand down very slowly to the area of the liver, which he touched with the points of his radiating fingers. He repeated the operation for a few minutes. I was surprised to observe that the dark cloud had become opaque as it began to dissolve little by little under the vigorous influence of this magnetizer on a mission of help.

The liver returned to its full normality.

A few minutes later we were before a pregnant woman who was in a seriously weakened condition.

Anacleto stood before her, highly respectful.

"Here," he said, touched, "is a sister who is in great need of our fluidic resources. Profound anemia has invaded her body. Due to undernourishment because of natural difficulties that have plagued her for a long time, her pregnancy is a clearly painful process. Her husband is very poorly paid and she has to stay up at night in order to help him sustain the home. Prayer, however, for this maternal heart is not solely a refuge. Along with spontaneous consolation, she gathers magnetic energies of substantial significance that uphold her in her present biological ordeal."

He then pointed to the womb and stated:

"Look at the dark spots around the fetus."

I could, in fact, see microscopic brownish clouds adhering to the sac of amniotic fluid, wandering in various directions within the sublime laboratory of generating life.

Letting me perceive his profound knowledge of the situation, Anacleto continued:

"If those spots pass through the liquid, they will cause painful pathological processes in the whole area of the epiblast. The outcome of the struggle will be a miscarriage."

Highly moved, I contemplated the divine picture of that self-denying mother, united to the spiritual organization of what would be her future child. The head of magnetic assistance then drew me out of my silent wonder:

"Despite the faith that adorns her character and despite her edifying sentiments, our friend cannot fully escape painful sadness in certain circumstances. She has been distressed and troubled for the last six days. Quite soon her husband will have to pay off a significant debt, an amount he does not have. Besides bearing the burden of negative thoughts she has been producing, the poor woman is also compelled to absorb the emissions of harmful mental matter from her partner, who leans on his wife's courage and resignation. Those dissolving accumulated vibrations are attracted to the organic region in abnormal conditions, and that is why they are congregated like tiny clouds around the generative organ, threatening both the mother's health and the development of the fetus."

Astonished by this new lesson, I noticed that Anacleto had called one of the helpers, asking something of him.

Soon thereafter, he acted very carefully by laying his hands on the sick woman's head as if he wanted to alleviate her mind. Next, he applied rotating passes on the uterine area. I could see that the microscopic spots gathered together, congregating into one and forming a small dark mass. Under Anacleto's magnetic influx, the tiny fluidic-brownish ball was transferred into the urinary bladder.

With even greater admiration on my part, my new companion finished up the passes and explained:

"We mustn't continue the magnetic action to remove the toxic matter all at once. By moving it into the bladder, it will be easily discarded, making the need of other procedures unnecessary."

At this point the worker I mentioned earlier approached Anacleto, handing him a small container that seemed to contain precious essences.

Anacleto took it carefully and said:

"Now we need to help the fetus. Due to circumstances beyond her control, the mother's nourishment has been insufficient."

Anacleto took a certain amount of a luminous substance from the vial and projected it into the uterine villi, enriching the maternal blood that was to provide oxygen to the embryo.

Expressing my deepest admiration for this efficient assistance, the generous helper considered:

"We cannot abandon our brothers and sisters in the flesh to the whims of the circumstances, particularly when they seek the help they need through prayer. By raising the mental level of the person who trusts and believes in Divine Power, prayer facilitates the exchange between the two realms and our task of fraternal assistance. Large armies of discarnate workers are active everywhere in the name of Our Father. In light of that fact, after the death of their bodies men and women of good will find new worlds of activity awaiting them, where they will continue to develop the seeds of love and wisdom they possess in their hearts."

Anacleto next began to assist a gentleman whose kidneys, due to the density of the fulminating mental matter surrounding them, seemed to be enveloped in black crepe. He very carefully applied longitudinal passes, and once finished, he remarked:

"Someday, ordinary people will understand the importance of thought. For now, it is very difficult to show them the sublime power of the mind."

The head of magnetic assistance was perhaps going to elaborate further on educational considerations, but one of the coworkers approached and said politely:

"I would be grateful if you could guide me in a 'tenth-time' case. It is our well-known friend, the one who has serious disturbances in the spleen."

Extremely surprised, I followed Anacleto, who went to one of the corners of the room.

In front of us was an elderly gentleman, whom Anacleto examined carefully. I too observed the liver and the spleen, which were showing great imbalance.

"What a pity!" exclaimed the head of assistance after a lengthy examination. "We can provide him only a little relief. After having received full assistance ten times, we must now leave him to himself until he changes his ways."

And addressing the assistant, he remarked:

"You can provide him with some relief, but you shouldn't remove the bulk of the destructive energies that our rebellious friend has accumulated for himself. Our mission is to help those who have erred – not to bolster their errors."

Noticing my surprise, Anacleto explained:

"Our efforts are also educational and we cannot disregard the suffering that instructs and helps transform people for the good. Amongst the service rules we must follow in this center, it is crucial to determine the causes as we extirpate peoples' ills.

There are individuals who actually induce suffering, disturbance and imbalance, and it is only reasonable that they pay for the consequences of their actions. When we come across people in such conditions, we save them from the enveloping harmful fluids, produced by their own decisions, for up to ten consecutive times as a gesture of spiritual benevolence. However, if the ten opportunities fly past without any benefit to the interested parties, we have instructions from above to let them be so that they may learn by themselves. We can give them some relief, but never free them."

After a short pause, and sensing that I would not dare interrupt his valuable lesson, Anacleto continued:

"Despite his sympathy toward our spiritual activities, this man has a difficult temperament in that he is extremely capricious. He likes to quarrel frequently, to engage in passionate arguments and to impose his points of view. He can't control his rage and constantly awakens anger and resentment in those who share his company. For that very reason, he has become a focus of intense destructive vibrations. He has come to our group in search of improvement, and for many weeks now we have been trying to guide him in the service of Christian love, striving to awaken his conscience to the practice of duties necessary for his welfare. Unfortunately, the poor man doesn't listen. He easily succumbs to terrible hatred and does not realize the dangerous position in which he has placed himself. He has been coming here for a little more than three months, and during that time we have performed ten sessions of full magnetic help, removing deadly burdens arising not only from the thoughts of resentment and revenge that he provokes in others, but also from the vindictive thoughts he creates for himself. Now we must halt the service of release for a while. Alone with his intense experiences, he will learn new lessons and acquire new values. Later on, he will receive our complete help once again."

Deeply edified by what I was learning, I dared to ask:

"What is the amount of time stipulated for these types of cases?"

Anacleto discreetly sidestepped the question and replied:

"It varies in accordance with the motives. The effect conforms to the cause."

Anacleto continued with his assistance, while I became absorbed in profound considerations of a higher nature. After the breaking of our corporeal bonds, we can understand more clearly and profoundly the function of pain in the field of edifying justice. My few minutes of involvement in the service of magnetic aid had renewed my ideas relating to assistance and correction. The Lord always loves, but he does not miss the chance to improve, polish, educate ...

Alexandre's return called me back to reality. The work was finished.

Giving me a farewell embrace, Anacleto pointed out:

"You are always welcome. Come back to our department whenever you wish. Your help will be a valued incentive for us!"

I could not find the words to correspond to his humble generosity, but I think that the devoted helper understood my look of profound gratitude.

Accompanying my instructor back to our spirit colony, I realized that my understanding was growing as if a new source of light were bubbling in my heart.

20
Farewells

I was looking forward to continuing my new studies with Alexandre; however, to my surprise, my friend Lisias was the emissary for an invitation sent by the charitable instructor. It was for a farewell get-together.

I read the small, graceful message and looked at the messenger.

"Farewell?" I asked.

Lisias explained:

"Yes. As happens with other instructors of the same hierarchical level, Alexandre from time to time goes to higher planes to carry out sublime tasks that we are still unable to grasp. I believe he is leaving tomorrow with some other like mentors, and he wishes to say his farewells to his coworkers and students tomorrow night."

"And what about the work down on the earth?" I asked. "Isn't Alexandre one of the direct instructors of one the large Spiritist groups known to us?

Lisias replied confidently:

"Of course, his replacement has already been arranged in accordance with the merit and improvement of the institution to which you refer."

And perhaps sensing the sorrow that had invaded by spirit, Lisias commented:

"What I can assure you is that our venerable instructor will not forget us. On going to the higher realms, his sole concern will be to serve Jesus, thus bringing improvement to himself so that he can be more helpful to us."

"We will really miss him, nonetheless," I objected ... "I feel as if he is leaving us in the middle of the task, when we need his valuable assistance so much for our learning."

Lisias perceived the passionate nature of my words and replied firmly:

"Now don't be selfishness, Andre! We know that Alexandre will be absent because of work, but even if his journey were to be very long and fully dedicated to rest and relaxation, it would still be up to us, his debtors, to share in the joy of his great merit. We need to examine the good that can still be done, pulsating with jubilation and hope for future accomplishments, so that we do not become lazy and unproductive. In order not to be ungrateful, we must not forget the good that has been done or received."

That remark had the virtue of awakening my conscience. I recovered the emotional balance I needed. I changed my inner attitude in response to the initial impact the news had caused me.

My kind friend understood, smiled and pointed out:

"Furthermore, we cannot forget about our own duties. Learning, in the various formats in which it appears, always comes to an end, although knowledge is infinite. We need to demonstrate in practice what we have learned. What better testimony of assimilation can we give our esteemed instructor than to follow the service we were initiated into through his kindness until he returns from his temporary journey?"

"That's true!" I exclaimed.

Reanimated by the enlightening words of my companion, we talked for a few blessed minutes, with Lisias promising me that he would return at sundown so that we could go together to the gathering.

My dear companion returned in the evening and we set off chatting pleasantly.

The night sky looked particularly beautiful from our spirit colony. Numerous constellations shone brightly, and the moon, appearing much larger than when seen from the planet's surface, looked even more welcoming and peaceful. Far from the bombardment of solar rays that incessantly renew life, the flowers exhaled a delicious fragrance as they danced gently to the whispers of the breeze.

"Many of Alexandre's students will come to visit him tonight," Lisias said happily. "Let's be up to their standards and maintain an inner attitude of gratitude and serenity."

I made an effort to agree, remembering the sublime lessons I had received. Alexandre knew how to make himself loved. Superior without affectation, humble without being subservient, he was an always receptive instructor, willing not only to teach but also to learn. He handled the highest duties entrusted to him without any delusions of the "self", and was deeply interested in fulfilling the Father's designs and in accepting and using our simple cooperation. Due to his blessed comprehension, this separation from him, although only temporary, distressed my soul.

With these inner feelings, which I was prudently keeping in check, we reached the beautiful residential building where the loving assembly would be meeting.

We went in.

I was surprised by the wonderfully illuminated hall. There was no decorative luxury inside; however, the star-shaped chandelier gave off a brilliant-blue light and bestowed on the ambience a mysterious beauty blended with higher spirituality. Delicate and symbolic arabesques of natural flowers decorated the walls, giving us a sense of well-being and happiness.

I was introduced by Lisias to several fellow spirits and I soon realized that there would be only a small number of students. Only Alexandre's disciples from our colony would participate: sixty-eight in all, including fifteen women. All referred to our loving mentor with laudatory words, as we were all deeply indebted to him.

With all guests present, our benevolent teacher made his entrance, extending the tenderness of his greeting to each one of us without any outward exaggeration. He was the usual Alexandre: admirable and simple. Linked to us like a brother and putting us perfectly at ease, he spoke with us individually about our tasks, studies and accomplishments. Next, very naturally, he began to speak to us in a paternal tone:

"You all know the reason for this get-together. I wish to say goodbye to you because of the temporary absence to which I am compelled by higher reasons of service."

I noticed by the looks of those around me that most of them were feeling as downcast as I was. We owed a lot to this wise and benevolent spirit.

After a short pause, he continued:

"I know the purity of your love for me and I'm certain that you are aware of the amount of esteem I have for you. It's only natural. We are friends in the same endeavor for the good and we are fortunate partners in carrying out the Divine Will. Companions in the constructive struggle, today's separation, despite being only fleeting, would weigh heavily on us if we did not have the light of understanding in our soul."

At this point, Alexandre paused longer, resting his eyes on ours as if scrutinizing our inner selves, and then he continued:

"Some coworkers to whom I owe much have begged me to remain in our colony of work, a kindness I am very thankful for. There is no vanity in what I am saying, only the mutual and loyal affection to which we devote ourselves. However, dear friends, it is imperative that we remember that this humble servant must not fill the space that only Jesus must occupy in your lives. It is very difficult to find faultless love and surrender ourselves to him without reservation. And because this difficulty is obvious on all the pathways of our evolution, we almost always fall into the old error of idolatry. It is very true that this is a gathering of simple and friendly hearts, that it is not the place for extensive and massive philosophical considerations, and that we should restrict ourselves to the blessed level of sentiment. But I cannot allow the opportunity to escape for serious reflection on the theme of the sacred links that unite us without shackling us to each other. Our road to perfection, as well as the way of progress for earthly humanity in general, has been a torturous path on which we must step over broken idols. Our reincarnations follow one another and civilizations repeat their course in long spirals of recapitulation because we have been unwatchful as far as the straight and narrow pathway is concerned."

There was another pause in his loving and momentous address, and I noticed that we all shared a profound respect at hearing his venerable words.

"We have created many different gods," continued the instructor movingly, "only to destroy them often times with profound desperation in our hearts when reality broadens our vision before the infinite horizon of life. In our search for individual comfort when faced with serious problems in our lives, we rarely find the solution; instead, we look for an escape route, which we use with all our strength to indefinitely postpone the action that is indispensable for our correction or redemption. Nevertheless, the day of the restoration of the truth, the moment of our personal testimony, will come."

We could see the reflection of his serene emotions in his eyes as he rested them on us, and after a long pause he continued with his farewell message.

"That is why, my friends," he continued in a fraternal tone, "an instructor who is aware of his task cannot escape the imperatives of the evolution of his or her wards. From time to time, it is necessary to leave them to their own devices, even if the sweetest thoughts of affection tell us to do the opposite. Usually, in the company of instructors, learners almost always only observe. But when apart from them, they experiment and act, applying what they have learned. It is indispensable to develop the unlimited capabilities that we hold as a divine inheritance in our inner world. The unconscious protection that keeps wards from accomplishments of their own kills the seeds of progress, elevation and individual redemption. To establish such dependency is to create a prison for the spirit, annulling our capacity for spontaneity and encouraging the stagnation of our thoughts. Let us break away from the reproachable conduct of reciprocal adoration, in which false tenderness causes the blindness of sentiment. Let us respect one another as brothers and sisters brought together for the same work for the good and the truth, but let us combat idolatry. Let us love one another as Jesus loved us, but let us help one another against the development of destructive exclusivity. We are depositories of great lessons of the higher life. To put them into practice by extending our hands of friendship to our neighbors is our main objective. Each one of you has different duties in the various areas of spiritual activity. For the past few months, as the situation allowed, we have been together most of the time. Partners in the same experiences, we have created holy bonds of love that join us to one another. However, we cannot rest on the comfort of affection. We must face the rigors of service, be familiar with the struggle and bear witness to our accomplishments. I would never use my position as an instructor to halt your mental growth. The earth, our common mother, demands enlightened children who partake in the divine task of planetary redemption. There are multitudes everywhere, enslaved either to their well-being or misery, happiness or suffering, ignorant of the temporary character of the conditions in which they act. They all live, but few spirits in our world have taken hold of life eternal. The field of work is enormous. In it try out what you have learned, awakening your sleeping consciousnesses along the way. The learning experience provides us with knowledge. Life offers us practice. Let us join knowledge with love in our daily activities, and we will discover the divinity that pulsates within us, glorifying the earth that is awaiting our effective cooperation through balance and understanding. There is no lack of benevolent and generous instructors; moreover, you must apply the lessons you have received, likewise guiding your neighbors in the struggle in addition to others who are still weak. Only the willing victims of idolatry convert an absence into emptiness. No, my friends, let us not foment any grievous nostalgia devoid of optimism and hope. An immense future of sublime accomplishment with the Father is awaiting each one of us. Let us uplift ourselves spiritually and accept the constructive experiences that are calling us to make a greater effort. I value individual consolation deeply, but above our own comfort, we must seek deliverance with Christ."

Undoubtedly, the talk was based on loving firmness, which at the moment did not feel amenable to our hearts accustomed to constant expressions of tenderness, but it did have the virtue of waking us up to the truth, evoking an attitude of genuine understanding. Even there, in that simple farewell gathering, Alexandre knew how to be great and generous, bringing us a balance that we would not have been able to preserve otherwise. Despite our understanding, our eyes were filled with tears. To be separated from good persons, even if only temporarily, is always painful. In his company we had learned sublime lessons. Strong and wise, loving and serious, he had exhorted our fragile wings to make grand flights of new knowledge. Compared to what we were previously, we observed an obvious overall improvement. How could we not owe him – our blessed friend of all hours – our unlimited recognition of love?

I felt that the majority shared my thoughts, because Alexandre, indicating that he was listening to our most intimate reflections, added:

"We owe Jesus Christ all our thanks! He is the Divine Intermediary between the Father and us. Let us thank our Master for his blessings, lessons and tasks. The spirit of gratitude to the Lord makes life more joyful and renders the work of fragile servants worthwhile!"

Next, the instructor stood up and embraced each one of us with a smile, speaking words of encouragement regarding the Good and the Truth, and filling us with courage and faith.

Strengthened by his enlightened words, the students did not dare express any words stemming from unbridled emotion. We were all uplifted into a position of serenity and dignity.

On our behalf, Epaminondas, the most respected disciple in our circle, conveyed to him our gratitude and most noble sentiments, sending our instructor and friend our most ardent wishes of peace and success in the continuation of his glorious work.

We could see that Alexandre received our vibrations of love and recognition in the midst of profound emotion. His venerable brow emitted sublime radiations of light.

After our fellow coworker's brief salute, Alexandre said a few words of undeserved thanks and concluded:

"Now, dear friends, let us raise our thoughts of jubilation and gratitude to Christ, consecrating to Him the unforgettable emotions of our farewell."

He remained standing, surrounded by an intense, bright sapphire light, and with his eyes turned upward, he extended his arms as if he were talking to the invisible but present Master, praying with infinite beauty:

"Dear Lord, may we render to your merciful heart
All our joys, hopes and aspirations!
Teach us to carry out your unknown purposes,
Open to us the golden doors of opportunity for service,
And help us to understand your will!
May our work be the sacred workshop of infinite blessings;
Convert our difficulties into saintly encouragement,
Transform the obstacles along the way into lessons renewed.
In your name,
We shall sow goodness wherever the thorns of evil appear;
We shall bring your light to wherever darkness persists;
We shall spread the balm of your love wherever there is weeping from suffering;
We shall proclaim your blessings wherever there is condemnation;
We shall unfurl your flag of peace in the wars of hatred!
Lord,
Enable us to serve you
With the faithfulness with which you love us,
And forgive our weakness and hesitation in the execution of your work.
Strengthen our hearts

So that the past may not disturb us and the future may not worry us,
So that we may honor your trust on this day
That you have given us
For our continued renewal until our final victory.
We are your wards on earth,
Confused by the memories
Of millenary errors;
But we now wish,
With all the strength of our souls,
Deliverance in your love forever!
Uproot evil from our hearts,
Free us from inferior desires,
Dissipate the darkness that obscures the vision of your divine plan
And help us to become
Loyal servants of your infinite wisdom!
Give us the balance of your law,
Put out the fire of passion that sometimes
Still erupts
In the depths of our sentiments,
Threatening the development of our higher spirituality.
Keep us in your redemptive inspiration,
In the unlimited love that you have reserved for us;
And may we, partakers in your work of incessant progress,
Be able to follow your sublime designs
At all times,
Making ourselves faithful servants of your light forever!
So be it."

Alexandre's moving prayer was the last note of the wonderful farewell.

We left. All around, the flowers exhaled a very pleasant fragrance under the silvery light of the evening. And far away, up in the heavens, the celestial bodies shined like brilliant hearts of light on distant shores of the universe, linked, as we were, to one another in the search for the supreme joys of union with the Divine One.

Publishing Committee:
Jorge Godinho Barreto Nery – President
Geraldo Campetti Sobrinho – Publishing Coordinator
Cirne Ferreira de Araújo
Evandro Noleto Bezerra
Maria de Lourdes Pereira de Oliveira
Marta Antunes de Oliveira de Moura
Miriam Lúcia Herrera Masotti Dusi

Publishing Producer:
Fernando César Quaglia

Translated by:
Darrel W. Kimble and Ily Reis

Cover:
Evelyn Yuri Furuta

Graphic Design and Layout:
Rones José Silvano de Lima – www.bookebooks.com.br

Photo of Chico Xavier:
Grupo Espírita Emmanuel (GEEM)

Cover Photo:
http://www.istockphoto.com / mediaphotos
http://www.dreamstime.com / Tasosk
http://www.dreamstime.com / Serp

Technical Standardization:
Library of Rare Works and Book's Patrimonial Documents

Printed in Great Britain
by Amazon

67710124R00208